AF428754

What She Heard

Liddycoat is also the author of:

A WANDERING MAN

"An entertaining and thought-provoking examination of Western vigilante justice" Kirkus

"…rough-and-tumble, high stakes Western provides a riveting read." Bookmonger

"…perfectly captures a moment in time for the great American West…A solid read…" Covertocoverpub

HIT AND RUN

"The author stamps the frenzied, exhilarating final act with an unexpected plot turn and a thorough resolution…An action-packed tale with likable characters." Kirkus

"…action packed, entertaining, and suspenseful…well crafted." Scribendi

THE EDGE OF EXTINCTION

"A diverting SF tale with a steady momentum and a remarkable cast." Kirkus

"…the development of the survivors identity and family was profound." Scribendi

"…the first of a two volume story…Fast fun read…" Covertocoverpub

SURVIVING EXTINCTION

"…an enthralling post-apocalyptic tale." Kirkus

"…a page turner of the first order." Eve Marx, National Journalist, and Author

"…enjoyed the development of the Survivors' lives after the Aliens." Scribendi

"You'll probably want to buy both books, just to see who survives." Covertocoverpub

THE EMMET WAR

"…inventive…fascinating…a personal and emotional story about a horrible, terrifying alien invasion of human-eating insectoids and the soldiers that fight them…" Kirkus

THE EMMET WAR Underground

"…an intriguing look at what an alien attack might be like…an effective portrayal of the human fight-or-flight instinct…impressive." Kirkus

This is fiction. The actual geographies and named businesses of the cities mentioned are used through the imagination of the author. Except as noted in the **Thanks from the Author** section at the end of the story, the novel is populated by fictional persons through the imagination of the author. No other actual persons are used. No private homes are depicted. The locations of those houses mentioned are vacant lots at the time of writing. Actual public businesses are described through the imagination of the author.

The cover art is the authors. Actual shots of the Prom at night and the shark mural on the Beach Club wall are used.

The author used Trick-or-Treating here for the purposes of the story. The truth is in Seaside most of it went on in the Malls, Outlet stores, and Rec centers. On this last Halloween, there were no Trick-or-Treaters on North Downing.

WHAT SHE HEARD

Was more than a name.

Seaside
Oregon
2020 Copyright © Ontheworldmap.com

This is dedicated to those who will not be intimidated.

Those who seek truth.

Those who try, fail, and try again.

"There are more things in heaven and earth, Horatio, than are dreamt of in your philosophy."

Shakespeare's Hamlet

Parasite: an organism that lives on or in an organism of another species, known as the host, from the body of which it obtains nutriment.

Dictionary.com

Prologue

The letter arrived in a nondescript post office box in the city of Talcahuano, Republic of Chile on Oct 1, 2021. It was in a plain white envelope. It had been routed from an offshore account, through a mailbox in Salem Oregon, then through a mailbox in New York, and finally to the sleepy seaside city. It sat in the local postal office's small ornamental lock box for almost a week.

No one paid any attention.

Then the man, who lived somewhere up off Avenida Tumbes, walked down and opened the box. He put the letter in one of his well-used pockets and started back up to his house. It was an easy half-mile walk down the Avenida and then back up for him.

There were times during his weekly walk when the man would stop at Café Marbella for a leisurely lunch. The owners would serve him carefully. The man was very insular and particular. He spoke rarely and with precision. He seemed to want only enough interaction with people to communicate the service he required. His words were clipped and exact. The service was expected to be the same. The owners thought that was just fine because he paid cash and tipped generously. Yet they did their best to make sure he stayed no longer than necessary. They did not want to have him around. He had a tendency to drive others away. His very being seemed to repel other customers.

Actually, it repelled everyone.

Yet the man's IQ was significant. His ability to plan and execute was remarkable. He had an eidetic memory. He could be an engineer or scientist if he were not so frightening to be around. A psychiatrist would not know what to call his disorder and would not know how to treat it. If any came into actual contact with this man, whomever it was would decline to opine and would move away quickly. He was not a sociopath. He was not a psychopath. He simply had no personality. Yet there was something animating and driving him. Psychologists could not explain it. Nor did any try who had to interact with him. They felt the aura of death when he was near.

He was unable to be around people for long. He had no marketable skills except one. He was an adept killer. Therefore, he was an assassin. This was suspected but ignored by the townspeople.

The people of Talcahuano did not try to look closely at this man. But when they did, they saw a larger-than-average, stiff, dark-haired man with big hands and dead eyes. Once a young boy said that he thought they were shark's eyes. His mother shushed him and said never say that again and do not look at that man. The boy saw the fear in his mother. He never said it again but he thought it. He did not need to be told not to look closely. He never did again. The first time was enough even without his mother's admonition.

There were times when the man would be gone for a time. He would get into his older Nissan and drive away. He would be gone sometimes a week, sometimes a month. During those times, the city would breathe easier.

But he always came back.

Today he did not stop at the café. He strode with his signature quick, precise measure back up the hill. He opened his unlocked front door and settled into his sparsely furnished dimly lit den and opened the letter. Inside was a picture, an address, a date, and instructions on accessing USD 100,000 from an offshore account.

He memorized the face, address, date, router, and account numbers. He put the letter into his fireplace and lit it. The small smoke plume went up unnoticed through the trees and drifted invisibly over the canopy overlooking the town, dispersing the remnants into the ether. The order that would end a man's life was no more. The action it started was assured.

In the assassination trade, he was unknown. If there were a name ascribed to him it would be "The Editor." There were several accomplished assassins available through the dark web. But only he did business by mail. And only one other knew the correct address. Other assassins used various weapons to accomplish their assignments. Guns, knives, poisons. Murders made to look like suicides. They required support. Their kills were recorded. Some were investigated, some were caught, and some were prosecuted. Some were not. Yet all were known to authorities. Except one.

The Editor was not even known to the people who hired him, but his work was.

Only he could make someone disappear with no trace. Every one of his 'edits' that were investigated met a dead end. Someone simply disappeared. These were not insignificant people. To make notable people disappear was an art. One he excelled at.

He required no logistical support. He used no weapons; he left no evidence - not even a trace. No detectable DNA, no hair, no fingerprints, no fiber. No nothing. He lived quietly while he performed his edits. The cleaners that went to the rooms or cars he used could find no evidence of use. The beds were untouched, the showers and toilets sparkling. He watched no TV and used no Wi-Fi. Yet he stayed there. The clerks saw him come and go. The card keys were used but had no fingerprints; if anybody even thought about it.

While on assignment he tried to tone down his aura. He shaded his eyes with contacts. He knew how he affected others and tried to be affable as he was taught. Still, the local hotels and restaurants that served him tried hard to not pay much attention to him.

And every time he acted, an important someone's story was edited to another's benefit.

He did not care. Nor did he care about the money. His several accounts in several banks in several countries were approaching a million in US dollars, the currency of the world for now. He could live anywhere he wanted. But he stayed in this town. Like a trapdoor spider, he preyed on unsuspecting people at the behest of those who could not do it themselves and who wished to keep far away from any suspicion.

Back in his den, he sat back and took a deep breath, he made a plan in just a few minutes, loaded his jacket with his needs, and went to his Nissan. He drove to the airport at Carrel Sur, parked the car in the long-term lot, and walked to a local café Wi-Fi station to access the accounts. When the transaction was complete, he went to the Southwest counter and bought a one-way ticket to Santiago. His ID there identified him as John Parnell. At the Comodoro Arturo Merino Benitez International Airport, he walked over to the American Airlines counter and booked a one-way passage to Los Angeles, USA. His passport there identified him as John Vassal. On the flight, he slept. It was best this way. Even with the contact lenses, people who saw his eyes were alarmed. On a plane, he could be taken as a terrorist. The contacts would be removed when he went to work. Their effect on edits was helpful in subduing them. The edits were the only people who saw those eyes. It was the last thing they saw in this life.

When he passed through customs at Los Angeles International Airport, with no luggage, he was asked the purpose of his visit. His answer was "sightseeing." The agent looked at the man and his doctored passport picture and looked quickly away. There was something there he did not want to know. He stamped the passport and waved him through.

At the Avis rental car counter, he produced a California driver's license in the name of John Cassell and drove away in a new Nissan. Twenty hours later he was in Portland Oregon where he stayed the night at a local Holiday Inn outside the Portland International Airport. In the morning he left the Nissan in the long-term parking lot, took the shuttle into the terminal, and rented a compact SUV at the Enterprise counter using an Oregon license in the name of John Masset.

He then carefully drove through downtown Portland on I84, through the I405 exchange to Oregon Highway 26, over Sylvan hill, through the flat Tualatin plains, and over the coast range summit to Seaside, Oregon. He arrived on a gray blustery day in mid-October. He checked in to the Saltline Hotel at First and Downing under the name John Bissell and waited for his appointment to show.

All transactions were in cash. Nobody wanted to remember him.

All the while, inside The Editor, a silent parasite waited and hungered.

Before it found The Editor, the parasite had waited in the void without time. Watching. Hunting. Hungering. It had no form and could not move of its own volition. Potential hosts passed by, some close enough to taste. It tried to spin its seductive web and enter them but it was always met with resistance and cast out. Then this host passed by and was instantly and easily entered without needing to be lured. There was no resistance. The host did not notice or care.

There was an upside and downside to this host. It did not have any appreciable negative emotions for itself. The parasite could not feed on it.

The upside was this host was a formidable provider of fear. With the parasite's power, the effect of the eyes on his victims was a feast.

The parasite was in its own heaven.

Others would call it Hell.

It waited within its host, savoring the last kill. Longing for the next.

The Editor was not truly alone.

Chapter 1

The evening of October 31, 2021. Halloween in Seaside Oregon. The westering sun belatedly peeked out from under the grey low scudding clouds bending over Tillamook Head. It lit both the mist and the seaward side of the iconic Promenade with weak yellow beams and a soft orange halo. Ghostly shadows briefly formed on the walkway through the balustrade. The sea and sky began to blend into one luminous pale palette at the horizon.

The Promenade, to visitors, was a wonderful eight thousand-foot straight wide walk bordering the Pacific Ocean with views over the surf and sometimes out to infinity. A great place to bike, skateboard, or stroll. The coastal climate provided a mix of ever-changing scenic clouds, storms, mists, and sometimes dazzling sunny days and brilliant sunsets.

To the people of the town, the Prom was either a noisy bother or a money maker. Today, however, it was neither.

This year, a few Trick-or-Treaters in Seaside proper would haunt the city's inner streets seeking free-for-the-asking booty that comes only once a year. They would mostly haunt the Malls and Rec Centers, but a few would venture into the city.

They would not haunt the Prom.

There was very little Trick-or-Treating on the eight thousand-foot walkway. Most of the buildings near the town center were commercial hotels, condos, and vacation resorts. The south Prom did have big, beautiful homes built in earlier times when having an expensive vacation home on the Prom at Seaside was prestigious. The surf then was right up to the sea wall and balustrade.

Now massive dunes were built up, courtesy of the North and South jetties at the mouth of the Columbia river, and a couple of landslides off the Tillamook Head. The latest landslide in 1987 had moved the south shore out a quarter mile. The redirected outflow of the Columbia River had altered the ocean currents and pushed landslide-spalled rock and sand onshore. Over the years the westerly winds pushed the sand higher and higher. Then invasive beach grass took hold. Forty-foot dunes, covered in beach grass, stunted beach pine, and scotch broom, now obscured the once famous views. The homes were largely expensive rentals now. Not inhabited for Trick-or-Treaters.

Nevertheless, Seaside waited for this year's Halloween onslaught patiently as the westering sun managed to light the horizon for a moment, turn to burnt orange, and sank into a misty cloud bank riding the rim of the Pacific Ocean. Darkness approached.

Political reaction to the Covid pandemic stifled the last few Halloweens and the city was still recovering. The weather was reluctantly cooperating. With no rain in sight, the afternoon wind calmed, and the temperature dipped to the lower fifties. As it got darker, the western horizon belatedly glowed with the silvery mist for a moment and then true night descended. The iconic ornamental lights on the Prom came online, one section at a time. Doors opened and small princesses, demons, witches, and pirates emerged. Bags and glo-sticks in hand. Mischievous glowing eyes headed for the local malls and parties. Mothers and fathers, some in their own costumes, paced their imps. The truth was not many ventured out on the streets. Local parties were now the fashion.

There may be no Trick-or-Treaters on the Prom but there was a party planned in a south-side rental for those who were too old and too smart for the annual sugar fest. This one was going to be a real blast. The planners knew what they were doing. The house they rented was a massive five-bedroom four-bath colonial revision beauty. The face to the Prom was an arbor with now dormant ivy covering it. Orange and blue lights were strategically placed. There were not too many ghostly decorations. The attendees were too sophisticated for that.

Inside there was a keg of beer, stacks of six packs, and a large bowl of gin-spiked punch. The back sunroom held a stash of marijuana. A professional DJ was ready with the latest style music. Over thirty select teens were invited. Some were new to the scene. Others were not. For those veteran hopefuls, the bedrooms were ready.

As the sky grew darker and the cloud cover lowered, the inside lights came on, the music started, and people began to arrive.

This was going to be a real blast.

Chapter 2

As the party house was being prepared, and the Trick-or-Treaters shot out their doors, up off the Huckleberry Street neighborhood in the western foothills, not far from the new high school complex, Johanna Bergstrom sat at the small desk in her room. She studied her image in the makeup mirror. Lame, she lamented. Who would believe this was supposed to be a witch? It looked more like a zombie.

The sky darkened in the window. It was almost time to leave. The makeup time was getting short.

Johanna was twelve, almost thirteen. Too old to Trick-or-Treat and too young for the unescorted scare-fest parties, or so her parents said. Still, she managed to convince them to allow her to go to her BFF's house for a tweener party. The house was across the river close to the city center, on North Downing Street, and well-situated for her alternative plans. Several of her contemporary tweeners had arranged to have an all-night *Halloween* movie franchise binge with a costume party, hosted by her BFF's parents.

Lots of Pepsi, 7-up, chips, and salsa dip. Cheesy scares and boyfriend gossip.

Her own parents were going to a friend's house for an adult get-together.

She looked at her image in the mirror and sighed. Someday…

"Hey!" the irritating voice of her irritating older brother blew up the stairs. "Get your fanny in gear, we're ready to leave."

She disdained to answer, put on a last dab, and checked the final result. She wondered if the greasy Vaseline stuff she put in her hair to simulate slime was too much. The pointed hat covered most of it. Too late now. One final assessment. Still not good but passable. She turned and went to the door.

Jack was waiting. The smug look on his face told her he was about to tease her. Instead, he turned and went out into the gathering gloom to his car and opened the door for her. Her parents came out and her mother came over. "Now you take care, Johanna. We'll be at the Brennans. Jack has the number. Call if anything comes up." Her mother had been a teenager once and remembered how things could go wrong. Still, this party was safe enough. She knew the Jorgensons.

Nothing was going wrong tonight alright, thought Johanna. It was going right for once.

"I'll be okay Mom." Johanna climbed carefully into her brother's worn Toyota, making sure the hat was not dislodged. Jack noted and snorted. He got in and started the car. For a minute he sat and considered.

"Alright sister. I know your plans tonight." There was no banter in his voice. This was his serious side talking. Before she could deny anything he continued, "You should know that there'll be guys there looking to take advantage of young witches." His voice began to be lighter. "Keep your feet on the ground, both of them."

Johanna was offended. "What? D'you think I'm stupid!"

Jack wryly smiled, "No. But you're a target now. In case you didn't notice. Others are beginning to think about you and it. That's what you're doing. Sneaking off to test the waters."

"How'd you know about this?"

"Been there. Done that."

"No. About me and the party." Johanna was suddenly worried that her parents might find out.

"I have my sources. Mom and Dad don't. But they'll sure know if you get pregnant." Snicker. He pulled out of the driveway, down the street, and onto Cooper. She reached over and hit his arm as they pulled onto Neawana drive to Broadway. They headed over the Veteran's bridge and past the American Legion building.

Johanna thought about what he said. She had an idea. "What did you mean 'Been there. Done that.' Anything Mom and Dad need to know about." Blackmail raised its ugly head. She was sorry even before the words came out.

Jack shrugged and shook his head, "Ancient history, Joh. All I'm saying is, keep your feet on the ground. I'm the candy man this Halloween so I'll be home. If things go south, call me."

Johanna looked over at her brother. He was serious. He was being protective. He was also fairly big and played football when the school let the team play. She felt a warm glow for a moment. She shook it off.

"Nothing's going to happen. I'm going to see what it's like to be older that's all. And I promise to keep my feet on the ground, both of them."

"Keep your pants on too."

"What! You cretin! God, you're insufferable. How could you think of such a thing?"

Jack laughed. "Got you thinking, huh? Keep on doing that. There are things out there that can be a surprise."

They made the light at Roosevelt, then to Holladay. At the three-way stop, Jack turned to her and said. "Look, I mean it. There will be guys there looking to score."

Johanna felt the glow again. "I got it, brother. Let's go."

He turned north to 1st crossed the Necanicum and north again on Downing. Where Downing ended and Franklin Street began he stopped at the Jorgenson's. The door opened and Johanna's BFF Katrin rushed out to meet them. She was dressed as a kind of princess fairy. Jack thought about another warning but kept silent, checked the charge on his cell, and drove away. Johanna ran with Katrin into the decorated house.

Jack drove back to their house. He worried for his sister. He knew how those parties went.

He had no idea of what things could really happen.

Chapter 3

Sitting in his room in the Seaside Saltline hotel, **The Editor** continued to execute his plan. He had watched his assignment for weeks now. He knew the meetings in the Seaside Convention Center were concluded. He did not care what it was about, only how the edit tracked and moved. October 31st, he knew that the edit would be celebrating his latest scoop with his partner at Finn's restaurant until late. This time when he returned to the Saltline he would be alone. His partner was staying at the Shilo Inn on the Prom. Whatever they were up to, they were cautious and stayed apart for most of the time.

During the surveillance, he pretended to sightsee and actually traveled to historical sites for show. He could not care less about Lewis and Clark. He did care about body disposal. He bought a small crabbing boat out at the Hammond Marina. The name he used was John Fogger. The boat, named High Adventure, was in sad shape but he needed it only once. This Halloween night there would be a terrible accident at sea. An unskilled would-be-crabber would be lost. People would question why this John Fogger thought he could be a commercial crabber.

He applied for a commercial permit in Astoria and planned a trip on the night both the edit and John Fogger would disappear. He would radio that he was doing a trial run. Shortly after passing over the Columbia bar, his transponder would fail. His radio would lose its antenna. No distressed signal would be detected. The edit and the boat would be scuttled in the trench dug by the Columbia river near the continental shelf. It was thousands of feet deep. Even if by some stroke of luck, the boat were discovered, the weighted body bag with the edit, would never be found. It would be jettisoned miles away and left to the ocean's depredation.

The Coast Guard would find no trace of him. It would be a story on the back pages of the Daily Astorian for a day, then forgotten. No one who met John Fogger cared. Most were relieved.

The small electric-powered inflatable raft he bought for cash in Longview would be used to return to Hammond and would there be buried in several feet of nearby sand under the dock. The inflated black raft was nearly invisible. If someday it was uncovered by the tides, no one would connect it to the High Adventure tragedy.

John Bissel would then drive the SUV south and stay a few more days at the Seaside Saltline to allay any suspicion. The edit's disappearance would hit the news for a few days and then go on the back burner. Then he would return to Portland International Airport, turn in the SUV, and retrieve the Nissan for the return trip.

Ten o'clock. Time to execute. He exited the Saltline and moved his SUV to the dark side of the Beach Club tavern. He waited – as still and as certain as the trapdoor spider. Eyes now unshaded, ready to unleash their power.

He had planned his trap at the corner of a small brick-walk mall-type passage between Broadway and Oceanway streets. He waited at the corner of the Beach Club Tavern. A dark corner. The street light there was not working. It was across the street from the mostly empty city public parking lot and within an easy drive to Highway 101. The edit would pass by headed toward the Saltline. It would not arrive there tonight. It would disappear without a trace.

Without needing to see, he felt the edit approach. The Editor exited the SUV and moved to intercept the edit. He snapped on his gloves. He waited. As still and hidden as the trap door spider.

When he was done, he would have no sense of achievement. He would not be proud. It would simply be another edit. A successful plan.

When he returned, the people of Talcahuano would feel the chill as the Nissan pulled up the Avenida.

The Editor did not know or care.

But something did. It would feed and be sated for a while. Inside The Editor, the parasite's need was growing. It had been a long time since the last kill.

It was now positively ravenous.

Chapter 4

At seven that night, the tweener party was in full swing at the Jorgenson's on Franklin street. The introductions were complete. The costume judging by Katrin's mother and father was done. The greasy witch won to Johanna's surprise. It was deemed better than the sprite, princess, zombie, alien and black cat.

The back room was set up to look like the Addams Family place. That was her BFF's mother's idea. Johanna thought it was pretty good and was impressed at how much effort the parents had put into this. The effect was to make the room seem like part of a haunted house, complete with dusty antiques and spiderwebs hanging off the walls.

There were rules. No bootlegged booze, ha-ha! And one Mrs. Jorgenson imposed: No *Halloween II*. The F-bomb, gore, and terrible ending were too much. Of course, the girls had pirated a copy and watched it first thing. The eject button ready.

On the porch, the father had set up a straw man, like those scarecrow horror movies. He used fishing line to animate it with twitches and jerks when the Trick-or-Treaters arrived. Her BFF's parents were having more fun with this than Johanna was. For now.

Every once in a while it got noisy. Some Trick-or-Treaters arrived with shouts and shrieks as the scarecrow moved. But there were not many. Seaside was not much for Halloween on the city streets. But this place drew a few. Cars actually came specifically for the Johanson treat.

Johanna and Katrin waited through the horrible *Halloween II* then snuck out. Katrin's Mom was right about that movie. It stunk. It involved a lot of stupid cussing, stupid people, stupid ich, and ugh but no real scares. The end was depressing. The girls turned to the original. At least that one killed Michael. Even if they had to reanimate him for all the sequels.

Johanna and Katrin planned their move. Their friends promised to keep their secret and make enough noise for six. Katrin's parents were attending to Trick-or-Treating duties. The father was gleefully teasing the few small beggars as they walked up. Katrin's parents were the real thing Johanna thought again. Munsters and animated scarecrows. She smiled. Then sobered.

This was the scariest thing Johanna and Katrin had ever done. Real scary.

And in retrospect, the stupidest thing.

The corner lot made it easy to go quietly out the back door and get on to 9th over the damp grass. Then down to Necanicum and up to 8th and up to the Prom avoiding any Trick-or-Treaters. They were on their way. When they got to the Prom the walk to the real party house became more and more anticipatory and exciting. Johanna and Katrin walked south past the Aquarium, the Lewis and Clark statue at the Broadway turnaround, and the big Wyndham and then the Sand and Sea Condo, Maggie's restaurant, and the Hi-Tide hotel. Each building as they moved south got smaller and lower. At I Street the older houses appeared. Pedestrian traffic waned. They were getting close. All the time they whispered and giggled and wondered who would be there and what it would be like to party with the seniors. And *they* would be there.

From three blocks away they could hear the thumping music. The sound rolled over the Prom, through the dunes, past the surf, and out over the sea. For a minute Johanna worried that it might be raided for noise pollution or something. But as they neared she saw that the was nobody home at the neighbors.' The party had been in full swing for a while now. If there were complaints it would have been shut down earlier.

They could only stay for an hour. The Trick-or-Treaters would be done at about nine. They would have to be back by then because Katrin's parents might be checking on them. For now, they carefully approached the darkly lit up loud house. Stepping inside the music hit like a blow to the chest. There were people dancing in the front room. The smell of dope wafted through the open door and windows. They were there!

"Look it's Derik!" Katrin exclaimed, "He's alone. I'm gonna talk to him."

Derik was a Seaside high school track star. He had been written up in the Seaside Signal and Astorian newspapers. He was going to graduate with honors this spring and was accepted into Oregon State University on both academic and sports scholarships. He was six feet two inches tall with Norse heritage. Blond blue-eyed and poised beyond his age. And right now he was standing next to the back door looking like he was lost.

Johanna was astounded at the bold assertation. "What do you think you're doing? He's taken for god's sake."

"Not right now, here I go." Before Johanna could say anything else, Katrin drifted over like the sprite that she was costumed as. She seemed to materialize in front of Derik. He took a step back in surprise. While Johanna watched like a movie, Katrin began talking. Johanna could not hear over the noise but Derik began to smile. Katrin took his hands and pulled him to the dance floor. Katrin was a good dancer, but Derik was not so good. Soon, however, he loosened up and they were in some sort of sync to a recent Justin Bieber hit.

Johanna did not know what to do. She stood uncertainly. The music was loud, vibrating through everything. Pounding in her chest. The salty chips she ate earlier caught up with her. She needed to drink something and moved to the punch bowl. A 12th-grade socialite was there. She was dressed as a princess and her makeup was smeared. "Well, hello newbie. What brings you to the senior party? Looking for someone older than eleven to service you?" She laughed and carried two paper cups of punch away. Johanna stood for a minute wondering what that was all about. Service? Someone she did not recognize came over and poured a couple of liters of 7-up into the lowering liquid in the punch bowl. Effervescent bubbles foamed the brew for a minute. She decided to try it and dipped a cup into the bowl and took a sip. It tasted different. She looked under the table and saw empty Mountain Dew and lemonade bottles. No wonder, this was a mix of several soft drinks.

She did not see the empty gin bottles in the trash can.

Johanna sat and watched while Katrin tried to spritely vamp Derik. It began to get funny. The small Katrin holding on to the tall

Derik, like ivy on the arbor. She had another cup of the punch. Someone had added a pink lemonade flavor.

And another bottle of gin.

This was good stuff she decided. Maybe when they got back she would try a mix in the bowl at Katrin's house. She had another. She sat and watched the dancers move slower and slower.

It was mesmerizing.

She was just beginning to relax and feel warm and comfortable when a boy came over and asked her to dance. She had seen him around school but had not paid any attention to him, nor him to her. She did not have a chance to say yes or no. He was not much bigger than her but was a member of the wrestling team and very strong. She felt it when he pulled her up and half carried half drug her to the dance floor. It was crowded and the DJ had switched the sound to some sort of heavy metal mash-up. The dancers began gyrating with abandon. She was crushed against his hard body and felt something she never had before. He was excited. Then his hands were on her hips. His mouth was close to hers. Her brother's warning came and triggered every young girl's instinctive nightmare. Her panic rose along with his hands up toward her budding breasts. But she was also feeling a sensation that brought a blush to her face under the makeup. She was having trouble moving and trying to stop his hands. She was not trying that hard.

He turned her so that her back was to him.

Then his hands reached under her shirt and pawed aggressively at her. That hurt. *"keep your feet on the ground"* echoed in her mind. It was still not enough for her to try to make him stop. He was now pressed up against her. He was hard.

Suddenly, *"looking to score!... surprise!"* came. Her brother's words this time hit like a wet snowball. Johanna panicked. She tried to turn and push him away but stumbled and nearly fell.

The boy then looked closely at her. "Shit, you're drunk. C'mon, let's go upstairs. You can lie on a bed for a while. His grin began to become borderline predatory. He had strong white teeth.

Where was Katrin? She tried to call but only mumbled. The boy held her up and started for the stairs. *"Score!"* sounded in her mind and gave her strength. Johanna managed to break free and head for the door. The boy laughed and let her go. There were enough girls left to go around and this one was hardly half-grown.

Johanna made it to the door; derisive laughter followed her. She turned and tried to find Katrin again but her eyes blurred and she stumbled. She had to get back to Katrin's house and let them know. Katrin was in danger. *"Score!"* She sure as hell was not going to call her smarmy know-it-all brother. She looked at the time on her cell. A gasp escaped her. Was it really that late? She tripped and fell down the steps and heard more laughter from the house. She was now a sort of deranged entertainment. Sound faded as she passed the lighted arbor and got to the Prom. She got her bearings and started north. A mist had rolled in during her time at the party, further cooling the air. She shivered and felt sick.

Get back, keep going, she told herself.

The misted Prom lights began to waver and dance demonically in her eyes, the long shimmering line of lamps seemed to go on forever. They were laughing at her. She could never make it to forever. She stumbled on, step by step. The lights invited her to try to catch them. Every time she passed one there was another and another, forever. The scene became a nightmare. Then she tripped on the curb at the turnaround and found herself blocked by the balustrade. She was suddenly facing the ocean. She could not take the lights anymore and turned east down Seaside's main street past the uncaring statue of Lewis and Clark. Yet now even more lights danced, and on both sides; those starfish lights added to the taunting.

She passed a tavern, with soft sounds leaking out, then past the brightly lit Times Theater. If there were parties going on in there she did not hear them. There were people but she did not notice them.

Time slowed. A car beeped at her, she was in the center of the intersection of Broadway and Columbia with the flashing street lights now laughing at her. She jumped clumsily to the sidewalk and continued down Broadway. She almost missed the turn at the Downing Park walkway. In the past this was an actual street, now it was a brick-lined compact park. A couple of barren trees were shedding their remaining leaves which crunched under her feet. A homeless man was sitting next to the Seaside Carousel Mall bundled against the cold. She drifted away to the far side of the walkway. Continued. She was on the home stretch now and her head was pounding. She neared the public restroom in the parking lot. The start of South Downing street proper was just on the other side. There was another homeless man camped at the restroom. She stopped just past the Beach Club Tavern, confused for a moment. Which way around the homeless man? The tavern door was open and music and voices leaked out. Oceanway street loomed before her like a river. The homeless man looked at her.

Which way?

She began to hear something. Someone was talking to her. She looked around. In between the tavern's back wall and away from the window, two men stood in shadow behind a medium-sized SUV. They appeared to be having a conversation, but it was all one way. The smaller man was trying to make a point. She heard the words but they made no sense. Then the bigger one reached up and took the other by his head. Holding his face like he was going to kiss him. But that is not what happened. The bigger man made a violent motion and there was a soft wet pop. The smaller man slumped. The bigger man pressed a key and the tailgate silently swung open. He smoothly lifted the limp body in and began stuffing it into a body bag. She heard a heavy zipper slide and hit the end with a final snap.

Johanna was frozen. She could not look away. The tavern's iconic mural of a shark swam above the scene. Then the worst thing that she could ever imagine happened. The man turned to get into the car and saw her standing there.

His head turned to her.

Like an insect might do.

It was mostly dark, yet the lights of the restroom partially lit the face of the killer. His mouth opened in a snarl over sharp white teeth. A terrible doom oozed, then radiated out from nightmare black eyes in waves of darkness. Johanna's mind was overwhelmed with a personal, inescapable threat of death. Never before had she seen or felt anything like this. She had seen all the horror movies, all CGI monsters. They were nothing compared with this... demon.

The area got darker. Her head pounded. Her vision swam. The mural of the shark teeth melded with the bared teeth and black eyes of the demon. The promise of a personal, horrible, painful death continued to flow from the demon. She closed her eyes against it, but it seemed she felt his hands clamp on her face, felt the violent crushing twist. She heard the pop and then nothing.

He closed the lid and turned toward her.

She was doomed.

Chapter 5

Something nearby growled. Then there was a loud barking. Time stopped. Johanna gasped and opened her eyes. Subconsciously, in that time outside of time, she knew. In the barking was meaning, and the meaning formed words.

Run! Run! RUN!

Time returned. Johanna's survival instinct kicked in. She ran. She made a staggering, weaving path around the remaining cars in the parking lot and then across 2nd street. The first house on the right was decorated with a giant spider eating a skeleton dog. In her panic saw and felt the spectral spider move. She dodged and ran harder.

An unrelenting horror, and something else, followed.

For just a moment The Editor had to recalculate. He had completed the first part of the edit. Now he needed to get rid of the body. But there was a problem. The girl saw him. She might have heard the edit say a name. Something inside him had slowed this kill. The edit had babbled and pleaded. There was a feeling of pleasure that he had not noticed before. But it was not his.

So, change of plan.

First thing, freeze and catch the girl. Then a double burial at sea. It would add mystery to the edit's disappearance and offer a red herring to the investigation. This he could do easily. The girl was slow by his standards. He aimed his eyes and unleashed his horror at her. She stood dumbstruck. He scanned the area. The homeless man was gone. He did not matter. Now for the girl.

But she ran before he turned back. She should have been stunned. How could she recover so fast? The answer came from something inside, unbidden. Some other had freed her, warned her. It did not matter. He let her run. He would use the SUV and look for an opportunity.

To the only witness, it looked like the man moved like an insect, maybe a spider, quick and deadly. Still one moment and on its prey in the next. He averted his eyes, and then quietly, and quickly moved away. And tried to forget.

The Editor calculated the geometry. The girl had run up Downing. She was weaving like she was drunk. If she found a haven he would simply continue with the plan. The only change would be that John Bissel would have to die at sea. Bodies would not be found. The edit would be complete and he could keep the money. He would return by a different route. The inflatable raft had a range of fifty miles. There were long lonely stretches of beach near Gearhart. And the Highway 101 bus stopped there. Within easy walking distance.

But if she heard the name, his employer could be compromised. Even though he did not know who that was, and did not care, it would not be good for him to not complete an assignment. Plan one: get the girl.

He drove around the parking lot and turned up Downing. The girl was struggling toward 5th Street. There were no other cars around. The Saltline was quiet. The outdoor festivities for the children were over. He sped up and caught her as she made the dogleg turn where the street made a right turn from Downing down 5th a short half block, then left back to Downing again. She ran across the corner and up on the sidewalk between a power pole and a supporting cable. He expertly ran the SUV around them, over the curb, and hit her. She fell. It was not a direct hit and now he was in the yard of a house. The lights were on inside. He must move quickly. He jumped out and caught the stunned girl by her hair. He hauled her up while he hit the key and the tailgate opened silently. But she fought free by twisting and falling away. Leaving him with a few strands of greasy hair. His gloves and her Vaseline makeup had saved her.

That time.

He then grabbed her by her wrist and jerked her to her feet.

Johanna felt her shoulder separate with a sharp tearing pain. Her mind went blank against it. She sagged. He placed his big, gloved hands on her face - as if he were going to kiss her.

She tried to scream but only whimpered. The eyes bored into her. There was something there that wanted to witness her death. She closed her eyes and tried to hide, but the eyes found her. Death was coming.

Then again, a growling, and barking filled her head. Again time stopped. The sound morphed into words. The words to action.

Fight! Fight! FIGHT!

Time returned. She lashed out. She kicked and fought. Oblivious to the debilitating injury. Then there was a blast of noise and she fell. She ran, and the memory of the dog was left behind.

To someone watching it would seem like just a few seconds passed from the time the SUV hit her until she scrambled away.

Chapter 6

Inside the house at 5th and Downing, Harrison Baker was getting ready to go to bed. He was fifty-five years old. A retired Airforce vet of 35 yrs.

He was now enjoying the life he had fought for and protected for others. At least as much as possible.

Harrison stood, stretched, and turned off the depressing evening 9 o'clock news, once again thinking that he should just quit watching it. Yet he knew this was a new addiction for him that was not going away soon. A consequence of having time on his hands now.

The Trick-or-Treating was over. He went to turn off the porch light and was surprised by a sudden commotion on his front lawn. Headlights flashed across his front windows as they sometimes did with turning cars. But this was different. These bounced and wavered, casting strange moving shadows across his front room wall. He went to the window and looked out at a surreal scene.

Harrison might be a little slow to process civilian things but this was immediately recognizable. It was a kidnapping. A tall dark man was fighting with a young girl in some sort of witch costume. Harrison was not one to be slow to act. If there was one thing that the military taught him it was to act first and justify later. He also knew the value of firepower. He grabbed his service pistol from the chair's pocket and went outside, stood in firing position on the porch, and yelled. "Halt!" It was all he could think of at the time.

The dark man now had the girl by the head. She dangled like being hung. Her feet were barely on the ground. She was fighting but he held her face - like he was going to kiss her. Harrison knew that was not going to happen.

The man turned to him. Only his head.

Like an insect might do.

In the porch light, the man's eyes were black. Fathomless. For a second Harrison looked into the abyss. And something looked back. He felt dizzy. He blinked and concentrated. But the scene was blurry. His gun hand shook.

Time stopped. From somewhere near a dog started barking. A deep-throated warning and challenge. Harrison heard the sounds as a meaning. Like a pet guard dog warning of an intruder.

Wake! Wake! WAKE UP!

Harrison was startled to awareness. His eyes cleared. He looked again. The man was calculating something. He did not wait to see what it was. He knew there was no negotiation here.

The dog barked louder. Urgently.

SHOOT! SHOOT! SHOOT!

Time returned. His hands steadied. He pulled the trigger. The bark of the pistol echoed off the nearby houses and the back of Beachside Inn across the street. The flash lit up the man's black eyes without reflection. The light was negated, swallowed in them.

The man grunted and his right arm dropped. Then in an incredibly fast move, he caught the falling girl with his left by twisting it in her hair and tried to break her neck one-handed. But he kept losing his grip on the greasy locks. He tried to shake her like a rag doll. But the action was without the ability to do what he wanted. The girl was very supple and was now fighting hard, kicking and scratching at the man but without effect. Harrison steadied and fired again. The girl fell away. The man still stood. Harrison fired a third time. The man incredibly still stood. He aimed a fourth shot at his head.

The man folded up, stumbled to the street, and fell. He closed his eyes. He did not move.

The girl scrambled up, stared at the body in horror then up at Harrison without recognition. She danced around the idling SUV away from both Harrison and the body and took off down Downing, her feet barely touching the ground. Her arm hanging. A fluttering make-believe witch without her pointed hat, which now lay crumpled on Harrison's lawn. She disappeared in the lowering mist toward 9th.

The entire action took only a couple of seconds, but for Harrison, it seemed like forever, even though he had reacted with uncharacteristic speed. The people who heard the shooting described it as "pop-pop-pop" very fast almost like a machine gun.

Harrison had never shot another human in all his travels with the Air Force or any other time. Yet it seemed to him that he did not just now shoot a human. This perceived gateway to Hell must die. He felt the need to shoot again, leveled the pistol, and placed the iron sights on the man's unmoving head. His hands began to shake again.

His arm was touched. A soft hand calmed him. He turned to his wife, and she lowered the pistol.

"I think you got him," she said.

But the growling dog did not believe it.

Jennifer Baker was a practical woman, who stood by this man through his several deployments from Iraq to Afghanistan to Germany to Japan and back to Afghanistan. She suddenly knew Harrison was going to shoot a downed person. Murder? Something that she thought was not possible.

"The police are on their way, best you put the gun down now," she said in his ear.

Harrison did not want to. The dog was softly growling in his ear. A diminishing whisper:

Finish! Finish! Finish it…!

There was an instinct, some feeling that this was not over. The man lay, not moving, but there was an emanation remaining. A black hole with an unimaginable pull of… evil remained. He expected for a moment that the 'thing' - not man, would stand up or more hopefully be pulled underground. He shook his head and let Jennifer take the hot pistol from his shaking hand. She put the weapon on the ground. And stepped back, pulling Harrison with her.

Sirens were getting close.

The growling stopped and was forgotten.

Chapter 7

The 911 calls to the police were relayed to the patrol cars as "shots fired." The first Seaside police car on the scene was the Seaside metallic grey "stealth" cruiser. The Dodge was that soft grey that screamed cop but the lettering was small and barely readable. It pulled up on 5th with its lights flashing. The siren went silent. The officer slid out away from Harrison, who was standing with Jennifer looking at the inert bundle laying in the middle of Downing street. The officer held his service pistol in his hands aiming over the hood. "Let me see your hands!" he barked. "Show me your hands." Repeating the command three times. Both Harrison and Jennifer turned with palms out. The officer lowered his weapon, came around the patrol vehicle, and approached. When he was near enough he saw the pistol on the ground and said, "Back away please. Turn around and put your hands behind your back. You first," pointing at Harrison.

Harrison was handcuffed and moved to the waiting stealth cruiser and pushed inside. The door with no inside handles closed and the officer went to Jennifer, cuffed her, and had her sit on the porch. He stood talking into his vest mic and waited for more cruisers to arrive.

More sirens approached and went silent as they neared.

Jennifer watched as yet another patrol car arrived, this was the traditional white with blue wave stripe Seaside vehicle. Its siren went silent. More lights began to flit, strobe and blink. That officer went to the body in the street, weapon out. He checked for a pulse and hurriedly talked into his comm. "Need a bus and supervisor at 5th and Downing." He waited there for a few minutes. Everybody also waited. A fire truck squeezed in past the stealth car and parked. EMTs emerged and went to the body. Yet another police car came up Downing from the north. This was a Clatsop County Sheriff. The lights were beginning to resemble a blue and red fire blazing off the 5th avenue Beachside Inn across the street. And out over the entire neighborhood.

Jennifer saw lights come on in the neighbors' houses. People were paying attention. Crime scene tape was spread from the house across Downing to the other side then across 5th. Another car arrived, and a tall man emerged and was escorted under the tape by a Seaside officer. This was a personal vehicle. The tired-looking grey-haired man took in the scene quickly and conferred with the original responding officer for a minute. Then he walked over to the patrol car that held Harrison. He opened the door and bent down, and looked inside at the resigned man. Jennifer became concerned.

At the cruiser, the man identified himself to Harrison. "I am Frederic Jeffers, Seaside Police Chief. You are not under arrest but anything you say to me now will be part of an official record. You understand?"

"Yes." Harrison had a sudden aversion to the man. A type of animosity had carried over from his interaction with the man on the ground. He was not about to say yes sir to a civilian cop.

"Okay. Who are you and you want to tell me what happened here?" he waved his arm at the flickering scene. A line of police was combing the area with handheld flashlights adding to the surreally lit scene. The pistol and casings were already flagged. Jennifer was sitting on the porch watching the exchange between the man and Harrison.

"Well, I'm Harrison Baker, this is my home, and I shot that guy they're hauling away." He almost added, "I hope he's dead."

The straightforward statement caught Jeffers by surprise. He expected a deferral or a request for a lawyer.

"Why?"

"He was beating up on a young girl."

"Look. Mr. Baker, help me out here. Start from the beginning and tell me what happened." This Baker guy was not ready for this. He looked like he might be in shock.

Harrison took a deep breath. The aversion brought on by the man he shot, ebbed. This Chief was just doing his duty. He took another breath and told Jeffers the story. The headlights, the sounds, the scene where the man grabbed the girl by the hair, slipped, then by her arm, and again by her hair. Then by her face.

"I saw an abduction, a kidnapping happening. I yelled and the man turned to me…" Here he stumbled in his thoughts. The dread he felt when the man looked at him returned. He pushed forward. It was going to come out sooner or later. Either during an investigation, deposition or trial. Somewhere, sometime for sure. "Alright, I'm going to tell you what I saw. This man I shot… there is something wrong with him. He has black eyes! When he looked at me there was no fear. Hell, I had the nine pinned to his center. All I saw was him calculating. Could he kill the girl and get to me before I fired? He was assessing me!"

"Hold on. 'kill the girl?'"

"Yeah. That's what he was trying to do."

"I thought you said you saw 'an abduction.'"

"Yeah at first. " He looked over at the SUV. The CSI techs were hauling out a bundle. It looked heavy. Now there was a police movie camera operating. White light arced over the ground, adding to the confusing scene, adding to the strobing red and blue effects.

Harrison swallowed. "That guy had no fear. Like he was just doing a job. But there was something more. If you interview him, I bet you'll see it. He doesn't hide it. I shot him once. It must have broken his arm. He was sideways to me. He still tried to kill the girl. He was twisting her head. I shot him again. He did not stop. Then again. Finally, he fell. And God help me, I wanted to shoot him while he lay there." Harrison then said what he did not before. "I hope he's dead."

"Mr. Baker, are you telling me that you tried to kill this man?"

Before Harrison could answer an officer came over and said, "Chief, something you need to see." A bundle had been wrestled out of the SUV by three men and laid on the ground. It was opened. Inside was the body of one of the journalists covering the recent political event in the Convention Center. Under him was a load of rocks. The entire bundle must have weighed three hundred pounds. The dead man's head was twisted at an angle no head could have achieved naturally.

"Call the Oregon State Patrol. Get their crime bus down here. Call the sheriffs. Get their Medical Examiner here. Find the girl dressed as a witch. Now!" Jeffers saw the beginning of a big problem. He called another officer over, "Canvass the area now, two blocks out, three blocks out. Look for lights on. Hell, knock on them all." The officers sped off to obey the orders. There was a flurry of activity as calls were made and patrol cars were sent out. Jeffers came back to Harrison.

"Turn around." Jeffers unlocked the handcuffs. "I am going to give you good advice. It's obvious that there's more to this than meets the eye right now. I think this is going to become a media event. So, Mr. Baker, get a good lawyer. Say nothing more to anyone without consulting a lawyer. If you need help contact my office." He handed Harrison his card. "There's going to be a full-scale investigation, by the city, county, and state. Maybe the others. Say nothing without a lawyer."

"I have nothing to hide."

Jeffers looked hard at this man. He saw someone who had some sort of military bearing. Maybe he just did not know how things like this could spiral out of control. "Okay. Try this. Tomorrow's headline is going to read: 'Unarmed man gunned down in the streets of Seaside.'"

"I've read the stories in the Signal and Astorian. That would not happen."

"Not here perhaps, but what about the Oregonian? The Associated Press? Get a goddamned lawyer and shut the hell up Mr. Baker. For both our sakes." He turned and stiffly walked away. Harrison slid out of the patrol car and walked over to Jennifer.

Chapter 8

At the Jorgenson's, Bjorn, the father of Katrin, heard a rapid series of gunshots echo up the street as he was taking down the decorations that might be stolen later. He stepped out onto the porch and looked up 9th. The shots had come from the south or maybe the Prom but it was hard to tell where. Now there was silence.

Bjorn was a foreman for a local construction company. He was a no-nonsense man.

Except when it came to Halloween.

He was also a hunter. He knew guns and gunfire. Best to call this in and go back inside. As he turned he saw movement out of the corner of his eye. A figure up near Downing. Running in the middle of the street. A girl in a costume. She was weaving, her costume flapping around like a windblown flag. One arm hung loosely. He stood watching the approach. She came within the glow of their street light and he saw that it was the Bergstrom girl, Johanna. Without her conical hat. What was this about? A prank?

She quickly arrived and ran straight into Bjorn's arms. "It's coming! It's coming!" she cried. This was Katrin's father. He was big and strong. He would save her.

"What? Who's coming?" Bjorn came quickly to the knowledge that this was not a prank.

"The demon! Shark eyes. Shark teeth. It killed that man! It's after me! Help me! Save me!"

Bjorn pulled her inside. It was not hard, she was not big and she had hold of him like on a life raft in a storm, holding on with one arm and incredible power. His wife, Janice, came over,

"What's happening? Give her to me." She extracted Johanna from her death grip on Bjorn. She was also a no-nonsense woman.

Except when it came to Halloween.

Janice came to the same conclusion as Bjorn. Whatever happened to Johanna was not prank-related. Janice was smart enough to see something really bad had happened.

"Johanna, what's the matter? What's happened?"

"It's coming! It's coming! Save me! It wants my head!" She began to sob and blubber.

Janice looked at Bjorn. He shrugged. "She's delirious. And drunk. I could smell her coming at ten paces. Her arm's broken or something. She's in shock. But something's happened up Downing. I heard gunshots. I'll call 911. We need to call the Bergstroms."

The horror then caught up with Johanna. Black eyes closed in. She shut it off. Closed the door to her sanity. And hid cowering in the dark of her safe room. But she knew the eyes were hunting her. Coming for her. To devour her.

Katrin came in from the back room, trying to control her breathing from running all that way. Earlier at the party when she was with

Derik, she saw Johanna fight with that boy and leave. Derik was a good guy but his girlfriend came and he left her without so much as a 'see you later.' She stayed for a minute watching the dancers come and go. The upstairs was busy. She looked at the time and gasped.

Then she tried to follow Johanna, but lost her. She did not know Johanna turned on Broadway. She hustled on the Prom up to 8th, retracing their original path, passing Downing just after hearing what she thought were fireworks going off moments before Johanna arrived there. She was tired now from the party and running but she forced herself to continue to run down to Necanicum and back up 9th. She managed to get in the back door just as Johanna was carried into the living room. She caught her breath and immediately went to Johanna and tried to hold her and warn her to stay quiet. But Johanna was now catatonic. Where there was once a look of blind terror, there was now a blank stare.

Katrin was stunned.

Johanna stood stiff and unmoving. Unaware of Katrin's embrace. Katrin was suddenly afraid. Not so much for being discovered but for her friend. What had happened between the time she left the party and now? She knew it could not have been that boy. Her BFF was hurt, and her arm was bent like it should not be. This was something else. The suspension of disbelief needed to watch the movies was blown away like leaves in the wind. This was something real. This was something bad, really bad.

Her mother gently pulled Johanna away from Katrin to the couch, cradled her arm, got her to sit, and began washing off the runny greasy makeup. Johanna sat like a statue.

Then the front of the house lit up with blue and red lights. A Seaside officer came to the front porch and asked for the girl in the witch's costume. He immediately saw Johana and noted her trauma.

He called for EMS. He then began to ask the Jorgensons about what happened. There was a lot of "I don't know."

Within a few minutes, a Medix arrived. The EMTs quickly, expertly and gently secured Johanna's arm, placed her in a neck brace, put her on a carrier, and put her in the vehicle. Johanna was compliant. She did not complain. It was like there was no life left in her. One of the EMTs thought the patient had that thousand-yard stare of some combat soldiers she had treated in Afghanistan.

The Medix left with a shriek of sirens and the Jorgensons looking at each other with confusion and concern.

Chapter 9

As Katrin watched the scene. She feared for her friend. At the same time, she feared for herself. The police were here. Whatever happened to Johanna was going to lead to an investigation. She silently hoped that Johanna would not tell about the party. Or that she would not tell about herself being there. She looked over at her concerned mother and shivered. This was bad, really bad. She resigned herself to the truth. If Johanna told of the party and her. Then so be it. She could weather the punishment but Johanna needed a lot of help. She would try to help. But if she could, she would beg Johanna not to tell about her. She got a sour taste in her mouth. Her stomach churned. This could not be contained. She resolved again to just handle whatever happens next. Her stomach eased.

Yes, whatever happens, she would deal with it. Her parents were straight as could be. She looked at them as they tried to navigate the problem that had been thrown into their laps. She knew they would not lie. She should not lie either. Could she just shut up?

Not a chance. Maybe she should just fess up. The sour taste and roiling stomach eased some more. Yes, that would be better. Not for her, but for Johanna. Johanna needed all the help she could get. And she could not contain this. Too many people knew. Including those at the party and the BFFs right here.

'*Fess up!*' whispered in her mind. She did not know where that came from, but she knew it was the right thing to do.

"Dad? Mom? I have something to tell you. And the police officer too."

Before she could say anything more, another officer arrived. The two officers began conferring, listening and talking into their shoulder comms. Bjorn suddenly wanted to see what was what before any further police involvement. He beckoned Katrin and her mother to the back room. The *Halloween X* movie was silently playing. He turned it off. The chips and dip were sitting on the coffee table. The girls had been watching and listening to the talk in the living room. He sent them up to the bedroom for the moment.

"What is it, Kat?" His voice was low and cautious. Full of warning. Her mother sat beside her on the worn couch and put her arm around her.

"It's okay, Kat. I have a hunch what it is." Her mother said.

Bjorn looked at his wife. She made a "leave it alone" motion. Bjorn moved to a chair and sat watching. He knew this was better handled by his wife – for now. But if need be, he would take it over. His daughter was involved somehow with what happened to Johanna and the police would for sure be asking about that. He would make sure his family was protected. To do that he needed to know what happened.

"Tell us," Janice said.

Katrin began to cry. "I'm sorry, I'm sorry," she kept saying between bouts of sobbing.

Janice waited her out. Keeping one eye on Bjorn who for the moment deferred to her. Katrin began to calm, She sniffled and wiped her nose and eyes.

"Tell us," Janice repeated.

Katrin let it out. She told everything she knew. Then sat back and awaited her punishment.

Out front, another vehicle arrived. This one was a Clatsop County Sheriff's car. An emergency call from the department dispatcher had a deputy pick up a social worker and deliver her to Seaside Providence Hospital ASAP. He had to wait outside her house in Warrenton while the social worker got dressed and then with running lights and siren he made it to this house in just ten minutes. The first instruction was to take the worker to the Seaside Providence Hospital but that was amended in route to transport her to this address in Seaside proper.

During the ride, the social worker listened and spoke quietly into her cell. The deputy noted that she appeared nervous for a moment. Then resolved.

He cut the siren as he entered the city, turned up 12th and found Franklin street and the address. There was a Seaside cruiser parked at the house with lights running. The worker got out and the deputy sat and waited. Being a glorified chauffeur was not to his liking. His shift was almost over and he wanted to get back soon. As he sat he figured that something big was happening. This had something to do with the murder just up the avenue. He sighed; it was going to be a long night. Then he thought, well, a little overtime never hurt.

Chapter 10

In the back room of the Johanson home, as Katrin finished her story, there was movement at their door. A woman in a hastily assembled outfit entered. She had bypassed the officers in the front room with sure authority. She was older; heavy with time-accrued flesh. She stopped and surveyed the room. Her wise, time-lined face seemed to cool the air. She went straight to Katrin.

"I am Evalyn Hanson, with Clatsop County Social Services. Pardon my mess," she apologetically shrugged addressing the parents. "I've been called to see if I can help someone who is indisposed right now, one Johanna Bergstrom."

"I've been briefed on the way down here by the police. Johanna is now in the hospital. Now, anything I can learn about what happened to put her into a catatonic state will help me to help her. And perhaps help Katrin." She turned to Katrin, "I've been told you are Katrin Jorgenson and her best friend." She then asked the parents, "May I speak with Katrin alone for a minute? Nothing she tells me will leave this room. I am here for Johanna's welfare only.

She is being taken to a trauma ward for the time being. I will be attending to her later."

"No!" said Bjorn. He had listened to this woman but had no intention of leaving Katrin. "The welfare of our daughter is our concern. Johanna will be seen to by her parents. What is said here we and they will know." For Bjorn, now was the time to assert his authority. He would be the broker of any information concerning his daughter.

"Mr. Jorgenson, I am bound by law to keep this confidential. You are not and may be called to testify in a court of law. How will you answer?" Hanson wanted to get information Katrin might not want her parents to know.

"With the truth. She has already told us everything." Bjorn was adamant. He was old school where family took care of family, friend took care of friend. He would see to Katrin. The Bergstroms would see to Johanna. He would see to the Bergstroms and they to him. This was like iron in him.

"What is your concern again?" Janice pointedly asked.

Hanson looked at them frankly. She had seen this before. Sometimes it was a façade. Sometimes it was meant to conceal guilt. Sometimes there was trauma. She came to the conclusion that these people were real.

"Very well. It seems the cat's already out of the bag, so to speak. So I'll speak plainly. There has been a murder and shooting up on 5th and Downing - involving Johanna. There will be an intensive investigation. I do not yet have the particulars, but this may have grave implications. So… I should advise you to get a lawyer before it gets out of your control."

"Whatever happened and whatever happens next we stand with our daughter. We have the story and will stand by it. Katrin has done nothing…" Bjorn stopped and considered. "She has nothing to do with whatever happened to Johanna."

"Admirable, but ill-advised at this point. Let me talk to Katrin. Let me help."

"So talk." Bjorn sat back down. Janice stayed holding her daughter. Hanson stood uncertainly for a beat, took a breath, looked around at the Halloween decorations, sighed, then sat across from Katrin. She then looked back at Bjorn with a further assessment. A quote came to her. It was ascribed to Maslow but said in many contexts and by many others since.

"To a man with a hammer, everything looks like a nail."

This father *was* a hammer. There was nothing to be gained by trying to be other than a nail. This was as good as it was going to get. She went into her professional mode. The air in the room stilled.

"Very well. How are you feeling right now?" Her voice became soothing, smooth, and unthreatening. Almost conspiring. Her eyes were on Katrin's, caring, comforting.

Katrin had watched as the drama between her father and this woman unfolded. She looked at her father, who looked back with a stoic demeanor. She turned to her mother who nodded with a small smile of encouragement. She gathered her courage, took deep breath, and said, "I feel bad for Johanna."

"Why?"

"Something bad happened to her."

"Do you know what it was?"

"No. But I know Johanna. It was bad."

"Maybe we should start at the beginning. Tell me what you guys did tonight."

Katrin told her the story again. Bjorn noted that it was the same as what she told him. With insignificant variation. It was the truth.

"This boy she was arguing with, did he assault her?"

"No. She just left."

"Why didn't you go with her?"

"I tried but I didn't notice that she actually left at first," crying, "maybe if I did whatever happened would not have."

Bjorn started to intervene. Janice made the "Leave it alone" sign again. He shut up but remained on alert. This seemed more about something else all of a sudden. How did this lady get here so quickly?

"Katrin, you did what you thought was right. You looked for her. Did you see anything that could help me help Johanna?"

Katrin was crying and could not answer.

"That's okay, Katrin. If you think of something else call me." She handed her card to Bjorn, turned to Katrin, and said "Thank you for your time. You are very brave. You have good parents. Be at peace with this." She stood offered her hand to Bjorn and left.

In the front room, the officers waited. It was Bjorn's turn to be questioned on the record. He debated whether to invoke a lawyer or not. Decided to let it out into the open. The sooner they got past this the better. He told what he saw but did not tell what his daughter said. That part would involve a lawyer.

Janice was next. She told the same story as Bjorn but from her point of view. The officers wrote it all down and seemed satisfied.

Then sergeant James wanted to interview Katrin. Bjorn again bristled. Janice stepped in before Bjorn could make things worse. "Officer James you may interview Katrin. I and Mr. Jorgenson will witness. There will be no interrogation. Katrin has told us the story and she will repeat it for you. Do not interrupt. Understand." It was not a question.

"Understood." James came to the same conclusion as Hanson. These people were the real thing. He did not correct her about his rank. He turned to Katrin.

Katrin repeated the story. She was dry-eyed now and dull-voiced.

"Ma'am, I need to ask one question," James said to Janice who seemed to be the one in charge right now. "Katrin may answer, or not, at your discretion."

Janice looked at Bjorn who nodded at the professional and respectful manner.

"Did you see anybody else while you were coming back? Anybody suspicious?" He had to ask but it was Halloween and there were plenty of suspicious characters wandering about.

Katrin thought for a moment. "No, just some partygoers, but I wasn't paying attention."

"Thank you." James put away his notepad and turned to Bjorn. "This will likely become a problem for your family. I advise you to get a lawyer now." Bjorn was tired of people advising a lawyer. But now he was considering it.

The police left. The night got quiet. Yet Bjorn could hear the coming of a legal storm the way he could tell it was going to rain. He looked at his wife and his daughter. How could he protect them from this kind of storm? And how was Bergstrom going to protect Johanna?

Chapter 11

Back at the crime scene, Harrison sat down heavily next to his wife on the steps. Jennifer looked over at her husband of thirty years. She was amazed at how quickly he reacted and foiled this supposed attack, but also worried about that too. "Harry, what the fork just happened?"

Harrison sighed and told the story again while looking out at the crime scene. Most of the police were gone. The lone Medix was gone and only the SUV was left sitting on his front yard, and the coroner's wagon, remained, shaking on its springs while the techs wrestled the bundle into the back. The EMT and fire engine had backed out. The small evidence tags were picked up. The scene had been recorded on tape and film.

The coroner's wagon left. The area cleared. A lone policeman remained to supervise a lone tow truck driver who came for the SUV. When they finished it went completely quiet. It was close to midnight and the crime scene tape fluttered in a weak wind. He was suddenly cold.

"Something big is happening according to the police Chief," he absently finished.

Jennifer had listened patiently. "That's not what I meant, Harry. Why were you going to shoot that guy when he was on the ground - after you'd already shot him - three times? Why were you going to shoot him again? I've never seen you move so fast. I've never seen you shoot so fast. I saw you run outside with your gun. That all happened before I could even get to my phone to call 911."

Harrison was not about to lie to his wife but he was not sure about talking about what he felt. "I don't know."

"The fork you don't. You knew exactly what you were doing. Tell me!" The mild expletive "fork" was as profane as Jennifer ever became. She was saying don't mess with me.

"Alright. Here's the thing. That… 'thing' I shot wasn't just a man. I don't know how to describe it. But I wanted it dead. I wanted to go over and shoot it in the head. But I was frozen. I didn't want to get close to it. I almost shot it from where I was standing. And I didn't know I was moving fast. It seemed slow to me."

"And I stopped you from shooting again. How sure are you that 'it' was something else." Jennifer was suddenly worried about what was going on with Harrison. This was so out of character. Harrison was a methodical bean counter for Air Force logistics. Throughout his deployments, he never showed any kind of panic. Even when his airfield in Afghanistan had come under attack. Yet she saw it now.

"As sure as I can be. There was no '666' on his forehead. He didn't have horns or a tail, but… it was as close to something from Hell as I have ever seen. Those eyes…"

"You see things from Hell often, Harry?" she tried to lighten up.

"Hah! Not often. Not ever before, Jen. I'll tell you though like I told Jeffers, you'll see."

"I don't want to. Let the law handle this. Stay away."

"I'll try. But I just shot something. The press will call it a person. Jeffers said to get a lawyer. I guess I should."

"First thing in the morning. Right now we need to get some rest. It's…" she looked at her cell, "It's past zero forking dark in the morning."

"Get out the forking Scotch, we need a hit before bed."

"Maybe two."

They set up at the porch table chairs in the cold air. Jennifer brought out the whiskey and two tumblers.

She could not wait. "Tell me more about the 'thing.'"

"Alright. I know you're not going to let this go until I spill my guts." Harrison sighed. "So here's what I saw that set me back. The 'thing's' eyes. They were black. Not just dark – black like Hell. There is something else going on here. Now I know it was more than flesh and blood. The bullets put him down but I felt it was hurt and just surviving," he paused looking at Jennifer for understanding. He saw her concentrating on his words but not getting the impact the 'thing' had on him. "Okay look. I can't describe it with words."

Jennifer saw the pain and felt the need to help but was at a loss. "Harry, I'm here for you. I know you can't handle this right now. So let's take a look at it in the morning. Things will look better in the light of day."

The scene in front of them now was empty save for the crime scene tape. It was cold. Even the whiskey could not make the chill go away. It was more than just the temperature that was dropping. It was Harrison's grasp on reality. They moved inside.

It was three more shots and three in the morning before they could sleep. They did not wake up until noon. To an insistent knocking at the door. And a building headache.

Chapter 12

Jessop Johnson, Clatsop county DA sat in his office in the Court House. It was now quiet on this Tuesday. On Monday afternoon he had a telecom with the Clatsop County Sheriff and the Seaside police Chief. An investigation into the shooting at Seaside was launched. Seaside police would take the lead for now. By nine he had already received the identification of the Seaside murder victim. One Waylon Billings a supposed freelance investigator.

Unanswered was: How did he die? Who killed him? Why?

At ten he had met with his prosecutors and reviewed the crime scene notes with them. This Baker person was alleged to have shot the supposed journalist killer in the middle of trying to kidnap or murder a young girl. The shootee was unarmed. The girl turned out to be one Johanna Bergstrom of Seaside. She was now under a doctor's care in the Providence Trauma unit. She was catatonic and of no help for now. He instructed his team to monitor the girl's condition and coordinate an interview when she was competent.

He then sat back and tried to determine how this was going to play out. He tried to replay the scene as it was presented to him. There were too many blanks. How did this wind up on Baker's front lawn? It had to start somewhere else. The Seaside police Chief had a detective, one Sheila Dennett. Hopefully, she would have a murder board and timeline going. The Chief had ordered a canvass of the shooting area, Dennett would hopefully backtrack Bergstrom's path from where the crime was reported to wherever it started. Right now there was too big a gap. He called his aide in and made an appointment with the detective and Chief in the afternoon, before the Baker interview. He ordered an escort for the drive to Seaside. Best to stay on top of this. The news hounds were gathering. It was going to be a big story for sure. In his experience, nothing good ever came from that. There would be no lunch today.

At one thirty the Bakers were sitting in a small room in the Seaside police station. They had been asked to come here the day after the shooting by a pair of Seaside officers. The meeting was to be the following day. They would be escorted at one o'clock. Harrison wondered why the personal invite and escort. He would find out.

They had been waiting for twenty minutes. The officers that escorted them were gone. There was no window. There was no reading material. There were only a couple of worn chairs and a table that could have been appropriated from a second-rate motel. There was a large mirror on the wall. This was an interrogation room. It was depressing. It was like being held as a prisoner. Was this the beginning of an interrogation?

The door opened.

A tall woman entered. She was straight as a milled two-by-four with a no-nonsense aquiline face. She wore a tailored business suit over a cream-colored blouse. She smiled ruefully. "Okay. Sorry for the accommodations and to keep you waiting. We're kind of busy right now and the station is packed. I am Sheila Dennett, Seaside detective sergeant. And you are the Bakers, Harrison and Jennifer. Come with me, we now have the conference room." She turned smoothly and walked down a short hall to a room with windows. The Bakers breathed a sigh of relief and followed.

When they entered the conference room, it was obvious that it had been in use. The smell of stale coffee, sweat, and deodorant hung in the air. Pale rings remained on the long veneered table top. Eight chairs were turned to the door, remaining in the configuration of people leaving. Jennifer noted that someone from the previous meeting smoked. Not here, but it was on their breath and tainted the room. She had a good nose for this. Harrison had managed to quit twenty years ago but the memory remained.

"Okay," said Dennett. "Sorry about the mess. We're kind of in a hurry here. Coffee?"

"Please," Harrison jumped at the offer. "Black for me, cream for Jen."

Dennett went to the door and yelled their order down the hall.

"Okay. Can I call you Harrison and Jennifer, I'm Sheila."

"Harry and Jen," said Harrison.

"Okay. Harry and Jen. Let's get started. I have an investigation to run here and you are an important part of that." She was indeed a no-nonsense woman. The coffee came from a smiling woman who could have been a waitress in one of the local restaurants but who looked very competent in a much different way. "Thanks, Darlene," Sheila said. The door closed silently.

"Okay. I have the reports from the officers on the scene. And the notes from the Chief." She watched Harrison for a reaction. There was nothing. "As you can imagine, this will hit the news cycle today. We would like to get ahead of any fallout." Again she watched Harrison. This man had shot another just a day ago and there was no reaction?

"Okay," she said yet again. "There are cameras up there and there," she pointed, "and a recorder here. I am going on the record now."

"Wait a minute," interrupted Harrison, "Before you start recording I want to know if you or the Clatsop DA are considering charges against me. If so then I will invoke my right to a lawyer. I know you're in a hurry, and I will make a statement, but only if charges are off the table. And that it is on the record from the DA"

"Okay. Wait here for a moment." Dennett rose and exited smoothly. The door closed silently. Another time passed. But at least they had coffee now. After about five minutes the person who delivered the coffee came in and offered more. Yes, please. More time, about twenty minutes elapsed. The door opened again.

Dennett and a medium-height older man came in. He wore a conservative tailored suit and tie. He was somewhat slumped and partially bald. He looked tired. "Okay. This is Jessop Johnson, Clatsop County DA, He will be running any prosecutions arising from the Seaside and County investigations. This is Harrison and Jennifer Baker." Dennett was more formal now.

Johnson stepped forward and offered his hand. "Harrison and Jennifer, I am sorry for this. I cannot make promises about where these investigations will lead. However, I will listen to you off the record. As a matter of fact, both Dennett and I need to hear your take. No action will be taken against you for anything you say here. But if it turns out you shot an unarmed man without cause I cannot promise anything."

"I want that in writing." Harrison bluntly said. "I had plenty of cause." Harrison was below the political radar in the Air Force, but he knew how that worked. Justice was often a casualty of ego and politics.

"Oh, stop that, Harry. We've nothing to hide. Go on Mr. Johnson." Jennifer admonished. Harrison was proud that she thought he was innocent. But he knew that would not matter if any shit hit the fan. It was pointed at him. He would talk only if immunity were guaranteed.

"It's on the record that I shot an unarmed man last night, Jen. If these people are in a hurry to find a way to shut this down I'm the perfect target."

"We need your take Mr. Baker." Johnson turned to Dennett, "Get the Chief." She smoothly left again. The door closed silently. "I can see your problem, but we have no designs on you. There are bigger things happening." They sat for a minute. The door opened and Jeffers came in with Dennett.

"Sorry to have to do this, Mr. Baker," Jeffers apologized again. "But we are not after you."

"So put it on paper." Harrison was adamant. "You advised me to get a lawyer, if I do that, this will turn into a circus. I want to be assured that I will not be prosecuted for shooting that thing."

The three officials looked at each other. 'Thing?' Was this going to be a problem?

"Done," said Johnson after a minute, "But no paper. We can't have a paper trail of this. You have our word. We will do our best to ensure accurate reporting by the press, but cannot promise anything about that. There will be hit pieces for sure. Like I said this is bigger than you. It is bigger than me, the city, and the county. Even the state.”

Harrison thought, “There’s federal involvement?”

“Yes, unfortunately, the victim was working for the FBI. On the way down here I was contacted by the field office in Portland. They want to keep his identity quiet for the time being. They have bigger fish to fry and want the bait left alone.”

“Shit!”

“Exactly.”

“Alright. I’ll talk to you, on your promise, but if the FBI comes in, I’m going to get a land shark for a lawyer and that will be the last anyone will hear from me.” Then he thought, “How will you handle any FBI questions about this meeting right here? I know about the lying to the FBI trap. I can just shut up. Can you?”

Silence.

“Okay,” said Dennett. That apparently was Dennett’s favorite opening statement Harrison noted. Maybe it was her way of processing information. “Please give me the room, Chief, Johnson.” There was a sudden tension between the officials. Then Jeffers said, “Come on Johnson, she knows what she’s doing.” They left; the door silently closed.

“Okay,” Dennett said, “What I’m going to do is this. I will listen to your account, off the record. If the FBI asks me about it, I will say ‘what meeting?’ There will be no recording, no paper trail. You will have to also say nothing about this - ever.”

“Don’t worry, if the FBI comes snooping around me, lawyers will be also.”

“Okay. Don’t be… do be aware that they may use other people’s words. Do not talk to anybody else, okay?”

“Okay,” Harrison said.

"Mrs. Baker?"

"Okay," she smiled.

"Oh shit!" remembered Harrison. "I already talked to Jeffers last night. What if the FBI questions him or subpoenas the police records? Get Jeffers back in!"

Once again Dennett moved smoothly to the door. The door closed silently. A minute later she came in with Jeffers.

"Okay. Mr. Baker is worried about the statement he made last night to you." Dennett said.

"What statement? He made no statement. Check my notes. There was no statement." Obviously, Jeffers was prepared for this. He must not have written it down; or destroyed it if he did when the bigger crime was found, he was protecting Harrison. Or maybe his investigation. Either way, the man seemed to know what he was doing.

"Okay. I saw no statement from you, Mr. Baker, in the Chief's notes," confirmed Dennett. They carefully danced around the words written and heard.

Harrison looked at the two Seaside police. There was no duplicity he could detect and what could he do about it anyway. "Alright, let's get to it." Jeffers left. The door closed silently.

"Okay. Just tell me off the record what happened."

Harrison thought it was pretty straightforward. "I heard a car crash in my front yard. I looked out the window and saw a man attacking a young girl who was dressed like a witch. He had her by her hair but she slipped away and gave me time to get to my pistol. When I got to the porch he had her by her face. I yelled at him and he turned to me." Here Harrison swallowed and looked directly at Dennett. "I saw he did not fear the gun or me. I saw him calculating times and distances. He was going to kill us both. I shot him three times. They were good center mass like I'd been taught. I wanted to kill him!"

Dennett paused looking at Baker with concern. Was that another glimmer of crazy there? "Okay. We'll get a timeline going. What time was that?"

"About a little after ten."

"Okay, Why did you get your gun? This will be a big concern and will be part of any trial for sure."

"I saw the way he acted. This looked like a kidnapping at first. I'm a capable guy, but I've been taught overwhelming force is the best response to deadly aggression. This 'thing' set off my alarms like nothing I've ever experienced. The way he handled the girl showed he was very strong."

"Okay. You say deadly aggression and he wanted to kill you. How did you know that?"

Now Harrison was in dangerous territory. If he began to sound crazy, his account would be discounted. This detective was already suspicious. "Off the record, when I looked at him there was something deranged. I can't explain it but I just knew." He lamely put his eyes down. "This guy… this 'thing' needed to be killed." He really did begin to sound crazy.

"Okay. Did you recognize the way he held the girl?" Dennett had to get away from this line of questioning. Baker was beginning to sound traumatized, 'thing?'

"Not specifically, but he was planning on killing her. When I first shot him his arm fell away but he tried to twist her head one-handed. He wanted to break her neck. That's why I shot him again."

"Okay. I think I have it. Now off the record, we have anecdotal evidence that supports your impression that this man is… something different." But nobody else had called it a 'thing.'

"From who?"

"From the girl's statements to the Jorgensons, before she froze, from the Medix EMTs, the doctors and nurses at Providence before he was life-flighted to Emanuel in Portland, and finally from those who transported him. I suspect we will hear the same from Emanuel personnel. He kept his eyes closed as much as possible, but part of the medical procedures required examining them. Everybody who did mentioned his eyes." This was the first time since the Jeffers conversation that Harrison heard her start a sentence without 'okay.'

What was it, she thought, about the eyes? She knew they were described as black, but that was not really possible.

"What color were the assailant's eyes again?" asked Dennett.

Harrison looked at her for a trick, but she seemed curious.

"Black. And I mean black, not just dark. There was no reflection from the gun flash. This 'assailant' is something more than just that."

There was time to see for herself. "You are free to go for now. Please speak to no one about this for the time being. I'll have a car brought around to take you back."

"We'll walk," said Jennifer. "It's not that far."

"Okay. I'll take you out."

In Jeffers's office, he, Johnson, and Dennett discussed the interview. "This is going to be a clusterfuck of media hype. There's no way to keep a lid on this. Lieutenant Dennett, I want you to ride herd on the Bakers. Keep them from blowing this up," Johnson said.

Dennett looked at Jeffers, and he nodded.

Johnson felt the air cool. "Sorry, Chief. This is your house."

"I'd have said that if you didn't, but we know what we're doing here."

"Got it."

Johnson left with his county sheriff's escort. Jeffers said, "He's right. This is going to be bigger than anything we've done before. You're the lead. But remember Johnson has to present the case to the courts. Let's button this down tight."

"Yes sir. But you saw this Baker guy. His use of the word 'thing' is a problem."

"Yeah. Well, get him straight. The wife seems okay. Maybe she can help."

"Maybe." Dennett went back to her desk. This Baker guy was going to be a problem for sure.

She began to look for a way to get around him with no hope of finding one.

Chapter 13

As the Bakers stepped out of the police station Harrison was locked in deep thought. Jennifer looked up at building clouds blowing up from the southwest. Rolling waves of rain were coming. "Let's get something to eat and wait out the rain," she said, pointing at Riley's across South Holladay Drive.

Harrison looked up from his thoughts and said, "Good idea, I'm hungry. I think we need to rehash what's happened. The police are not believing about the danger in the 'thing.'"

They crossed the street and found an open table near the front window. It was afternoon but it felt like morning. The first waves of rain blew in. The street turned slick and shiny. The window fogged and then ran with windblown spattered drops.

Harrison ordered the bacon and eggs and Jennifer had the pancakes. And coffee, black and strong. Nothing bad to be said about the police coffee, but this was much fresher and better. They ate in silence. When the plates were cleared, Harrison ordered more coffee and they sat for a while. He started getting his thoughts together. "We… I stepped into something here. This is going to be a problem."

"Yeah? Yes, you did and yes it will. Tell me again how this… 'thing' affected you so much. You've been around. More than thirty years in the Air Force, traveling through pretty ugly places. I know you've seen pretty ugly stuff. What was it about this guy that made you want to kill him?"

"Like I said. I… felt something… evil in him. I've been around alright. I've seen some brutal events and brutal people. You've been with me most of the way. Nothing that happened before was outside of human possibilities. Even the mass murderers in Afghanistan and Iraq. Those people were demented for sure. Some actually thought they had the blessing of God. But they were sadists, psychopaths, sociopaths, and assorted other 'paths' who only thought about themselves. War brought them out in spades. They were opportunists." Harrison paused. Breathed in and out. "But this… I have no words to describe him. There was an emptiness, a lack of humanity. He's not any kind of 'path.' Yet he was animated by something bad. Maybe demon-possessed. There was no human emotion in him. At first, it appeared to be just a job to him. Almost mechanical. But… when he turned to me, I saw… I felt a horrible cold presence, the promise of an end. Total end. No afterlife. No hope. No nothing." Harrison was looking out the window, but he saw only a dark abyss.

Then he snapped back as Jennifer took his hand.

"Hey," she said, "I'm here, Harry. Harry! Look at me."

Harrison tore his eyes away from the blackness that descended and looked into the concerned eyes of the woman he married so long ago. They stood together through some tough times, some sad times, and many good times. God, she was strong, but she didn't see the… 'thing's' stare.

"I'm okay. I'm okay.

"Yeah? Well, I think you need help. Remember, Dennett said others saw what you saw. There's support."

"Let me work this out first. The DA is probably going to charge this 'thing' with some heavy legal stuff. The 'thing' won't say anything. He won't do anything. But he's a hitman. There's somebody out there willing to pay him to kill that man and he would have killed the girl and me if he could. Why? Why kill this journalist? The girl and I were simply a glitch. Why kill us? More than that, what did they turn loose in Seaside?"

"Well, he's not loose. He's locked up."

"For now."

"Let's go. The sky's clear for a minute." Outside the air had cleared. But to the southwest, another bank of rain moved toward Seaside.

They hustled up Holladay past a rental shop and bank, and through the Broadway intersection to 1st. They walked quickly up the street past the Convention Center and turned right on Downing. The rain began to catch them and they sped up. They hit the porch just as the wind picked up and the rain gusted sideways up the street. The crime scene tape fluttered. The blood stain in the street disappeared under the slick sheets of windblown water. They stomped their shoes on the mat and went in.

The day closed in.

"I think I need a Jameson."

"Yeah? I think you don't. Let's listen to some good music for a while." Jennifer went to the stereo and got out one of the CDs they had collected during their travels with the Air Force. She bypassed the Reggae, Tesh and Soca albums. She passed Summer Place, Frenesi, and opted for Moonlight Sonata. The sound filled the room. Harrison sat down in the chair he was in when this started in what seemed just a few hours ago and tried to feel the peace evoked by the master. Still, his shoulders burned, and his gut churned with the recent meal. The image of the 'thing' grew. The eyes, the blackness seemed to beckon him, to doom him. He looked out the front window at the flapping crime scene tape and did not feel good. Not good at all.

And suddenly Jennifer was there rubbing the tension away. She felt for her man. He was in pain. And something else. He had been affected or maybe infected by the encounter with the killer. This obviously was something that had not happened before. She tried to understand but could not see what he saw. All she knew was that he was hurting. She felt the tightness in his shoulders and worked to ease it.

"Let go, Harry. Let me help you." Jennifer had been with Harrison for most of his service time. There were times he spent deployed in "conflict" zones and she could not follow. They had no children. She had been diagnosed early in their marriage with an inability to conceive. Harrison understood. That he loved her anyway was a great feeling for Jennifer. She loved this man for it. She wanted to help him now. He seemed so lost. She willed her hands to cure him. To ease his pain.

Harrison sighed. The blackness subsided. He began to get a grip on what happened. As time went on the effect of the thing's eyes faded. Slowly. Yet in the back of his mind, he knew, the 'thing' must die for him to live. Both physically and mentally.

For now, as Jennifer relaxed him with her massage, Harrison wondered about the word 'bait.,' the police used. That meant there was someone else out there. Someone the FBI wanted to be kept in play. To catch someone else. It was not him. He was just a side issue. They were still hunting. If the FBI was snooping, who else was in the background?

"Jen. We have to be prepared for more. I'm a witness if nothing else. This could go on for a while."

"Yeah? It could. So we persevere. We've done it before. Meantime, Harry, don't obsess. Let the system work and do our part as required. How about I cook up Korv stroganoff for dinner?"

"Deal." Harrison's mouth watered. Yet his thoughts went forward to the morning news. What were the media going to report?

The furnace came on as the temperature dropped. "I'll start a fire. It's a good time for it."

Outside the crime scene tape tore loose and fluttered down the street.

Chapter 14

The next day at nine o'clock the Bakers sat in the homey office of a local law firm. The clean, orderly room had a direct view of the busy traffic on Roosevelt Drive. The day dawned foggily but was clearing up nicely. The walk from their house north on Necanicum and across the river on the 12th Street bridge was invigorating and felt good despite the circumstances. They walked up to the modest office building and entered.

They were met by a sharply dressed aide who exuded competency. "The attorney will be just a minute would you care for coffee?" she asked. "Sure," was the obvious answer. It came from a new single-cup machine stationed in the lobby. It was the best they had tasted here in Seaside. As good as *Burly and the Bean's* premium brew. Jennifer asked where they got it. Before they finished the attorney came out and introduced himself. He had a firm dry handshake and a sincere demeanor. "Bring your coffee," he said. They were led down a hall into his office.

Inside Harrison thought the lawyer looked awfully young. But they had to start somewhere. He was at a loss here and needed advice.

"How can I help you, Mr. and Mrs. Baker?" Miles Schiefer started. He had a deep cool voice. He sat back and waited with complete attention on Harrison. He knew the story as reported in the Astorian, but did not know if he was up to the task. His trial experience was with tort litigation.

"Well, Mr. Schiefer, we're in a bit of a bind here," Harrison blandly started. "We have been advised to get a lawyer. Seaside doesn't have a lot to offer. But we want to stay local. You obviously know about the shooting and murder. All we need is someone to protect our rights. We have nothing to hide. But we don't want to be taken for a ride."

"Yes, I've heard and read about the incidents. I'm not sure I'm the best choice for protecting your rights. This is out of my area of expertise. I know how to advise you to keep silent but I am not a criminal lawyer."

"We're not criminals. Do you have access to a partner, perhaps, or another lawyer who can help you? We want to stay local. I want to see the person who is representing me. I'm not interested in recruiting an 'online' lawyer."

"We can call in consultants. Though I must warn you, that could get expensive."

Harrison thought. "Well, we can mortgage if necessary. We own our home. We have savings. Right now I would like to offer a retainer."

"What we want is to be protected from further questioning from any except the Seaside detective," Jennifer said. "Sheila Dennett."

“Good idea, Jen.”

“Before I commit to anything, I will consult with the firm’s partners. This is bigger than anything we’ve handled before.”

“How long will this take?”

“It’s Tuesday. I’ll be ready with an answer by Friday.”

There was nothing more to be said. They thanked the attorney and aide and left. The walk back was a leisurely stroll up 12th to the Prom and south to 5th and back to the scene of the crime. Harrison picked up their mail which included the Astorian paper. The story of the shooting hit the front page. He read it carefully over a fresh pot of coffee, which was not nearly as good as the attorneys.

The story was generally factual. The headline was “Murder in Seaside” and the sub-headline was “Seaside police investigate the murder of a journalist.” A secondary story was headlined: “Murder suspect injured in shooting incident.” It included what the reporter could glean from the police and statements from witnesses to the aftermath. In a subsection, the writer noted the incident was on Baker’s lawn. The “who, what, where, when” were weak but factual. The “why” was unanswered. The police were investigating that. The police had not released their names but the reporter noted the address of the incident and who lived there. Well, it was public knowledge and would come out eventually, thought Harrison.

He sat looking at the rutted lawn and noted a passerby also looking at it.

“We’ve become items of interest, Jen,” he said pointing at the latest gawkers.

“Yeah? Let ’em look. It gives them something to talk about. Which reminds me, we should get our lawn service to smooth it out.”

"I can do that!"

"Then get to it, my he-man," Jennifer grinned. Anything to get him back on track.

"Do we have any tools here?"

"Check the garage, but you know where Ace Hardware is."

Harrison was about to get a taste of civilian life. He began to understand how easy life in the Air Force was. His food, shelter, and clothing were taken care of by others. It might not be comfortable, and sometimes in dangerous areas, but the care of service personnel was always someone else's problem. His duty was to make sure the equipment and armament needs of the front-line pilots and techs were attended to; while others took care of him. Even off base, Jennifer took care of him. This house had two bathrooms. He had his own. It was a new thing to have to clean up after himself. And there was a new respect for what others had done for him.

Now he was also a gardener.

And part of a murder and assault investigation. More than just a part. He was a main part. But first, tend to the lawn.

After he somewhat successfully smoothed the ruts by beating on them with a shovel he found in the garage, he read the story again. The clinical discourse did not begin to tell the unbridled horror of it. He realized that no amount of words could make anyone understand the feeling. He also knew that of the hundreds of similar incidents he had read about; none could be told with actual feeling. Maybe a novel could approach it, but newspapers and media were superficial and sometimes a lie.

Let it go, Harry, he admonished himself. Deal with this in reality. No one truly knows how another feels. No one sees what another sees. No one hears what another hears. Like the military: suck it up buttercup!

Friday they again walked to the attorney's office and had more of that good coffee.

Schiefer greeted them and again they sat in the office. He closed the door and started right off.

"My partners and I have looked into this and have noted the interest of several federal agencies. We will do what we can within the strictures of Oregon law, but if the feds want to do something you can bet we'll get tossed aside like an afterthought. There are not many law firms that can stand up to the feds if they invoke any of the National Threat Acts and start using the secret subpoena and indictment protocols. Federal agents will simply show up on your doorstep and will make life miserable. They don't have to let you remain silent. They can put you behind bars until you talk and then use it to prosecute you. There is no effective recourse."

"Will you be available to try if they do?"

"Yes. You can invoke your right to an attorney, but again, if the Terrorism Risk Protection Act is invoked, you will be forced to comply with any of their orders and answer any of their questions under threat of fines and/or imprisonment. We will not be able to help except in court. If it even gets that far." Schiefer saw the sudden set of Harrison's jaw. "Do not try to resist, Mr. Baker. You can stay silent but any aggression will be met with greater aggression. The federal TRPA powers are great."

Jennifer looked at Harrison, then back at Schiefer. "He won't. So what can you do?"

"Here's the reality. If it continues to be a county action, we can and will be active in protecting you. If it becomes what I fear, then we will be of limited use. That being said, our senior partner has access to more formidable law firms. These can mitigate any actions by the federal powers, but not blunt them. They are expensive."

"How much?" Harrison said between clenched teeth. There was a bitter taste in his mouth. This is the country he fought for?

"It can run up to a $10,000 fee for felony defense plus $200 to $500 per hour."

"And your cost?"

"Having discussed this with the board we decided to ask for a retainer of $1,000, then $200/hour for billable hours for civil and criminal defenses. We will not use the high-priced spread unless we are outgunned. Which may happen."

"Harry, let's do this. I don't think we're going to get anything better and I think it will not come to the 'high priced spread.'"

"I should have killed him." Sourly said.

"Yeah? Maybe next time. Well, here we are anyway. Get out the checkbook shooter." Jennifer said.

Harrison heard the hurt. "Jen?"

"I'm okay, Harry. I won't stop you next time."

"Jen, I don't blame you. I could hardly stand much less shoot again. I'm just mad at myself."

Schiefer listened as they talked. He felt for them. This was going to be a messy legal problem. Also, although this was a privileged conversation and not recorded, he knew if the federal government wanted any of his records the FBI would simply take them. If they pulled him in, he would tell all or be indicted. Still, he felt the pain of these people and wanted to help.

"I'll have our paralegal draw up a contract. For what it's worth, I think you people are handling this better than most would."

Harrison and Jennifer looked at each other. He leaned forward and kissed her. "You just stopped me from becoming a cold-blooded murderer, that's all."

"Anytime shooter. But next time for this 'thing' I'll help."

Schiefer wished he had not heard that.

Harrison got out the checkbook.

Chapter 15

"Who sent this guy? We had the deal ready to go. At least the documents are gone. But there's somebody else involved. This was a heavy hitter." The speaker was an impeccably dressed tall stiff man. His hair was fashionably graying at the temples. He was checked into the hotel by an aide. He entered through the back door.

"I don't care. He got caught and knows something. He must not testify." This was a well-muscled man. His dress was casual military. His past training with special forces was evident in his manner.

"This is somebody else's mistake. Let them deal with it. He won't talk. I've talked to the court-appointed lawyer. He is scared shitless of this guy. The lawyer will fold up like a wet napkin and toss this guy to the wolves. We can't afford to meddle. The deal is almost done. "

"What about the girl? If she doesn't hold up, the guy will walk." Clipped short words.

"So what? He will just disappear. He's the least of our worries. The Clatsop County DA is now investigating. If he makes a money connection to this guy... They could trace it back to whoever sent him and cause an investigation through the journalist." Then he added, "Could we have this guy shanked in the Seaside jail?"

"Hell, no! It couldn't be done and even if it could, it would just bring more heat. I might be able to take him out if he's set free, but that's unlikely."

"Our money trail is almost impossible to unravel. Whoever hired this guy needs to cover their own ass. We should just lay low for a while."

"Easier said than done. We've made obligations to a bunch of very volatile people. They have resources of their own. Maybe they hit this 'journalist' for another reason. We owe them and better deliver."

"What are they going to do? Hit seated Senator? Not likely. Nobody knows what's happening but us. If we go down the Russians will not benefit."

"You mistake the Russians for giving a shit. They will bury us and move on to another Senator. They know the system is in place it just needs new players who respond to easy money."

"Yeah. But it won't last. Nothing does. The Ukrainian war and how the President reacts will be old news in another year. The Russians will be on to something else. So what's the plan?"

"I'll find out what the girl knows. If it's nothing then we're okay. If it can lead back to us then make sure she doesn't or can't talk. The guy walks and disappears. We write off the cost and continue. The journalist is gone and that connection is broken."

"Too many things could go wrong. That journalist has an employer."

"No, he was freelance. His cohort, our aide, conveniently lost all his notes. He's on his way to the Bahamas until this is over. We managed to purge the online accounts of those moronic bird and face things. You are either in or out. And by out I mean you are all the way out. Got it?"

"Yeah. So how do we get to the girl?"

"Sideways. I have already handled this end. I have a person inside the Clatsop sheriffs. She made sure the DA uses our therapist to influence the girl."

"How? Whoever it is can't just insert themselves."

"This person is a certified trauma expert. My operative made sure she is in the proper rotation. She is used for rape victims and will be used here. I have no idea how, but she says it can be done. Memory is a funny thing when alcohol and near death are in proximity. A little nudge here or there can make the girl unreliable. That's all we need."

"So what are the moving pieces here? Seaside has the unknown hitman in custody. So far he is saying and we think he will say nothing. We have the only witness to the hit. She will be made unreliable. The DA and Seaside police have this guy Baker to use to prosecute the hit man for assault. We know how the courts will sentence that. He'll be out in a short time. Hopefully, he'll have to retire."

"One step at a time. Let this first act play out."

"The Russians aren't going to wait."

"You're right we need to move now. Get that cohort back. We need a mule."

"It won't be enough."

"Yeah. We have to open the pipeline now."

"Problematic. The source is not paid yet."

"We'll have to push it. Pay from that Swiss account. Take the financial hit for a while. The Russians will be happy. When they verify, the profit to us is still there. Just a little down the road."

"Where are we going to put this? It can't be on any radar. And there is plenty of that. FBI, NSA, and a plethora of competing agencies are lurking around like a clan of hyenas on a dead gnu."

"These SIM cards are easy to move and hide. It's our advantage. Voice recording on SIM is old technology. Our guy has devised a way to put a gig on it. The phones are wiped when any Cabinet meeting is done. But the SIM is intact. What the Russians want is an ongoing pipeline of the POTUS plans for any Ukrainian response. That's what we have. No matter what he blusters to the press. Straight from the presidential Cabinet meetings. One SIM at a time. That's what we must protect. Look at it this way. Putin has his finger on the nuclear button. This info shows we have no intention of provoking that. From the horse's mouth. Despite what the war dogs want. We're actually keeping the world safe."

"Yeah, and making ourselves rich in the process."

"That's the best part."

Chapter 16

Sheila Dennett had set up a murder board and timeline above her desk. It was pretty straightforward so far. She had a rough timeline. The two incidents needed to be pinned down. She had a time and witnesses to the assault. She might have a time and a witness to the murder. What she did not have were *reliable* witnesses. The girl was catatonic now and was remembering nothing. The Baker guy sounded like a nut. If a defense lawyer got wind of that 'thing' word, Baker would be torn apart on the stand.

She now had a chance to avoid all that. A meeting with the murderer himself. Now she could see for herself if the eyes were black.

As unpredictable as this two-part entwined criminal investigation was becoming, she must collect and analyze all evidence. She must develop a theory and validate it. Means, motive, and opportunity. So far she had identified and arrested the assault perpetrator and now must develop and present a case to prosecutors. She must assure that her analysis would stand up to cross-examination by both her superior, the DA, and then in the brutal cauldron of trial. She had been there before. In her experience, some attorneys were soulless sociopaths. Winning was put before anything, except money. Sure the defendants deserve to have their rights protected. But there were those who would destroy others to win and sometimes just for the fun of it. For some, it was simply a game. The rights of the witnesses were basically nonexistent when on the stand. They were merely weapons to be used or a target to be destroyed. She knew of a serial murderer that was let off on BS technicalities. This would not happen on her watch. She wanted to take this guy apart. A confession was not bulletproof but carried a lot of weight in a trial.

The suspect was recently transferred from Portland Emanuel to Seaside Providence hospital. He was healing faster than the doctors expected. Emanuel had rushed the return. Dennett had seen the medical report. This guy was one tough bastard. He had not voluntarily opened his eyes during his hospital time but still held an aura that repelled anyone near.

She arranged the interview meeting in a 'secure' ward. The court-appointed attorney was falling all over himself to be cooperative. She met him the day before. He was a big man, solid and sure. He had all the points of law in play. Yet when asked about the suspect he simply said, "See for yourself." He had seen the eyes.

The room was now wired for video and sound. Surveillance was set up. The defense attorney had okayed it. Jeffers, Johnson, and the attorney waited in the hall with the video and sound feed. The recorders were ready.

The hospital did not have an actual secure ward. At the demand, not request, of the hospital administrator, Seaside police set up a room off the Emergency area. It was essentially a supply room. The supplies were taken out. Nothing remained except the bare concrete walls. The suspect's bed and monitoring equipment were stuffed in. The door was guarded by taser-armed security personnel, who watched like it might crash open. It was locked by a brand new manual three-bolt system. It had no windows. The hospital personnel remembered this man and wanted nothing to do with him. The surveillance station was in the hall. Wires and cords snaked around from various outlets from rooms away.

Dennett wanted to interview the suspect alone. But Jeffers overrode that unconditionally. He believed the reports of the psychological danger this man carried. Not one, but two of the biggest and strongest Seaside officers were to back her. Their orders were to use lethal force at any aggression not because he thought the man would attack her but because he wanted them to be armored against it.

Dennett was not offended but wondered why all the fuss. Obviously, this guy was deemed as dangerous as Hannibal Lecter. Even wounded and handcuffed to a hospital bed? Even with all the fear evinced around her, she was sure she could break this guy like a cracker. The lawyer had waived the accused's rights. The entire time he had been in custody he had not said a word, nor done anything other than be still. He accepted no orders. He moved only when the hospital bed moved. The men who moved him stayed out of his sight as much as possible.

She had not met him yet.

She had not seen the eyes yet.

Lock and load.

The hospital security moved the bolts. Heavy metal slides scraped on unoiled guides. The officers held their hands on their weapons.

The door opened. Dennett went in before the officers, determined to appear unafraid.

And stopped dead.

The temperature in the room seemed to drop twenty degrees. It was not that the man on the bed was suddenly freed or rose up like a zombie. He simply turned his head to her and stared.

Like an insect might do.

Black eyes fixed on her. An overt threat of death oozed out. She wanted to put her hand on her weapon but could not move. She suddenly knew why she was allowed to carry her firearm into the cell, it helped like a talisman to lessen the impact of the stare, even though she could not move for a moment.

During her training, she had been tased. It was a minor charge to let cadets know what it was like. This was exponentially worse. It was like being tased in the face. The lights went out for a second. She froze.

The two officers squeezed in past her and took positions at the corners of the small room. She was suddenly glad they were there. The stare seemed lessened by their presence.

Dennett stiffened her resolve. So they were black, so what? She would not succumb to the fear the assassin tried to project. She took two more steps to the foot of the bed. Her legs felt wooden. She began, forcing her voice to be authoritative. "I am Detective Dennett of the Seaside Police." The man's black eyes stayed fixed on her. She began to lose her train of thought. She coughed and continued. "I am told you have been given your rights. Is that true?"

Nothing. No movement. No acknowledgment. Except for the stare he could have been dead.

The guards nervously shifted. Outside the open door, the security guards stood ready with their hands on their tasers.

"Okay. I would like to hear your recollection of the Halloween events that led to you being shot." Sometimes that would provoke a heated response, including accusations and denials. All of which could be used against him in a court of law.

Nothing. No movement. No acknowledgment. Except for the stare, he could have been dead.

It seemed to get even colder. Dennett involuntarily shivered. Yet she forged ahead. She had access to all the identifications this man had. None were authentic. He had been booked as John Doe, which seemed to be appropriate as all the IDs were in John 'various' names.

"Okay. You are charged with the murder of Waylon Billings. You want to tell me about that."

Nothing. No movement. No acknowledgment. Except for the stare, he could have been dead.

Dennett suddenly wanted to leave. "Okay. Thank you for your time." She backed out with the guards on either side of her.

The door closed. The heavy metallic bolts slammed shut. The temperature rose. Dennett found she was holding her breath.

Jeffers looked up at her from the video feed. "Damn. I wasn't even in there but I felt… uneasy. This guy is going to be a problem."

Dennett breathed in and out. She looked at the lawyer and nodded. "I see what you mean." This Baker guy was not crazy. In fact, that he managed to shoot this 'thing,' was becoming impressive. She was not sure she could have pulled her weapon in there.

She got no confession. But, on the upside, for sure they were going to get a conviction. The prosecutor would not have to say anything. Once the jury was in the same room and saw this assassin's eyes they would vote to hang him today - not tomorrow.

Then she reconsidered. A conviction in circuit court would be appealed to judges who would have no contact with the assassin. All they would see was a bunch of paper. She better cross the t's and dot the i's. He cannot be allowed to escape justice. She was sweating, her hands were clammy.

"Okay. The suspect is not talking. I need to get going on the evidence. We need to get this guy. Airtight."

She suddenly realized that if the murderer had not been interrupted, he would be gone with the body. She would only have an open missing person case if that. Now it was getting complicated.

She turned to leave and almost ran into a man coming in.

Chapter 17

The emergency doors had opened and Dennett was stopped in front of a short overweight man who came in like he owned the place. He was dressed to the nines. The suit and shoes probably cost more than the entire clothes rack of the police department. He was flanked by two very formidable men who looked vaguely military. He looked at Dennett and stepped around her, strode up to Johnson, and handed him some papers.

"I would like to see my client now." His voice was deep and would be well suited to a courtroom proceeding.

The court-appointed lawyer looked over Johnson's shoulder in relief. It was an order from the United States District Court designating one Hynd Ozio as counsel for one John Doe held by Seaside police. It was also a release of the said John Doe to the NSA.

Johnson was neither deterred nor intimidated. Any tiredness he felt slipped away. He had been around this block before. His radar picked up this incoming problem the second it hit the door. When he was a young man, he had a background working for a defense contractor during the initial Iraq campaign. He saw the people his employer called 'spooks' come and go. He was young and saw things in light of that. He learned that what you saw is not necessarily what you got. He learned that there are all kinds of agendas out there. What the public saw was what the current powers wanted them to see. It was partly the reason he came to Astoria after law school and service with Portland's police. Things were simpler away from seats of power. At least until now.

What he knew with certainty was that this was his prosecution for a crime that occurred in his county. It was not going to be taken by an unknown agency. What you saw was what you got with him anyway. He stepped closer to Ozio.

"Identification," he said.

Ozio waited for a beat, then wordlessly produced an NSA-certified ID. At least it looked authentic. "Detective Dennett, run this will you."

"That is not necessary, I assure you, Mr. Johnson. And causing a problem will not be in your best interests."

Johnson saw the threat. It could be real. The best way to test that was to confront it immediately. He looked at the two bodyguards, "Identification," he said. The word was spoken conversationally. The men tensed. Johnson stood pat. Ozio looked at Johnson with undisguised malice. Jeffers moved forward. Both Seaside police officers paid attention. The hospital security watched with interest but had no dog in the fight. Dennett stepped forward and waited in front of the men. Hand out.

"You are making a mistake," Ozio growled.

"You waltz into *my* county, into *my* prosecution, and say *I'm* making a mistake. What does NSA care about a murder in Seaside?

Who are you really? Who are these men behind you?" The air began to crackle with tension. Hands went to weapons. The hospital security backed away. You don't bring a taser to a gunfight.

Johnson was unarmed but stood like a solid oak tree against a flood. There was no give in him. Something about the people in front of him rankled. If there was more going on than a murder he would hear it directly from his line of authority, the Oregon Attorney General. Not from this pretentious bastard. He was not going to move now. He knew the FBI was interested; he was going to see what other alphabet agencies were afoot. If this were that big, let them fight it out amongst themselves.

Dennett waited. She looked at the men and at Ozio. This was a shit bomb and the fuse was lit. And she was in it now. She felt Jeffers move to her side. She felt the two police officers spread out behind her. What the hell? This happened so fast. The word clusterfuck came to mind. Jeffers had used it when this first hit the fan. But he was talking about the media. She felt the tension continue to rise. Any spark now would result in a bloodbath. She had her hand out waiting. The other was involuntarily on her Glock. The snap to her holster opened with a crack that she thought could have been heard in Seaside Town Hall a mile away.

For a moment it was like a picture in time. Frozen for posterity. Nobody moved.

Ozio suddenly smiled. Dennett thought he looked like a snake just before it struck. She expected to see his forked tongue slip out testing the scents around. There was nothing behind the smile. Nevertheless, the fuse went out, and the air cleared. "Very well," said Ozio with obvious disdain. "You will hear from us later. Perhaps with a contingent of Marines."

"I don't think so. Marines I know wouldn't have anything to do with you. The military cannot be used to enforce civilian laws."

Ozio continued to smile like a snake, "Think you so? We shall see." He tried to grab the papers he gave to Johnson but missed as Johnson deftly flicked them away. He then turned abruptly and nearly ran into his guards. He angrily shoved his way out to the limo waiting in the emergency lane. The three supposed NSA representatives climbed in and it sped away.

Dennett and Jeffers followed them out. "Did you get that license plate?"

"Got it!" answered Dennett.

Johnson turned to the hospital security guards. "Get the admin. We're taking this guy right now. Jeffers, can the Seaside jail handle this?"

"Yes, sir. We have that capability. I'll call Medix for transport. I think we should sedate him first."

The security detail was only too happy to help rid the hospital of this problem and spoke into their comms. "She says 'take him.' A sedative is being prepped. We need your guys to stand by during administration."

A few minutes later an orderly came down. The door was opened and the two Seaside officers went in weapons ready. The man on the bed watched with black-as-death eyes as the orderly, eyes averted, nervously inserted the needle into the IV drip line and pushed the plunger. The man closed his eyes. There was no change in his mien. Nothing to suggest he was relaxed.

No movement. No acknowledgment. He could have been dead.

"Is he out?" asked one of the officers.

"Damned if I know, that stuff I gave him would knock out a rhino, but I'm not touching him to find out."

Johnson was suddenly animated. "This is turning into a shit show. The spook intervention makes this guy as high an assassin as can be bought. There is money here, and power. Anyone who wants out better leave now. We are about to get a first-hand look at interagency cooperation."

"What?" asked Dennett.

"Exactly," said Johnson. "There is no such thing. People are going to be ruined. Let's make sure it's not us. At least not all of us. I will check the NSA docs and license plate. You will stay out of this," he addressed Jeffers. "Concentrate on the murder, nothing else."

Chapter 18

Back at the station, 'clusterfuck' came to Dennett's mind again. Ugly political infighting. With overtones of hidden danger. A shadowy landscape of agencies competing for prestige and power. Sociopaths and psychopaths with agendas incompatible with justice, gleefully wielding power just to see what happens, with no care as to who gets hurt. Vendettas and revenge dredged up and chased. Players with advanced degrees in subterfuge having fun applying them.

Yet she knew some of those people from her cross-training at Quantico. Not the top brass, but special agents from the FBI. They were really trying to do a good job. But they were following orders from those with power. So was she. What happens when justice departments are at cross purposes? When each wanted a single asset under their control.

Infighting.

There was another thing. She knew and had done it herself, that criminals were used to trap other criminals. The law tried to get the bigger fish and toss back the smaller. The smaller fish then became the bigger. It was rare that law enforcement could wrap up an entire criminal enterprise. In fact, she had never seen it happen. But that did not stop them from trying.

What she knew from personal experience was that all these agencies were run by and populated with obsessive, and aggressive people. People with their own political ideas of justice. Just as she had her own ideas. She also knew that most people who sought positions of power thought they were God's gift to the world. If they were just left to run the thing, all would be well.

To be honest, she knew she did too. She knew how it should be. The difference was that she knew there were limitations to the use of power and others believed there were none.

She needed to know the landscape here. She thought back on her training. There were three general policing departments under the president. The Department of Defense, who oversaw the NSA, the Department of Justice, and in the cabinet the Director of National Intelligence. The DNI oversaw the National Intelligence Program and the Central Intelligence Agency. Each had their interests overlap. Who was actually running things now was in question. She was pretty sure POTUS was absent. Without an iron ethical hand at the top, the underlings would have a field day lunging for the ring. Nobody at the top would pay any price for whatever clusterfuck went down, they were masters at deflection. But those at the bottom would feel the pain. Some would be prosecuted. Some would be hurt. Some would die. The word clusterfuck did not cover the coming pain.

At the bottom of the hierarchy were state, county, and then city forces. These were insignificant and expendable when it came to federal power.

This guy Ozio said he was from the National Security Agency, who answered to the DoD, who answered to the doddering politically correct obsessed president. If that were true then Johnson and Jeffers would be run over like roadkill. And she also would be right there under the wheels of that unbridled power. If it were not true then something else was afoot. Another agency? CIA? Certainly, someone with connections. It would be too easy to check for fraud. Johnson held the papers.

For now, she had her orders. She quit musing and started analyzing. She went back to the station ahead of the Medix wagon and sat at her desk, thinking. What came to mind was that this supposed NSA intervention gave her a hint to work with. She looked at her murder board. At the timeline blanks and again thought that this was going to be… no. It was right now a plutonium clusterfuck.

Okay, she reflected. When it all looks so confusing, find a thread and pull it. Follow the money or follow the power? The safest thing was to just stand back and watch the show. But she could not do that. Nor could she look at the money or power actors. All she could do was put together a simple murder and assault case. Just the facts, ma'am, just the facts. The killer was hanging himself. And the lawyer was letting him.

She picked up the phone called the coroner and made an appointment to see the body. She then sat and wondered who would want the FBI informant dead. Maybe it was the journalism's cover that someone wanted dead. Maybe it was a mistake.

She called sergeant Miller over. He was a competent field officer and the resident computer guy. Miller was as sharp as could be with the department equipment and net connections they had. He came over to her desk from the air-conditioned server room next to his cubicle. He was not a nerd-looking guy. He was a football quarterback in college. He was tall, strong, and handsome. Dennett was always surprised at the contrast with what was the nerd stereotype. He was also a competent public relations officer.

"Yes, ma'am?"

"Sergeant, I told you before, just because I'm so damned together and a lieutenant doesn't mean you have to call me ma'am. Find all you can about this victim," she continued, "Who was he? I want to know what he ate for breakfast, what side of the bed he got out of, what he was working on, and who the hell he was working for."

"Sure, detective," Miller laughed. "I don't know about his breakfast or sleeping arrangements. I've found some other info though. He was divorced last year. No big court fights. He left his job at the Oregonian three years ago. He was self-employed earning a little over fifty grand a year. Fancied himself a whistleblower. He was involved in several previous attempts to implicate the Oregon legislature and governor as being incompetent or corrupt. Nothing stuck and he was branded as a..." he pulled out a notebook and found the correct words, "'Right-wing Trump-loving piece of shit.' According to a PDF, I managed to find from the Salem office of Senator Krantz from Oregon's 1st congressional district archives. "

"Hah! You've been busy. Why'd you pick Krantz? And what kind of blowback could you get?"

"This was part of the legislative log. Found it in a search for Waylon Billings. Krantz had it in for this guy. It was pretty open."

"Okay. You should know that we've been instructed to stay on the murder track and out of the fed's way. What I'm looking for is motive. Why kill this guy? But... you should be aware we are on thin ice here. If the motive the killer had was money for assassination, we are out of bounds according to Johnson."

"Not me. I just follow orders. But if I stumble across something, I'll let you know."

He went back to his cubicle. Dennett started thinking about motive. Could Johnson prosecute without a clear motive? Sure he could. The killer would be enough. She plowed on, gathered the canvas notes and began to search for other witnesses.

Before she forgets about it, she puts a suicide watch on the thing. Not so much because she thought he might actually try to kill himself as she wanted to observe him. She activated the cell cameras and microphones. She activated the recorder. She would review the thing's first day and night at the Seaside jail.

Maybe there was a clue in there.

Chapter 19

As Dennett pursued the case, in another section of the Providence Hospital, Johanna lay unmoving. Her dull blue eyes stared at nothing, while monitors obediently recorded her vitals. Temperature, blood pressure, heart rate, respiration, and oxygen saturation were all within acceptable limits. Her brother was with her now. Her parents were in the coffee shop waiting their turn in the rotation. They were taking eight-hour shifts. Keeping her eyes moistened. Talking to her. Hoping.

Outside, the Medix containing the suspect pulled away and headed to Wahana road. The 'thing' rode alone in the back. The men in the cab nervously watched the window. Police cars met it in the lower parking lot. At the Wahana intersection, the convoy turned and sped off with cruisers fore and aft, flashing their lights and clearing the way.

The demon had left the building.

Johanna suddenly spasmed under the bed covers. The monitors jumped. Her heart rate and blood pressure shot into the danger zone. Alarms sounded and a nurse rushed in. Then a doctor. Then more personnel. Jack was pushed out and stood impotently with the police guard.

The eyes had breached Johanna's door. They were in her safe room. She could not hide; she could not run. She again prepared to die. Was this the way of her life now? Preparing to die?

She went into a helpless screaming panic.

Then she was adrift. Outside of her safe room. Somewhere else. Something had slowed the eyes. But she knew they would breach whatever it was and find her again.

There was a flurry of activity that Jack could not follow. Hospital personnel surrounded the bed. After what seemed like a long time, one of the figures detached from the cluster. He removed his mask and walked to Jack. His face was unreadable.

"What happened?"

"She's had a panic attack. One of the most severe I've ever seen. But she's stable now. I will call for psychiatric help at this point. The sedation is no longer working for her and is becoming detrimental. She needs help that I can't give her."

Jack saw the concern in this doctor, but he had his own. "What about me, can I have a chance to see if I can reach her?"

"You've been here the entire time. What can you do that you haven't done?"

"Well, there's always been others around. What I can do must be done alone."

"You cannot abuse her!"

"God no! I know things that are somewhat sensitive to her and not for our parents or the police. Or you for that matter."

"We aren't sure she can hear you, or anyone at this point."

"Call the shrink, but let me try. Right now, before my parents get here."

"No! Her parents… your parents must agree to anything like this."

"They'll be here in a few minutes. They're just taking a break in the cafeteria. Wait here." Jack sped off down the stairs to the small cafeteria. He found them sitting with their heads together talking at a small round table near windows to the outside parking lot.

"Mom, Dad, come on. I need you to talk to the doctor for me."

"What's happened?"

"She's had a panic attack and is still in a coma. The doctor doesn't know what to do and I want to try something."

"What?"

"Come on," Jack pleaded.

Holding hands the parents rose and followed Jack who was practically running. They kept up, even up the stairs to the waiting doctor who motioned them over to a vacant room. They stood around expectantly looking at Jack who suddenly felt unsure of how to say what he wanted to do.

"Okay. I think I can get through to Joh. But I have to do it in private. She can't be afraid to talk. Something happened to her that's bad, but she carries a lot of other stuff right now. I can help with the other stuff."

"No matter what, we love her and can forgive any teenage mistakes," said Pamela.

"She knows that but she's got that tangled up with whatever happened to her."

"Look, we know she was drunk. We know she was at a party that we did not approve of. That can be worked out," Tye said.

"That's not it Dad, let me try!"

"I think the boy may be right," put in the doctor. "You seem to be a close-knit family. But the bond I see between him and his sister is… different than the parental bond. There is no authority, no judgment from him. My advice is to give it a try. As a doctor, I have done all I can and the patient is not responding. I have called the county for psychiatric help. But in my opinion, that is useless unless the patient is awake and aware." Spoken wryly.

Tye and Pamela looked at each other and came to the same silent conclusion. Both nodded. Jack bolted for the door. The doctor followed. "Please clear the room," he ordered. There were nurses and attendants still present, still monitoring the equipment as if waiting for another attack. They thankfully left with the doctor who held them in reserve in the hall.

Jack pulled the privacy curtain around the bed. He stood looking at Johanna's pale face. Her open eyes stared at nothing, or at something really bad. There was no movement. No sign of life other than the soft raise and fall of her chest. The monitors were silent.

Indecision gripped him. His heart began to beat faster, and his face beaded sweat. He shook. It was as if he felt her fear. This was going to be harder than he thought. Nevertheless, he plowed on. Carefully, he took her hand. It was cold and clammy. He bent forward and placed his head next to hers so he was speaking in her ear. He wanted no one else to hear. Softly he whispered, "Keep your feet on the floor, Joh. And your pants on." It was an attempt to rewind the last days and elicit a snide sisterly response. Nothing. "Joh! Tell me you didn't!" Nothing. He had to risk the elevated sound. "Okay. So I'm going to be an uncle, huh? Who's the father? Do you even know?" he got louder, scoffing. "So you didn't know what you were doing. I thought I warned you. I thought you were smart. What a mistake!" Jeering, laughing.

That did it. Her eyes blinked, closed.

"Leave me alone you cretin," she mumbled.

"Can't do that this time, Joh. We need to have a serious talk about the birds and the bees. Look at me. Use your eyes, look at me!" Jack moved from her ear to within inches of her face.

Her eyes flickered, opened. Her body twitched. The monitors showed an increased heart rate that the sedatives could not suppress. Jack sat further back and squeezed her hand. "I'm right here Joh," he said aloud. "Look at me!" He moved closer again.

Her eyes flicked closed, open, closed, open. Jack was the only thing in her field of vision. Light leaked in. She tried to focus. Her eyes watered. She tried to wipe them but the IVs and arm sling got in the way.

"It's okay, Joh. I got that." He used his fingers to wipe the tears away. She managed to focus on his face. He saw her eyes clear up. "You did keep your pants on didn't you?" he chided, prodded.

"God, you are insufferable! What are you doing in my room?"

Her room? Alright, Jack thought, now what? Go with the truth – partially. "Joh, this is a hospital. There's been an accident. You've been hurt." He pulled back so she could see.

"What... what happened?"

Jack was now in even deeper water. What indeed? More partial truth.

"You were hit by a car on your way to the Jorgensons. Your arm was broken."

Confusion crossed her face. She was moved out of her breached safe room and into this hospital. A feeling of safety came. Then the eyes followed. Then terror. The monitor's heart rate rose. Jack saw and leaned close. "Whatever happened. You're safe now, here, with me and Mom and Dad. Joh - they want to see you. Don't worry about the party. They love you."

The eyes retreated. Johanna sagged back into the bed. "God, I'm sorry."

"Don't worry. It'll be alright."

"No, there's something… else. I can't remember. Something… Demon!" she cried. Her eyes turned inward. Her face contorted.

That caught Jack by surprise. But before she could relapse, he butted in on her thoughts. "One thing at a time, Joh. Mom and Dad want to see you."

Johanna began to cry. It started as a low sobbing and turned into a loud wailing. That caused the room door to open, the curtain slid aside and Johanna's mother and father closed in like a protective blanket.

The doctor was amazed. The patient's turnaround was nothing short of miraculous. He sent the responders back to their stations. He stood and watched for a time and started formulating a paper in his mind. This needed to be told. This needed to be preserved in print. But not yet. The story was still unfolding.

What happened here, just now, was outside his medical knowledge. He would find out what that was.

Chapter 20

The Editor sat on the edge of the bed in his cell. The pain of his gunshot wounds was forgotten. Ramrod straight, his dark eyes staring straight ahead at maybe something only he could see, or maybe nothing at all.

The night watch entered the block. He looked at the man in the cell. Then looked away.

Nothing. No movement. No acknowledgment. Except for the stare he could have been dead.

The guard's job was done for the moment. In another ten minutes, he would have to do it again. He was not looking forward to that. He was wishing the time would go faster but the man in the cell seemed to slow the progress. He entered the visit on the log "No change," and went back to the safety of the front desk.

The Editor might sit like he is comatose but inside the façade, he is thinking. This is a first for him. Being in a cell. But that is not burdensome. Something else is working its way into his consciousness. In his life, for as long as he could remember, he had no past and no future. He had no wants, no needs. All was taken care of by an anonymous donor who only required that he perform an edit once in a while. The training and means were supplied.

He should not care. There was only now. That included waiting, then when the letters came, there was planning and executing an edit. There was never anything else.

But now there was. He remembers a man, a gun - pain. Mostly he remembers that his edit was foiled. That was unacceptable. It must be reversed.

But the past cannot be reversed. The edit was partly successful. The target was dead. But he did not disappear.

The Editor could not reconcile this. His ordered mind was incapable of accepting failure. There was always nothing but planning and execution. Now there was an interruption. To maintain his sanity he must complete the edit. It was too late to dispose of the body. It was on an autopsy table somewhere. But the edit must be completed. How? The solution came. The man with the gun, the man who interrupted the edit, must disappear. In his fevered mind that would satisfy the edit.

He did not think about escaping. That would be easy but would attract too much attention in this country. Without his contacts, he would be easy to identify. He set to planning. Comfortable back in his standard operating procedure. Back in the way it should be.

Inside The Editor, the parasite waited and anticipated. The host's eyes were now untethered. It had gleefully fed on the fear of the various people who tried to talk to its host. It was delicious. But not filling. It needed to taste that last hope as a soul was extinguished. It needed to feast. Reading the host's simple thoughts it knew that feast was coming.

At that exact time, the monitors picked up just a flicker in his eyes. Then the watch came in the block. The guard looked and then looked away.

Nothing. No movement. No acknowledgment. He could have been dead.

The guard entered the visit on the log "No change," and went back to the safety of the front desk.

Inside The Editor's mind, a plan was forming.

Inside that plan, the parasite's anticipation and hunger were growing.

Chapter 21

Dennett arrived at the county morgue early the next morning after the interview with the suspect, the… 'thing.' She decided to stay with Baker's description. It seemed apt. The Medical Examiner Division of the sheriff's office was located along with the county jail on a dead-end road off 19th in Warrenton. The drive was easy.

The rain had stayed to the north and the sky was thinly overcast with a little blue showing through. The sun had yet to make a steady appearance.

She got out and walked to the building. Inside she presented her credentials and was escorted to the autopsy room. It was colder here than outside.

The medical examiner waited with the body covered by a surgical blanket. Dennett had seen bodies before. Some were a mess after traffic accidents. And some were on autopsy tables. She never could understand why she was repulsed by an autopsy. Someone's body being deliberately sliced and diced to determine the cause of death was different from damage caused by an accident.

The smell of decay, antiseptics, and internal organs could not be completely eliminated by the air conditioning. A dead body remained. The examiner, Lisa Benoit, stood almost protectively across the stainless steel table.

Dennett put on her mask stepped up to the opposite side and said, "Thank you for seeing me. The DA wants this wrapped up quickly." She had been in this room before and knew Benoit professionally. She liked the way Benoit was compassionate, especially with grieving relatives of accidental deaths. Murders were rare but Benoit was an expert at handling those people who were affected. Her reports were concise and accurate.

Benoit nodded. "Yes. I've been notified. What do you need to know?"

"Okay. Whatever you have so far."

"The blood work is still out being processed. But I see no evidence of impairment. The deceased ate a full meal just minutes before death. There was alcohol indicated in the stomach contents but again the blood work is still pending."

"Okay. I guess I need two things right now: cause of death and time of death."

"Let me show you the cause of death," Benoit pulled the blanket down to the victim's chest exposing the sutures and more importantly the neck. "See here," she pointed and turned the head so that the separation of the spinal cord to the skull was apparent. The head wobbled without support. "This is called Atlanto-occipital dislocation. Internal decapitation."

Dennett bent to see. "Okay. How much force is required to do this? Any sign of a struggle?"

"No indication the victim fought back and the force required is not in my area of expertise. But I am told by those who know that with the proper technique, not much, depending on the fight put up by the victim. Again there is no indication he fought back. But the pressure exerted in holding the victim's head was extraordinary. See here, the bruising from the perpetrator's hands indicates that he was standing in front of the victim gripping the head. Both hands were used. The hand size is larger than average." She put her hand over the bruise to show the scale. She was an average-sized woman but her hand looked like a child's next to the bruise. "The strength and speed of the perpetrator would have to be more than average to prevent someone from protesting being decapitated," she finished.

Dennett knew as much, to get a man to stand still for it would be hard. Unless he was paralyzed with fear. Something the assassin could do. Something she knew firsthand. She involuntarily pictured the murder. The twist, the sound. She fought her way out of the fog.

"Okay. Time of death?"

"Now we're into an area you would know more about than I. I received the body within an hour of discovery. It is my opinion that death was within an hour before that. It is as precise as medically possible with liver temperature. The body was reportedly discovered at 10:26 after a 911 call by a civilian. I received the body at 11:43 pm on October 31st of this year. Time of death estimated between 9:30 and 10:00."

That gave a little help to the timeline. The assassin had not been driving around with it for a while. Did the Bergstrom girl actually witness the murder? It sure followed. Her trauma from witnessing a murder and the 'thing's' eyes could have sent her over the line.

"Thank you. If anything else comes up, let me know."

"Sure. You should know that the DA wants the report to be held for his review. There is to be no electronic recording without his approval."

"Okay. Then thank you for the heads up."

"You're welcome. Nail this creep."

"Okay. I'll do my best. You should probably know that federal agencies will be sticking their noses in soon."

"Yeah. I've been warned. But all I do is make reports. What happens after that is out of my hands."

"Okay. Right up until you're called to testify and the report needs your provenance."

"I've found the truth is a good shield. And a copy is a good thing to keep."

"Okay. Things are going to be messy for a while. I've got a feeling the truth is about to be challenged. The alphabet agencies have a kind of interest in this case. Keep your head down."

"You too."

Dennett drove back under a clearing sky. A cold wind had picked up from the north and traffic spray from the recent rain kept her wipers on low. Upon arriving at the station she was notified that the Chief wanted to see her ASAP. She hustled into his office through an open door.

"Don't sit down detective." Jeffers started right off. His voice was low and urgent. This was a personal communique. "Johanna Bergstrom has regained consciousness. I want you to get over there and interview her now. Make sure the parents, and a lawyer if they want, are on hand. This is an interview not an interrogation. Nobody else can be there. All notes will be on paper. You will control the paper. Take a picture of the suspect with you.

You know we want a positive ID. If she happens to remember any words spoken, get that too. The FBI and NSA are on their way. Get this done before they muck it up. Go now."

Dennett had no chance to say anything.

She went back out to her cruiser and used the lights to clear a path to the hospital. Three minutes later she parked with the ambulances and hurried in. Johanna was in a private room. She spoke quickly to the guard, "No one gets in while I'm here." He nodded and put the chair aside, and stood with purpose.

Inside were the Bergstroms with their son. Johanna lay pale and quiet. Dennett suddenly remembered she did not know their names, nor did they know her. She took out her shield and showed it to them.

"I am Seaside detective Sheila Dennett." She took out her notebook. "Who do we have here?"

The Bergstroms were surprised at the sudden appearance of this tall straight woman and the urgency expressed but Tye recovered quickly. "I am Tye Bergstrom and this is my wife Pamela. This is my son, Jack," pointing to a well-built teenager who looked on with an interested gaze. Nobody offered their hands. "What do you want?" guarded tone.

"Okay. Pardon my hurry here. I have to do several things as quickly as possible. First: please do not talk to anyone about this incident. Second: there will be federal agencies who will be asking questions. Know this: every word you may say will be vetted six ways from Sunday. There are penalties for offering misinformation. These agencies have agendas that are not in your best interest. Third: get a lawyer. One who knows his way around this type of…" she almost said clusterfuck, "problem. Fourth: anything said here stays here. I have no recording device right now unlike the other agencies.

Only paper. I need to investigate and charge a man for the murder of a journalist. Your daughter may have information critical to that. I am now asking to interview her." Dennett stopped and looked at the perplexed faces as they processed her remarks.

Again Tye was the first to recover. "Detective Dennett, what's the rush? Why the secrecy?"

"Okay. I can't comment on the secrecy but I need to get ahead of the publicity. Your daughter, Johanna, may have seen and heard a murder. May I please interview her? I guarantee none of this interview will become public knowledge. But… you should know there will likely be a trial for the murderer and her testimony may be required." Dennett was on shaky ground here. She was supposing and guessing. Any other time she would simply ask questions. But time was short.

"And if Johanna doesn't remember what happened?"

"Okay. There may be court-appointed counselors to try to get her to remember. Look, as much as we want to keep you out of this, that is not possible. The assault and attempted kidnap of your daughter and shooting of the perpetrator are going to be in the news big time. All I need at this time for probable cause to hold the perpetrator is for Johanna to identify the… this man as the one who murdered the journalist." She showed the picture to Tye. Pamela and their son looked over his shoulder. The doom seemed to lift off the picture and fill the room.

"This is moving too fast," said Pamela and looked quickly away. "We need time to think."

"All I need is an identification. Please, just the one question,"

The Bergstroms looked at each other. Then at Johanna, who was listening but not reacting. Jack went to her side. "Joh?" She turned her eyes to him. "Remember when we talked before?" she nodded weakly. "I will protect you; you know that." Nod. "I want you to look at a picture and tell me if this man killed another. Can you do that?"

Johanna tensed up. Her eyes darted around the room. She began to make little whimpering sounds. Jack grabbed her hand. "It's alright Joh. It's alright. You're safe. I'm here. Mom and Dad are here. You're safe."

Johanna calmed down and spoke for the first time, "It was the demon. The shark."

"Joh, what did he look like?" Jack had taken over the interview and Dennett let him. Her parents were close but did not interfere.

"Demon, shark, teeth… *eyes*!"

Dennett flashed back on her interview of the thing. Yes, the eyes. She got an idea. She used her pen to block out the eyes in the picture she brought. The face was bland without those black fathomless eyes that not even the photo could calm, and there was no smile to show teeth. "Jack? Please try this," she showed it to him and the parents. This would never stand up in a court of law but all she needed was confirmation that she was on the right track.

The three looked at each other. "What do you think, Jack?" asked Pamela.

"Joh, will you look at a picture for me?" Johanna weakly nodded again.

"Alright. I'm right here, Mom and Dad are right here. Nothing can hurt you here." He carefully held the picture up with he and his parents close.

The reaction was startling.

Johanna's eyes went dead. She stopped fidgeting. A calmness surrounded her. "That's him. That's the demon. But now he is without his teeth and eyes."

Dennett wrote that down word for word. "Okay. Thank you, Johanna. Can you remember if there were any words spoken?"

Johanna's face twitched. Her eyes moved with her thoughts. "I know one of them said something. He was trying to explain something… but I can't… I didn't understand."

"That's okay, Johanna. You've been a big help."

Dennett turned to the Bergstroms, "Okay. If Johanna remembers, call me. Tell no one else." She handed Tye her card. "And thank you, Jack, you are an amazing son and brother."

Jack actually blushed. "I just did what I thought was right."

"You did that alright." Dennett turned to leave.

There was a commotion at the curtained glass door.

Chapter 22

Dennett saw shadows moving against the opaque curtain. She slipped around the curtain and slid open the glass door. The Seaside officer stood with arms crossed in front of him facing three dark-suited people. These were of the federal type she noted. Who now? The center person was a medium-height woman with short black hair and piercing brown eyes. She was confronting the Seaside officer who stood six feet tall and was probably twice her weight. She was not deterred. Behind her stood two tall men in the same government-type dark suits. They both had sidearm bulges under their coats. If the woman were armed Dennett could not see it. The woman was talking in a low official voice, expecting to be obeyed.

"Stand aside. This is a direct order from a National Security Agent." The officer did not answer or move.

Dennett stepped out and stood next to the officer. "Who are you?" politely asked. One damned thing after another.

The woman looked at Dennett and said. "I am senior agent Mara Walker of the NSA. I have full authority to question the person known as Johanna Bergstrom. Who are you to question me? Stand aside!" This was spoken as a declarative statement. Expecting to be obeyed.

Unnoticed, the officer quietly spoke into his comm.

"Not yet agent. I am Seaside police detective Sheila Dennett. I am holding Ms. Bergstrom as a material witness to a crime committed within the Seaside city limits. May I ask what your interest is? And why there was no courtesy call to us. And why your agency sent a lawyer for the accused." This was flatly spoken and accusatory. Dennett watched the reaction to the last statement for recognition. There was none. This agent had been around the block and knew her stuff. There was no way to tell if she did or did not know of the fake NSA agent.

"That is not your business detective. Stand aside." Again spoken tiredly as if Dennett were of no consequence.

The men move closer. The guard dropped his hands to his side. Dennett grew nervous. This had the makings of an incident that would reverberate through her investigation. Similar to the one when the phony NSA tried to take the 'thing.'

"Show me your credentials and warrant." Dennett wanted to assert dominance in this meeting.

"The NSA does not need one. This is a matter of national security." Ignoring the credential request.

Dennett was thinking. "What about the FBI and your other agent, Ozio? Should that not be a part of this? And yes you need a warrant. It may come from that secret bunch of judges that validated the Russian hoax, but it is necessary." Dennett pushed ahead with the Ozio gambit.

"You know nothing detective. If I make a call you will be held in a dark ops room until this is over."

For the first time, the Seaside officer spoke aloud. "Try it!" His dark eyes flashed with overt hostility. Walker did not step back. Her agents stiffened. The officer put his hands on his belt.

Dennett coughed. "Okay. No need for force here." She heard sirens coming. She saw more people walking down the hall. Two women dressed casually and a man dressed like a sort of neo-hippy in jeans with a long blond ponytail and a three-day beard. She recognized one woman as a reporter for the Seaside Signal newspaper and the other as a columnist for the Daily Astorian newspaper. The third was the man carrying a lightweight camera which swung up to point at the group standing in front of the hospital room. This was a big story and reporters were on standby.

Agent Walker noted the arrivals and the sirens and was not deterred. "Detective, if I am not allowed to question the witness this will turn into something you do not want."

"Threats will get you nowhere, agent. This is *my* witness; however, *I* will allow *you alone* to enter and ask your questions. The news crew will have access. Your men will not. Note that the parents and son are now with the witness and will remain. If they ask for an attorney or to stop at any time you will stand down."

"You do not dictate to the NSA."

"Yet I just have." More officers were arriving. "Unless you want a war. Like Ozio threatened. Do you have a Marine unit near?" She almost sneered. "Do this the easy way. No rubber hoses or drugs. Understand." It was not a question.

The hall filled up with police. Through the crowd came an older heavy-set woman, briskly pushing through the congestion. She came directly to Dennett and said, "What is going on here, detective?" She did not look at agent Walker.

Walker interrupted, "Who are you?"

"I am the director of this hospital and will brook no violence, nor intimidation." She turned to Jeffers, who had also pushed through the crowd. "Please tell your men to leave."

"Yes, ma'am. As soon as this situation is resolved."

The director turned back to Dennett, "What will it take to resolve this, detective?"

"Okay. There is an offer on the table to agent Walker. She may enter and question *my* witness. The parents and news people will attend that questioning."

"What say you, agent?"

There was a long pause as Walker assessed the situation. There was no good way to use force or threats at this time. She did not think for a moment that the agency could not silence or cancel these small-town newspapers in an after-action. But it would be a failure on her part and compromise the mission with exposure. Especially if the name she thought could have been heard came up and was published. The people responsible would disappear and the espionage case would be compromised.

"Stay here," she ordered her people. "No news people," she looked at Dennett.

"Agreed." Dennett did not want that problem yet either.

Dennett slid the door open and poked her head inside. "There is an agent from the National Security Agency who would like to ask a few questions of Johanna. I and you will witness this. If at any time you feel threatened or uncomfortable, I will suspend the questioning. But you should know the NSA will eventually get an interview. I think this is the best we can do." She saw the look Mr. Johanson gave. Another war waited inside the room. One that Johanson would ultimately lose. If Johnson tried to interfere, she would need to pick a side. It would be Johanson's but she also would ultimately lose. It would take a court order but she was sure the NSA could do that with ease. She would not even know from where it was issued. Only that it was accompanied by US Marshals.

Johanson would be arrested. The girl would be destroyed.

Then she suddenly had a brilliant idea. She turned to agent Walker. "Agent, I have a request."

Chapter 23

"What, detective Dennett, do you want now? This will just get heavier if you stall."

"Okay. I ask that you interview the suspect first. A confession from the principle suspect would be far better than this traumatized young woman. And you will need to do this interview and get his statement to go forward in any case."

Walker thought. This offer was a way around the impasse. She could get what she wanted without undue force. The NSA management ordered her to focus on the victim. It was thought that the assassin was too tough a nut to crack. She had no doubt that she could prevail. The name coming from the assassin would be the best evidence. Success would buy her forgiveness for circumventing the process.

"Accepted. Will you allow me to bring my drugs and rubber hose to the interview of the suspect - without all the witnesses?"

"Of course."

Maybe there was hope for the NSA after all. Dennett poked her face in the room and explained what was happening. She let them know the NSA would probably be back, and so would she.

"Okay," Dennett turned to Walker. "We small-town folk have had no luck with this man. Maybe you can crack him. In my opinion, you will need the rubber hose. Follow me."

The procession left. The hospital parking lot emptied out. The hospital breathed a sigh of relief. Tension ebbed. The assassin was placed in the station's secure cell. The men who moved him carefully avoided his closed eyes. In the cell the assassin opened his eyes. Something wanted to feed on what was coming.

The Seaside police building parking lot filled up. Tension rose. Dennett led the NSA agents through the hall to the jail. Outside the door she faced Walker.

"All kidding aside. I suggest you take both agents in with you. I will have men positioned to help mitigate the man's psychological effects."

Walker would have none of it. This was her chance to break the case. "That will not be necessary. Guard," she called "Open the door."

The room door opened. To agent Walker it was as if the temperature in the cell block dropped, she shivered, and her agents stiffened. The police guard went to the cell door and stood uncertainly. Dennett said, "I caution you to stay outside the cell."

"Open the cell," Walker said through clenched teeth. She would show these small-town pussies how it was done.

Dennett did not try again. Let the agent's education begin.

The guard unlocked the steel cage and stepped back. The man who had sat like a statue until now turned his head and stared at Walker.

Like an insect might do.

Walker went blank for a moment. She stood motionless at the doorway. Once during a bust of a cyber net at a house in DC, she had been surprised by a man with a double-barreled shotgun. The two bores had pointed at her face like portals to hell. Her partner had taken down the man but for that moment she was paralyzed.

This was worse, much worse. For a moment she could not see, she could not move. There was no overt threat, just a sure promise of coming Hell. She blinked and tried to get her bearings back.

Then like Dennett before, she forged ahead. She was not a pussy. She took one step. Then another. She felt like her feet were mired in concrete. She suddenly wanted the rubber hose. Or maybe a nuke. She stopped. Breathed in.

"I am agent Walker of the NSA. You will answer my questions."

Nothing. No movement. No acknowledgment. Except for the stare he could have been dead.

"Who hired you?"

Nothing. No movement. No acknowledgment. Except for the stare he could have been dead.

"Answer or there will be consequences," her voice involuntarily went up. Almost a squeak.

Nothing. No movement. No acknowledgment. Except for the stare he could have been dead.

The NSA agents behind her shifted nervously, their hands involuntarily went to their pistols. Walker then did what Dennett had done before. She retreated. "Very well. You will have time to think about this. It has no happy ending."

The cell door closed and locked. The contingent left the cell block and that door was locked. The air marginally cleared.

"God! Fucking! Damn!" muttered Walker.

"Okay. You see what happened to the Bergstrom girl. I'm walking a thin line here. I can get you your information, but if you try to forcibly extract it she may be pushed to insanity. Let me handle her. She has identified the killer. She heard something. That's what I have now."

"I cannot stand down but I will let you take the lead if I can attend as a full partner. I am charged with getting the name of who hired this assassin. Or whatever else I can get from the witness."

"Done. Let's get out of here."

Back in the conference room, Dennett sat across from Walker. "Okay, let's assess. I've managed to get the hospital report on the assassin's wounds," she said.

"So what does that tell us?"

"This Baker guy is a good shot even under that pressure exerted by the assassin. He was using a military-style Sig Sauer nine. He put three into what he called the 'thing' at about twelve to fifteen feet. The first passed through the 'things' arm and entered the chest cavity… one-inch penetration." She let that sink in. "The second and third were direct center mass. All were within a six-inch circle. None were a killing shot. None penetrated a vital organ nor hit an artery. As a fact, none penetrated more than two inches. In an ordinary man, these were killing shots. If they didn't hit a bone they would pass through an ordinary body."

"What was he shooting? Practice rounds?"

"Okay. We checked the pistol. It was in fine working condition. The rounds left in the magazine were full-power NATO 124-grain brass jacketed bullets. The same as were recovered from the body of the suspect. The bullets were flattened like they had hit wood."

"Was the 'thing' wearing armor?"

"No."

"What the hell do we have here?"

"Okay. We've been beating around the bush, but we've both seen the assassin up close. This 'thing' is an unknown… 'thing.'"

"Yeah. But how does that help? We can't be calling him a 'thing' out loud."

"Okay. Yeah. Not for the public, but it seems apt for casual use. And like Baker said, the next time shoot for the head."

"Bad choice of target, detective. Center mass is what's taught."

"Okay. It did put him down. After three rounds. But the paramedics said he was conscious and whatever bleeding happened had stopped by the time they got there. He was just surviving. Eyes closed. Not wanting to be shot more. Baker was right on target. Even the enhanced assassin could not survive too many hits. And Baker said he was zeroing in on the head."

Walker thought for a moment. "Baker was going to shoot him on the ground?"

"Yes, and he was not afraid to say that. And we know why."

"Then we need to put this 'thing' away. Whatever prison he's put into will have a few less predators anyway. Anyone who challenges him will be dead meat."

"Okay. Let's put him there. Here's what we have." Dennett went to the timeline posted on her corkboard.

The discussion went on for most of the afternoon. Walker was carefully avoiding discussing her "interview" with the assassin. Finally, she asked for that issue to be buried. She now needed to interview the Bergstrom girl.

Dennett agreed to forget the 'thing' interview, but Johanna was still off-limits. They would have to find another way.

In the end, Walker wrote up her notes that described the witness as unresponsive, and had her second agent run them up the ladder. She wanted to know what the 'thing' was. She had been briefed about the assassination that was thought to be about a security leak at the White House, but nothing more. The 'thing' was either unknown to NSA or was being covered up for now. Then she remembered the orders not to interrogate the suspect. The brass knew what it was!

Inside The Editor the parasite gleefully chewed on the fear of the latest visitor. It was gathering more and more freedom to reach out for food as the host became more and more unstable. A feast was coming. It could still taste the terror of the edit. It could still taste the wonderful terror of the young one and then the muted terror of the shooter. But both had been saved by an unknown other. In the meantime, it was sustained with the various food presented and it could smell the fear. The last two were delicious but unfilling. It sensed more to come. But it sensed another at work during the last feast. It saved the young one and the shooter. It was vexing. The parasite knew it would have other chances. Many more.

It needed a feast. It needed to taste the dying eyes as they see the blackness of death coming. The other could not save them all.

If it had a physical form it would have drooled.

Chapter 24

Harrison woke from a troubled sleep at one in the morning. **It** was darker than usual. The street light that normally leaked through the bedroom window was out for some reason. He looked at the bedroom door. And froze. The 'thing' materialized out of nothing; its black eyes fixed on Harrison. The apparition approached. Silently scuttling. Its arms stretched out, with massive hands curled like talons.

Waves of horror washed over him. Harrison was paralyzed. He could not move. The hands closed on his head. He felt the hot oily grip.

A rage filled him.

He twisted and jerked away grabbing for his gun. But the Sig was not there. In a panic, he scrabbled around the bed clawing at the confounding covers. It was here, it had to be here. He fought, grunted, and moaned. He could not find it.

Jennifer was pushed out of bed. She hit the floor with a dull thud. "Fork!" she mumbled. What just happened? She rolled upright and went to the bedroom light and hit the switch. What she saw startled her. Harrison was thrashing around moaning and grunting, all tangled up in the bedspread. She heard the word "gun" slurred several times.

"Harry!" she yelled. "Harry!" She was afraid to get near him. He was fighting an invisible monster. He was a strong man and wildly lashing out. Then the sound of her voice and the light seemed to calm him. His eyes opened. She again saw a residual panic there that she never could have imagined in her man. They darted around the room and finally settled on her. Recognition came.

"What! What!" he muttered. "What happened? Where is he?"

"Harry! Calm down. It was just a nightmare. You're okay. You're okay."

It took Harrison several minutes to regain his sanity. Finally, he sat on the edge of the bed breathing like a quarter horse after a hard race. Jennifer came to him.

"Damn, Jen. That was so goddam real."

"Tell me."

"He's coming, Jen. He's coming for me."

"Who?" she asked but she knew the answer.

"The… 'thing.'"

"He's in jail, Harry."

"For now. Look, I don't know how I know, but we… I have to be ready. I need my gun back now. I can't wait. I need a concealed carry permit." He was shaking, his eyes darting around. He was not completely back yet.

"Well get it. Now relax. The man is still in jail. We'll get ready. We'll be ready. Please, Harry, get a grip." He was still jittering and his eyes darted around. This was not Harrison. How could she bring him back?

"Harry! Do you remember our wedding vows?"

"What's that got to do with the 'thing?'"

"Do you remember!?"

Harrison pawed at his head as if to clear off a web. "Yes, Jen."

"You said you would honor me always."

"Yes, and I do."

"How are you going to do that when you're acting like this?"

"It's not an act!" Almost petulant.

"Yeah? Well, it sure seems so. Nightmares? Really, Harry? If the 'thing' is so dangerous shouldn't you be thinking about me?"

"God, Jen. Of course. But it wants me, not you."

"Yeah? And what's going to happen if I'm between you and 'it'? Because that's where I'm going to be. I will honor you!"

Harrison slumped. He wanted to cry. Then he pulled up the rage he felt when the phantom gripped his head. "The 'thing' will not survive any attempt on you. I will kill it. I will protect you."

"Welcome back and thank you, Harry. I believe you that you are the target, but you are part of me. I will not stand by."

"God, you're beautiful. How did I get you?"

"Luck. Or something else." Harrison had stopped shaking. Jennifer saw the feral gleam come into his eyes again. But she knew that the 'thing' was still there too. Haunting him. The thought that this 'thing' could get loose and be hunting him was debilitating. She saw him try to push through but there was an impenetrable wall inside, a wall he would need to keep his sanity. She let him keep it. For now.

"Back to bed, shooter. Tomorrow we get armed."

Harrison stared at the ceiling for a long time before sleep claimed him. He did not dream again. Instead, a type of steel formed in the wall he built. He would not succumb to fear. That was the best weapon the 'thing' had and Harrison would negate it. He had no doubt it would be back. He had no doubt that he would kill it. His confidence slipped away sometime during the night. But the steel remained.

Chapter 25

Harrison and Jennifer sat in Jeffers's office at nine the next morning. Detective Dennett attended. The day was bright. The sky to the west was clear. A few fluffy white clouds drifted over the Tillamook Head and on toward the coast range. Mists formed in the valleys.

"Can't do it, Harrison. It's evidence until the case is resolved. But I can recommend the gun shop in Cannon Beach." Jeffers looked carefully at the man who had managed to shoot the suspect. After he himself had seen what they had in the cell, and seen the reactions of his detective and the NSA agent, he had an inkling of what Harrison felt. Still, "So why do you want another piece? The suspect is in jail. With what we have now, he won't get out for a long while, if at all. When he does it will be for transport to Oregon State prison. Dennett is building a case that will put him on death row."

Jeffers saw that Harrison's eyes were bloodshot with dark circles under them. The man was having a hard time sitting still.

Jennifer held his hand like he might bolt if she let go. Then Jeffers needed to get back on track. There was a murderer to prosecute. "Harrison, don't be offended, but you need professional help. We need you straight. The county has resources – use them. Also, don't go to the gun shop in your current condition. The man there deals with police both from here and Cannon Beach. He will flag you. Get straight first."

"I hear you. But I'm not crazy," the second he said that Harrison knew it was not the thing to say. "Look, I've seen this 'thing' up close. The next time I will shoot him in the head."

"Won't be a next time, Mr. Baker. Take my advice. I have a duty to protect the people of Seaside. Don't become a problem."

Jennifer butted in, "Harry is the straightest man I know. If he says he needs a gun, he needs it. I'll make sure he gets any help he needs. But be sure, the man you have locked up is dangerous to us. We are the witnesses to the assault. If you cannot get the girl's testimony for the murder, it's possible he will walk or get bail. You know what happened on Halloween even if you can't prove it. If he gets out he will try to prevent our testimony. That's what he was doing in our front yard. For all you know about the murder even I could present a reasonable doubt to a jury. Maybe he got the car that way. Maybe someone else is setting him up."

"We are doing our jobs, Ms. Baker. Do not become a part of the problem." Jeffers again warned.

"Yeah, you do your job and I'll do mine," interrupted Harrison. "I will testify. I will be straight. But I don't trust this process. Or in this case, the law in general. There is something new going on here. I know there'll be probable cause determination in a circuit court. The judge there won't know the thing. Then there'll be a bond hearing and arraignment. Lots of lawyerly power will be on display. Lots of motions before the trial. Years down the road. This 'thing' is something different. It will wait."

"Well, you have the gist of the process. The suspect will have counsel, but it will not be robust for the 'thing.' I've seen the effect on the lawyer assigned to him. He will go through the motions but will not be working hard. Go ahead and get a weapon. I will clear your history. Just don't shoot without cause." Jeffers had no doubt that there would be no necessity for Harrison to shoot. He was also sure that Harrison would not mistake anyone for the 'thing.'

"That I will do, Chief. I didn't before and I won't in the future. Thank you for your time."

Jeffers was still a little nervous. His judgment was on the line, but this dispelled the worry. Harrison was scared but aware.

The Bakers left. Jeffers sat and thought for a minute. Then went to the electronics room and watched the cell monitor for a while. After a minute the suspect's head turned to the camera. Only his head.

Like an insect might do.

Jeffers felt the dread ooze out even through the camera. The tech was deliberately not watching it. The officer who went in to do the required suicide watch did not linger and only glanced at the man. Jeffers shivered and left the room. Everything Baker had said rang true. The Bergstrom girl was not yet coherent and even if she did begin to recall, any defense lawyer worth his salt would make her trauma the main point. Did she really see what happened? Did she really hear what was said? Or was it an alcohol-induced hallucination?

There were other considerations. The NSA was snooping around. Dennett seemed to have that under control for the time being. The FBI was in the wings. He was sure they had an agent or two watching. There was the fake NSA lawyer. Who had disappeared. He knew that Ozio was not gone. The man had something at stake here. His tech had found no trace of him in their database. The credentials were an exceptionally good fake and the license plate phony, indicating a high level of interest. Foreign power? CIA?

Johnson had told him to stay away from this. But he could not do that and still investigate.

"What do you think, detective?"

"We have problems with the limits on evidence gathering. And no credible witnesses."

"Yeah, we do. Well, get to work and find a provable case, detective. Get the witnesses straight."

"Yes sir," Dennett said and left.

This was spiraling out of control. He went to his office and called the DA "We need to talk."

Outside Jennifer took Harrison's hand. "Nice going, shooter. We now can get some firepower. Let's eat while we can."

"Jen, that was awesome what you did for me in there. The Chief worries that I might go off halfcocked. If not for you, he'd be right."

Jennifer smiled. Then wordlessly accepted the compliment and the responsibility. "Let's eat. And plan."

At Tom's restaurant, a plan was made over old-style hamburgers, fries and coffee. Like all plans, it was doomed to failure. Harrison always thought readiness was important but he knew it does not win battles or wars. Logistics did. The right people at the right time, in the right place with the right weapons. Trained, equipped, and supported. And like he had been taught; he knew no plan survives the first shot.

The best he could do was stay armed and alert. The 'thing' would be here eventually. He needed to be ready.

In the meantime, he would be straight and sane for Jennifer's sake. The wall inside built up a little higher. A little more steel was added. The cost was significant. It sealed off a part of himself. A void was created.

A formless nightmare-fueled rage filled it.

Chapter 26

Sheila Dennett, sergeant James, and Mara Walker sat in a Seaside police station interview room. Across the table, an unshaven, nervous man sat uncomfortably. His eyes darted around the room but did not make contact with any of the trio. The odor of stale beer, stale body, and stale breath filled the room. The fear he exhibited was palpable.

It was morning on another overcast day. A light mist coated the window. This was an interview, not an interrogation.

Dennett had invited Walker as a sign of good faith even though there was nothing here for her. Sergeant James was the one who found this man and had brought him in. Since he knew the interviewee and had a connection, Dennett thought it wise to have him help out. Indeed she gave him the task of running this interview. James had detective potential.

"Okay. This interview is with a witness to a crime. Case number S2022-10-31/part 6," Dennett said. "There will be no recording. Hand notes only. Detective Sheila Dennett, NSA Agent

Mara Walker, and Officer Bret James are in attendance. The interview is with Harvard Crenshaw, currently homeless. Officer James will conduct this interview. Go ahead." This introduction was for the interviewee. To show his importance.

"Harv, do you know why you're here?" James began.

"I saw something," Harv mumbled.

"That's right. It was Halloween. You were camping next to the restroom at the parking lot. You were there because the Mill Pond camp was full."

No acknowledgment from Harv. His eyes were shaded.

"What did you see?"

"Fight. Girl."

"What kind of fight? Tell me like you said before."

"Bad man, quick like spider, grab another man. Drag him behind car."

"And the girl?"

"She saw. She ran."

"Would you recognize the girl?"

"Yes. Saw her picture."

"Did you hear anything?"

"No."

"The bad man, could you recognize him again?"

Long pause. "Don't want to. Bad man."

"Did the bad man see you?"

"Don't know. Didn't look."

James turned to the women. "This is as far as I got before. He identified the Bergstrom girl from a photo. My gut says he could identify the perpetrator but he's afraid. He will not be a credible witness. But he puts the girl at the probable murder scene. It fits in the timeline."

Dennett said, "I know that place next to the tavern there. They have a mural of a shark on the parking lot side. The girl was drunk. Her blood alcohol was .09. I think she saw the murder. According to the Jorgensons, she kept saying "demon, shark, teeth, *eyes!*" We know the effect the assassin's eyes have on people. I can only imagine the effect on a twelve-year-old drunk girl." She suddenly thought and said, "Even peripherally, the effect on Harv must be the same. That's why he spiraled."

"You've got nothing," butted in Walker. Three 'witnesses' that'll be discredited on the stand by any half-brained lawyer."

"Maybe. But we now have a crime scene and timeline that we can work. James, work with Harv here. Maybe we can straighten him out enough to testify. Have him tested for drugs. Maybe get a psych eval."

"It's a long shot but I'll try. Harv has been in Seaside for a few months now. When I first trespassed him I saw a man who knew the vagabond life. He had the instincts of the predator/prey game. He was wary and savvy. I could see him assess each incident with an eye to exploit or avoid it. He was not impaired. As time went on and I trespassed him several more times. Like you said he seemed to spiral into what you see here after the incident. My guess is drugs and booze. We aren't going to save him."

"We have to try, James," Dennett said and turned to Walker. "Okay. The only other witness is Bergstrom. There were probably words spoken just before the murder. Even if she can't remember, maybe I can leverage it."

"You mean leak it that there was a name spoken, and see what flushes out," Walker smiled. "You could be an NSA agent, Dennett."

Dennett was suddenly not sure. "Maybe we can't handle what flushes."

"You're talking to an NSA agent. We can handle it."

"Okay. You saw the thing. Can you handle that?"

"Don't have to. His handlers will be of that same caliber. This has the Russian Main Intelligence Directorate, GRU, written all over it. The 'thing' is their assassin. They will try to break him out or hit him. If either of those happens, you will have either have an unsolved or will have closed your cases and I will be pulled out. The FBI will be left to investigate. If not then the game is afoot, as they say. And the CIA is here now."

"Okay." Dennett was thinking and talking mainly to herself. "The NSA is under the DoD. The FBI is under the DoJ. The CIA is not supposed to operate inside the U.S. Did I say clusterfuck before?"

"You did and it will be even more so. Don't forget Russian political influence. If I'm right and the assassin is Russian, they will be active. Their hit squads are formidable. And will have diplomatic immunity."

"Okay. How do you know the CIA is here?"

"The NSA eats CIAs lunch - inside the USA. But their budget makes ours look like pocket change. They do have their own assassins. I have been apprised to stand down if the assassin gets hit."

"Will you?"

"Sure. I'll be ordered to another hot spot. I'll give you some advice if that happens. Run, don't walk, to the nearest exit. The GRU and CIA kill with abandon. They have more ways to kill than fleas on a mongrel. Car accidents, fires, heart attacks, strokes. They'll burn down an apartment building to get one man. They'll use a

Hellfire missile on this place. Collateral damage at any level is acceptable if the target is neutralized. And they can scrub the media like you scrub a burnt pan." She wanted to scare Dennett.

"Okay. I get the point, but a Hellfire missile is a little over the top. Thanks for the heads-up but I can't run."

"Then watch your back. People you know may not be or remain what you think. Money and power are here. I'll tell you that your police are so far unaffected. The Chief is straight. The DA is too. But any other players are unknown and suspect. Especially that counselor the county sent."

"Okay. Too many variables. I'll continue to investigate the murder and the thing. We'll get a conviction."

"Don't be too sure," Walker said. Her cell buzzed and she answered. "Agent Walker." She listened for a full minute. Then "Understood." She thought for a minute. "Detective Dennett, I will give you information, that also has been passed on to the Chief and DA, a delegation of Chilean diplomats has landed in PDX. They have booked the entire top floor of suites at the Elliot Hotel in Astoria. The Hampton and Holiday Inns are filling up with FBI and DoD agents. And I'm in the Holiday with two junior agents. This is turning into a daddy of clusterfucks."

"Shit."

"Exactly."

When Walker left to report, Dennett called in sergeant Miller. She had an idea. Chile? That's a piece of the puzzle.

"Can you trace this John Doe bullshit name trail back to Chile?"

"Not without a bunch of warrants, detective. I'd be in databases of airlines, car rentals, hotels, and foreign places that will be flagged by the big boys."

"Okay. We have all his IDs. We'll stay local and on foot. Personal interviews with the car rental, Saltline hotel, and restaurants."

"Should I be looking for a new job too?"

"Okay. You're right, forget it. I'll do it. It's my job."

"Detective, I can do some of this online. Legally."

"Okay. Best not. I appreciate your offer but you're right, the 'big boys' are gathering. You can bet their surveillance is extensive."

"What about you? You're going to be out there in the open."

"Okay. I'll just be doing my job. Checking the timeline with local citizens."

"Detective, I have managed to get the surveillance feed from the Shilo beach camera. I've sent it to your inbox. It shows the Bergstrom girl pass through at 9:58 and head down Broadway. The Johanson girl followed at 10:02 but continued north. Whatever happened was after that time and before she got to Baker's place."

"Good work. We have the time pretty much nailed down. Any other potential witnesses?"

"We found most of the tavern patrons. Nobody saw a thing. Nor anybody suspicious."

"Okay. I'll be checking with the citizens."

"Take a uniform with you."

The first place Dennett went to was the Saltline hotel. She did not take a uniform. This was not a time to involve too many others. She parked in the mostly empty lot right in front of the lobby. She walked into the posh lobby. And approached the desk.

The attendant concierge politely and sourly told her that the John Doe surveillance tapes were confiscated by the FBI and wiped from their servers. They also told her that she was the third person to be asking about them.

"Who was the second?"

"Some jackbooted SOB. Said he was from Homeland Security," groused the attendant. "He got all pissed off when I told him the FBI had them. DHS? Screw 'em."

"Do you have surveillance of that SOB? And the FBI?"

"Sure do. I'll make a dupe. Miguel!" she called. "Give me the shot of that asshole that was here yesterday. You know the one. And the FBI guys too."

A few minutes later Miguel came back with a flash drive. "You gonna cook this DHS guy? The FBI guys had the sense of humor of a rock, but the Homeland asshole was akin to a snake."

"Maybe. Were there any threats made?"

"Only to not talk about this to anyone. I figure you are not anyone, detective," the dark-headed woman behind the counter winked at Dennett.

"Okay. Thanks. You should know these guys are serious."

"You were never here. The tapes will prove it."

"No, don't do that. These guys will know. Don't lie to anyone. I'll be okay."

"What's going on here, anyway?"

"A clusterfuck. Best to stay out of the way."

The next place was *Finn's*. This was a guess from the fact that the victim stayed at the Saltline. He had to have come from somewhere on Broadway. She talked to a hostess who gave her the name of the server who was there the night of Halloween. She broke for lunch where she was. She had the wonderful Steamer Clams. That afternoon she managed to talk to Margie Genova during a lull in the crowd. They sat on the outside patio next to a warm fire pit.

"Okay. Thank you for talking to me, Margie. As you may know, I am looking for information about the man who might have been here before he was killed on Halloween night."

The server remembered.

"Did he say anything that you can remember?"

"No. But he sat with another. They were very friendly. They had their heads together for most of their time here."

"Okay. Can you describe the second man? Did they pay with a credit card?"

"Paid cash. But did not leave together. The second man was white, average height. Short white beard. Maybe fifty."

"Friendly how?"

"Not like that. Conspire you know. Sharing a secret. Not really happy. More like satisfied. I got the feeling they were done with something."

"Okay. Thank you. If you can think of anything else give me a call." Dennett handed her a card. The second man was another mystery. Who was he? Where did he go?

Dennett went back to the station and commandeered a couple of patrol officers to canvas the local hotels for a single man with the description Genova gave her.

Before they were even out the door, Jeffers stopped them.

"Belay that order. Go back on patrol." Then he turned to Dennett. "Don't go there, detective. Stay on track. There is nothing there that can help and plenty that most likely will hurt. Understand?"

"Understood." Dennett sighed. Maybe it was better to keep this as straightforward as possible. Now if she only had reliable witnesses.

Nevertheless, she queued up the recorded surveillance. The jack-booted SOB turned out to be one of the men with Ozio. The NSA/DHS phony was still around and trying to cover up. Dennett was kind of happy the FBI got there first.

And determined to beat them both.

Chapter 27

Harrison and Jennifer sat in their living room on a misty early morning. Dew covered the grass where the wheel marks of the SUV were flattened but still apparent. A slight breeze ruffled the laurel hedge that ran the property line to the north. The morning dishes were in the washer and coffee steamed in their mugs. The morning had been quiet. Now Harrison came to a conclusion. The wall inside was lowered for this exchange.

"I need to ask you to do something I don't want you to do."

"Yeah? Well, fork, Harry. That was about clear as mud. You want to try again."

"Okay. Here's the problem. I know that the 'thing' is going to come here. I know it like I know the sun is out there, like now, even when it's cloudy. I need you to know it too."

"Harry, I believe you."

"Yeah, I know that for sure. But you just think that I believe it, not that it's true. I need you to be ready."

"So, what can I do that I'm not supposed to do?"

"I want you to come to the arraignment with me."

"Well, that's easy enough."

Harrison let out a long slow breath. He was not breathing well during this exchange. He was putting his wife in the same dangerous position as himself. Along with that Bergstrom girl, who still had not fully recovered. Not dangerous physically so much as mentally. He still felt the pull of those eyes. Now his wife would too.

The coffee cooled.

The DA was pressing forward as fast as the law would allow on the assault charge. The defense lawyer was cooperating. But Harrison could see the case is getting complicated. This 'thing' was an assassin. He was hired by someone the FBI was interested in. There were legal storms ahead.

"Look, it's Wednesday," Jennifer lightened up. "The *Bistro* in Cannon Beach is hosting the *Thistle and Rose* singers. I made reservations. Let's go there and relax for a while. If we leave now you can pick up the pistol from the gun shop." Jennifer saw the haunted look Harrison had when he asked her to go to the arraignment. He felt he was putting her in some kind of danger. Did he think she was a Lilly to be protected? For a moment she wanted to challenge him but she saw the sincerity in the look. He believed it. That was enough for now. She would go to the arraignment and stand tall. He would see her strength. She would pull him out of this funk.

That late afternoon they drove the seven miles over the Tillamook Head and snaked down into Cannon Beach on the old 101 highway. The day had cleared somewhat and they found a place to park on Spruce Street and walked up the short mall to the *Bistro*. Inside the small bar, the *Thistle and Rose* singers were sitting on the bench under the front windows. They were into a tune from the sixties and looked like they enjoyed it as much as the crowd at the bar. The harmony was remarkable.

They were escorted to a table for two in the small bar area and waited for service. The place was crowded with a mix of tourists and locals.

The young man running the bar came over and Jennifer ordered wine and Harrison a whiskey. He came with the drinks and passed out menus. While they studied the menu, Jennifer began to think about the thing.

"Harry? Do you really think I doubt you?"

Harrison tossed back the whiskey and said, "No. But you don't know the thing. You can't know without… seeing it. Seeing those eyes."

"You know his person we are calling a 'thing' is just a man. I know he scared you. I know it was not without reason. But he is not the devil."

Harrison sighed. "I know it's not the devil. But it's damned close. You can't know without actually seeing him… in person," he said again.

"Got it, Harry. I'll go with you. You know I love you."

"I know, and you don't know how sad it makes me to ask you to do this. I love you too. Let's order."

They had the Local Dungeness Crab Cakes with wilted greens and lemon sake butter sauce, while they listened to the singers happily harmonize through some oldies.

Then they drove back to the growing legal storm.

That night the Bakers sat in front of a dying fire and savored the calm feeling after the evening at the Bistro. Harrison sighed and settled on the couch in front of their fire. Jennifer came over and snuggled up. Memories came to the couple, separately and communally.

"Remember when we met? There was a fire like this," Jennifer reminisced.

"Yes. But not exactly. It was a beach fire off Bruce's Beach. We were cold and wet from surfing. I wanted to hold you but I was afraid. We had just met." Harrison watched the dying flames wistfully.

"I wanted you to cuddle too. But… "

"Yeah. I was on a forty-eight-hour pass before shipping out the next day and had to be at the base by nine."

Harrison Baker met Jennifer Mason while he was on leave from the Los Angeles Air Force base in 1991. It was summer, just before he was deployed per UN Resolution 678 to Operation Desert Storm.

He saw a Nordic beauty. One that he could not forget. Harrison was twenty-five and single by choice. The service was his partner for now. But suddenly did not wish to be alone any longer. A hunger was triggered. A chemical action that drove him to want this beautiful woman. His gut ached and he almost thought about going AWOL. But that was not possible for him. He was almost five years in now and it was as much a part of him as anything else.

He vowed to find this girl after this deployment. There would be time.

"Wait for me!" Harrison had suddenly blurted.

"What?"

"Wait for me. I'll be back. I want to get to know you better."

Jennifer was shocked at the suddenness. Then she was flattered. Then she was intrigued. Then she felt the same chemical attraction. "Don't take too long," she said. But she was ready to wait for as long as it took.

Jennifer was a beautiful slim blond haired blue eyed girl at twenty-two when they met, though she would not admit that to herself. This guy Harrison had affected her. So she waited a year for this guy. There were only letters and telephone texts to sustain her. But it was enough.

There were other boys who tried to woo her. The attraction to Harrison did not wane with time or distance. When he finally got a thirty-day pass she met him at the airport and felt the full impact of a need. A need he could provide a cure for.

They spent time together and he met her parents. They were suspicious at first but even the father could tell this was going to last. She found out Harrison was an orphan and had no family.

After a while, they talked about having children. Harrison wanted a son. He wanted to give what he did not have. His parents were killed in a car crash when he was too young to remember them. He had been raised in a few foster homes. He was taken care of. The foster parents were good people but often had more kids than could be cared for individually. He wanted to give that. To have that.

He even said he would retire from the military and get a regular job. He was sincere. She went off the pill. But nothing happened except she no longer had regular periods. Time went by. While they had fun trying it finally became frustrating for her. Harrison did not notice.

Then when he was deployed to another conflict zone she stayed on base and went to the hospital for consultation. After a battery of tests, it was thought that she suffered from PCOS, polycystic ovary syndrome. The treatment involved several types of therapies. She was thirty by then and did not want to be treated like she was defective.

She confided in Harrison when he came back from his latest deployment. She saw the disappointment cross his face. She also saw that he did not blame her. She cried; he sniveled. Eventually, they got past it. Mostly.

Then she spent thirty years of her life with this man running around the world while he counted bullets.

Thirty-five years in, he was ready to retire. Now she was a beautiful blond-haired blue-eyed woman of fifty-one. Maybe a little heavier and with some grey streaking her hair, but Harrison did not care.

When it became clear that Harrison was going to retire, she began looking for a place to call home. America was a big open book. For the majority of her life, she lived on bases strewn around the world. She knew a few languages and many customs, but little about the country she called hers. Or of her ancestry.

At the time of his retirement, things were not quiet on the world front. He could not abide the way Afghanistan was abandoned. Not just the material but also the people. The drawdown, he said, was hasty and inept. He was denied proper accounting of Air Force equipment. His records were classified such that even he, who entered them and was responsible, could not see them once they left his hands.

She knew he was offered a substantial bonus to stay. He would not. She was happy about that. Now they could actually see the U.S. they protected for so long. Of course, the news of ANTIFA riots was widely reported. The January capital riot was forever being resurrected in response. That left out many big cities. Where could she and Harrison go that was relatively unaffected? And more than that, where would she feel at home. Harrison could be at home anywhere. He was a military man and an orphan.

She went to work studying maps and websites. Slowly it became apparent that she was zeroing in on real estate located on ocean-side properties. Then on those north of the fortieth parallel. The coasts of Maine, Oregon, and Washington lit up her imagination. In a sudden burst of memory, she remembered Astoria, Oregon. Her mother's father had lived there. Both her parents were dead now but Astoria called to her. She read up on it while they stayed in a furnished rental not far from Bolling field. Harrison was adrift now; it was up to her to anchor them.

Astoria was a port city on the Columbia River founded in 1811, the first permanent American settlement west of the Rockies. It had a rich history of Norse influence.

She decided to visit. Dragging Harrison along, they flew to Portland and rented a car at PDX, and drove over the coast range to the intersection at Highways 101 and 26. The drive was easy compared to many where he was stationed. The road over the summit was scenic with forested landscapes. A lot of logging was evident but the areas were planted and had dates of when on signposts. The weather in this April was cool and misty.

They headed north on 26 and passed through a town named Seaside. She had seen it on the map and paid no attention at the time. They got stopped at the intersection signal at Broadway. She looked at the old city hall, now a craft beer restaurant. The brick façade was well preserved. The original iron bars on the jail were preserved.

Harrison paid no attention. The light changed. Then they were on their way to Astoria. The twenty-mile drive on the two-lane highway was crowded but easy. Nobody drove fast.

This was a unique landscape. They drove past up-scale golf courses, and rolling grassy hills, through mixed conifer and deciduous forests. Elk herds, and black Angus cows dotted the Clatsop plains. Then Warrenton appeared. Mostly a new big open mall-like place. Lots of fast food and a massive Home Depot store, Costco, and Walmart were there too.

They hit the Youngs Bay bridge and saw the Astorian hillside dotted with houses nestled in the fir trees on the steep slopes. They spotted the Astoria Megler bridge towering over the city.

This was beautiful to Jennifer.

They passed the SUOMI hall in old town and found the Holiday Inn hotel and checked in. After catching their breath they pulled up the city map and found the real estate office. It was an easy but crowded drive and they went in on a dull overcast day.

The receptionist was ready. The agent was ready. The tours and visits began. The city had more historical homes than any other of its size. Most were well-kept impressively adorned mansions built on steep slopes. It was apparent right away that much Astoria was out of their price range, and the parts that weren't were not to her liking.

For a week they toured the city. It was a wonderful, history-loaded place. It had a proud history of filmmaking. *The Goonies* movie was highlighted by the agent. The hikes up and down the hills were invigorating. The Astoria Column on Cockscomb hill was majestic. The views were unparalleled. The city restaurants and bars were great.

But… the prices were high. Most of the homes were too big for them. Harrison noted that the hills were in landslide zones. Even so, they walked the Riverwalk along the Columbia River from Pier 1 to Tongue Point one clear day. They stopped at the Nordic Park for a few minutes. Jennifer remembered her Grandfather telling tales about Trolls. The statues in the park were not like those tales.

They ate at Pier 39 an upscale place with a country-like free museum honoring the fishing industry. But there were no houses that caught her imagination. And Harrison was not interested in any of the new apartments that lined the east Riverwalk.

They thanked the agent, and then Jennifer and Harrison walked back to the Holiday Inn to think and rest. They checked out and stayed one more night at the historic Elliot Hotel which they noted during their walks. They watched a brilliant sunset from the rooftop deck that evening. Then they prepared to return.

Their return flight was booked for the next day. They left Astoria and started to retrace their original route. This time when they got to the Seaside Broadway light, Jennifer suddenly said, "Turn here!"

"What?"

"Turn, turn, turn!" she pointed to the right.

Harrison turned past the old city hall and jail. The street was made narrow and awkward by random door openings from cars parked on both sides. They came to another intersection that began a one-way grid. Harrison went forward past a bookstore, art, and collectible shops. Then over a hundred-year-old stone and concrete bridge that spanned the Necanicum river, then past the Bridge Tender saloon, which looked something right out of the old west. Past more restaurants and then an arcade at another intersection. It took Harrison a second to understand the protocol at the flashing red-lighted intersection and randomly crossing civilians, some of whom apparently did not know either. Then up a two-way street to a turnaround and a large bronze statue of Lewis and Clark.

As they made the turn, Jennifer looked out at the vast Pacific, the endless view, and the rolling surf. She felt the turning of the world. The far off horizon beckoned. Then she looked up and down what was called the Promenade as they finished the turn. She felt a twinge of longing. Then they were in the shadow of the Windham again

"Turn here, turn, turn!" Jennifer pointed to the ramp for the Shilo Inn. "Stop, stop, stop!"

Harrison was having an interesting time obeying all these commands. He smiled; Jennifer was on the hunt now. She jumped out and ran into the lobby. A few minutes later she came out with card keys for a room on the third floor facing the ocean.

"What about our flight?"

"I canceled it. I want to explore this place. I called the agent to look here."

There was no arguing with that. And Harrison did not have anything planned. Why not? Two days later she found the place on 5th. The price was well within their means and Jennifer had grown to like the town. Two weeks later they were moved in.

For Harrison the move was easy. Jennifer took care of everything.

When he retired he was a Chief Master Sergeant. He mustered out after the Afghanistan withdrawal debacle from the 11th Mission Support Group Logistics at Joint Base Anacostia-Bolling. He was then adrift. Jennifer took care of the house hunting. He was just tagging along.

After a period of looking for a place to live, Jennifer found the cozy two-bedroom two-bath cottage on 5th and Downing in Seaside. It was affordable and as close to the perfect life as possible. The town was a small bustling resort. There seemed to be something always going on. From the 4th of July fireworks, soccer matches on the beach, the Oregon Rose Queen finals at the Convention Center, a national Volleyball tournament on the beach, the venerable Hood to Coast relay and party, beach runs, and many happenings at the Convention Center. There was the summer Wednesday Farmer's market near the Visitors Center that offered local goods and music.

Even though all this went on, the house they picked was mostly quiet. It was an easy walk to quality restaurants and the Fun Land arcade. Harrison liked the game called Fascination. Jennifer watched his concentration as he tried to hit that last hole for the win. Laughing and joking as someone rang the bell one second before his ball went in.

There were a couple of dark clouds troubling the retirement. War had broken out in Asia as Putin sought to reclaim the glory days of the Soviet Union. NATO was in a dither. There was a danger of recall. Nuclear war was threatened.

But the Bakers made it through the summer without those problems. Then came Halloween.

And now here they were, Harrison thought, enmeshed in a murder investigation where I shot a 'man.'

Harrison had a favorite Eisenhower quote he liked to say.

"You will not find it hard to prove that battles, campaigns, and even wars have been won or lost primarily because of logistics."

It validated his service. He also liked to say that behind every man on the front lines, stand a dozen or more supporting him. He knew that he and Jennifer were about to test that quote and that saying. It was going to take a lot of support to weather this storm. And plenty of logistical preparedness.

In the meantime, they would keep living the dream. But the Halloween nightmare was never far behind Harrison. He felt the weight of it getting closer each day.

Chapter 28

"**We have a problem,**" said Johnson.

"*A* problem?"

Seaside police Chief Jeffers and Clatsop County DA Johnson sat in Johnson's small office inside the Court House. Outside a winter storm blew the bare tree branches around and battered at the windows with fat raindrops.

"One big problem," amended Johnson. "Comprised of many parts. I'm trying to keep the prosecution of John Doe on track. NSA is helping with a real name. I've got two actions going. First: Prosecute him for the assault of the girl. A conviction will put him in the Oregon State Prison. That will hold him for a while. Second: Prosecute him for the murder of Billings. To do both I need witnesses. Reliable witnesses. This is where you come in. Keep Dennett and this NSA agent working on it. There is another player here. One Evalyn Hanson. This is the crisis counselor being used to help the Bergstrom girl." He stopped and let that lie for a moment. "I need you to watch this Hanson person. She was picked out of the rotation by one of my aides and sent to 'help' before the Bergstrom girl was even admitted to the hospital. She was interviewing the Johanson girl even before your police. She was there much too quickly. There's a reason for that. I want you to find it out. When you do, I will handle the aide.

"Understood. Dennett is suspicious of Hanson also. She has managed to befriend the Bergstrom girl and brother. The parents are being very open but protective. It seems that the counselor is focused on Johanna moving on. Not so much remembering. I am told this is not a preferred method for dealing with this type of trauma."

"We need Johanna to remember. We need her to be believable on the stand. Now, I can use her for the assault and attempted abduction charges without her remembering the murder. In fact, I have prevailed in court to exclude mention of the murder during the assault trial. The NSA is actually helping with that, for now. The big boys are hashing out who's who. My sources say the CIA is interested. Which means foreign powers."

"Yes. Russians."

"I did not say that. But… yeah, probably. Once the hierarchy is established, the real fight begins for us. I want this John Doe in prison before the shit hits this courthouse. Get our ducks in a row. We are set for arraignment soon and trial as fast as I can make it."

"Maybe the John Doe lawyer will plead guilty."

"Without the consent of the accused, the judge will not allow it. And we know the John Doe will not say any goddamned thing. Get prepared Frederik." Johnson paused. How much did Jeffers need to know? "Another thing. The FBI has frozen me out.. Something is happening up there."

"Yeah. They have their hands full with the political fallout from some public raids, and lack thereof."

"Not that. This is local cover-your-ass stuff. There is a sort of espionage event they have missed and are trying to rectify. They will be no help here and may get in the way if we head in their direction with the investigation. Let Dennett know to stay on track."

"Yes sir."

"But, Fredrick, if it does go toward international issues, let me know at once. We have to know what kind of monster we're dealing with. And I don't mean the assassin. We are not equipped to handle multiple fronts. Especially with the feds."

"It's already there. Maybe we should step back and wait to see who becomes the top dog."

"In my experience, there is never a permanent top dog with the bureaucracy. Just a lot of noise, barking, and fur flying. But these are big boys. And they don't care who or what gets trampled in the fight."

Jeffers walked out into the gusting rain to his cruiser with a bad taste in his mouth. He sat for a moment as the car warmed up and then called Dennett.

"Detective, batten down the hatches. Move all evidence not directly pertaining to the case to Clatsop county. All your notes of any outside influence should go to the library. Make a folder to be archived there."

"What about the murder board?"

"Leave it. We need it. The NSA has seen it. What we need to do is scrub any mention of the assassin's origin. Or of any foreign involvement. The Ozio incident. Let the NSA and FBI have their field day. We need to stay out of it if we want to keep control of the case."

"Got it. Anything else?"

"Yes. Keep your head in the game. There are a lot of moving parts here. And a lot of sharp edges."

"Yeah. I can see that. I'll get on it."

"How is the NSA agent doing?"

"I think she's coming around."

"Don't bet on it, detective."

"I won't."

Jeffers clicked off. No matter how he manipulated the evidence handling it would all come out sometime. That was not the most of it though. The assassin was a target for powers he could only imagine. He was sure there were agencies that just wanted to cover this up. Make it go away. And they had the power to do that on paper. But if the assassin were to be "outed" to the media all hell would break loose. Whoever produced this abomination would be on the warpath.

A sudden thought came, who was this Baker guy? How did he get involved? Jeffers made a note to pull his service records.

He then sat for a long time in the cruiser in the Clatsop County parking lot in the misty rain and tried to get his mind around it all. A deep foreboding end loomed on the grey horizon. Nothing good was going to come of this. His experience with federal power was limited but he knew that when activated, it became a freight train with a hundred cars to be filled with reports and no way to stop it.

He started the car and pulled out into the uncaring traffic. Back to work.

Chapter 29

Sunlight filtered through the slatted windows in the small deliberately bland, unthreatening office of Evalyn Hanson. The therapist sat serenely in an overstuffed chair facing the therapeutic couch on which Johanna Bergstrom lay. The girl was fidgeting. Her eyes were unfocused. Her arm was still bound.

Hanson had thought about prescribing a type of narcoleptic. But the father was having none of it. Maybe she could dose the girl here. That thought caused her to nearly cry out. What was happening to her? She tried to think of another way. But there was no other way that would not destroy her.

The only course was set. Get the girl to forget.

"Joh, we've been through this before. There's no gain to be made by trying to remember. It just causes you pain. You need to move on. To make peace with the trauma."

"I can't. The demon haunts me." Johanna had taken to calling the assassin a "demon."

"Yes, it will until you let it go. What you need to realize is that the 'demon' is just a man. It is the alcohol that caused the trauma."

Johanna shifted uncomfortably. The scene came back. The teeth, the eyes. The blackness. She shivered.

"Joh. Let it go."

"I'll try," Johanna lied.

"It is the only way. Time is up. I'll see you next week. Be at peace Joh." Her parents waited in the lobby.

For several sessions now Evalyn Hanson had tried to make the Bergstrom girl forget and move past the incident. It was not something she wanted to do but her practice depended on it. Her livelihood depended on it. Now her thoughts about not doing harm were becoming debilitating. She was becoming desperate. There was no way out of this that would not cause pain for either her or Johanna. Or probably both, since the path was set and she had traveled too far on it.

One mistake, she lamented, just one mistake in her past had caught up with her. How that piece of dreck had found it was confounding. It was over two decades ago when she plagiarized just a portion of her master's thesis. Just a portion. To do a document search after all this time was expensive. Especially to get into Boston University records. Hanson had been around law enforcement for a while. She knew the way they worked. But this was outside of anything from before. There were obviously powerful forces at work here. The threat was fearsome, overt and direct.

Get the girl to forget or lose her license.

To complicate things, the Bergstroms were getting suspicious. Especially the father. Hanson could not keep this quiet for much longer. The girl was fighting her. She knew that the girl lied and would continue to try and remember. Perhaps it was time to retire before she was destroyed by this failure or the hidden truth.

This was sickening to push the girl to forget. And it was becoming impossible. Whatever she saw and heard was more than what met Hanson's eye.

She heard from people who saw the assassin that he was very frightening. In a sudden inspiration, she would get an interview with the assassin. It was a last-ditch attempt and hope for an answer to make Johanna forget. She decided to see for herself. Maybe there was a hint there to how to approach the girl.

Hanson made an appointment to see the Seaside police Chief.

The weather forecast was for low clouds and fog. The reporter in Portland got it right this time. Monday Hanson drove down to Seaside on the slick wet highway and parked in the station's front lot. She entered the front doors and asked to see the Chief. She was escorted back to a conference room and asked if she wanted coffee. She declined and asked if they had tea. "Coming up," said Darlene. Hanson idly thought that the woman could have been her aide. She was professional and friendly, without any artifice, a rare combination.

After a few minutes, Frederik Jeffers came in holding a cup of steaming coffee in one hand and a cup of hot tea in the other. He set the tea down in front of Hanson and the coffee in front of himself, sat, and said, "Ms. Hanson, it's nice to see you, but what you ask is not advisable. There are legal implications of course, but if that's all there were I would allow it to help you help the Bergstrom girl."

"What else is there?"

"I can't explain it. It defies words. I understand your efforts here to help your client. I let you come here today because I know you will persist. I am now trying to caution you and dissuade you if possible. Take my word that this man is something you will wish you did not see first-hand."

"Thank you for your consideration, but I have to see why Johanna is suffering so acutely. Why her fear is so profound? I have dealt with dangerous and violent men before."

"This will be different! I again caution you. Be prepared." Jeffers turned and called down the hall. Two big armed police officers in full armor entered. "These men will accompany you. Do not come between them and the assassin. You do not need to fear a physical attack but there will be trauma. These men will mitigate that somewhat."

The implication was clear. They were a buffer against some sort of psychological attack. Hanson began to feel concerned. What could have affected Jeffers so much? He was a solid experienced police officer. Nevertheless, she had dealt with psychotic individuals in her practice. There were times when she was uncomfortable, knowing that the only thing between her safety and their violence was a modicum of restraint. Sometimes the restraint was more formidable, handcuffs and shackles. She had not met a career criminal she could 'cure.' The most she could do was evaluate them for the courts. Now she would do that for herself.

"May I speak with him?"

"You can try but I advise against it. I will observe through the monitor," He turned to the guards. "Let's go."

Hanson was led through a large steel door into the jail area. The guards became tense. Hanson took a step into the area; the guards flanked her. One said, "This is far enough ma'am." Hanson stopped. She was fifteen feet away and she still had not noticed the man behind the steel bars. Then she did. The assassin sat staring at nothing. There had been no movement. He could have been dead.

Hanson steeled herself. Jeffers's warning sounded in her mind, but she had to try.

"John! John! May I talk with you," she called.

The man turned to her, just his head, like an insect might do.

Evalyn Hanson was stunned. This was like nothing she had ever seen. Even through the bars, the stare was paralyzing. But the warning from Jeffers had prepared her. She immediately closed her eyes, took a step back, and stumbled. An officer caught her before she fell. The man turned away.

Then there was again nothing. No movement. No acknowledgment. Except for the stare, he could have been dead.

Hanson had seen just a glimpse of what Johanna must have seen. She turned to the guards and said, "Thank you. That's enough."

They left and Hanson came out to meet Jeffers again. He said. "May I offer my sympathy? And perhaps another cup of tea before you drive back. I hope that helped you to see what Johanna saw."

"Ah! Tea and sympathy. Yes, I need both. And from what I just experienced; Johanna needs more than what I can offer. I am going to tender my resignation to the county."

"I'm sorry to hear that. May I ask why?"

Evalyn Hanson thought for a moment. The tea and coffee came. "Chief Jeffers, may I speak off the record?"

"Yes. Most of our work at this point is off the record. Nothing you say here will be recorded and I will not remember anything - unless there's a crime involved."

"What I have to say is germane to your investigation. It also is the reason I am retiring. At this point, it is of no further consequence to me." Hanson took a breath, "I was approached by one of Johnson's aides. She wanted me to insert myself into the counseling of Johanna Bergstrom. I was to assure that the girl did not remember any words she might have heard. I am now unwilling to do that for a number of reasons. One of the most compelling sits in your cell. This girl needs to safely remember for her own sanity. And another is that I find that I can't betray my principles. Even at the cost of my job." She put her head down and sighed.

"Thank you for that. I am not going to ask you what they have on you, but I need to know who approached you. That is a crime I must investigate." Jeffers had gotten nowhere on this until now. Sometimes fortune delivers a gift.

Hanson sighed again. "I suppose it will come out sooner or later. The woman's name is Beth Stringer. She has evidence of a past mistake I made. One that would ruin me."

"I won't promise anything, but let me see what I can do before you officially tender your resignation. It would be better if you were the one to control your future."

Hanson looked up. "What?"

"Wait a week. Continue to work with Bergstrom. Use preferred techniques. I will work with Johnson. This aide can be of use to us and can be controlled with threats of prosecution for interfering with an active murder investigation. Johnson will want to know who is behind the attempt. And he can use this to open a line of inquiry into the assassin's motivation."

Hanson left and Jeffers called Johnson. The DA was in court on another matter so Jeffers left a message to have him call when he could. He did not leave a voicemail with any information that leaves a documented trace. The phone call was probably not monitored. Maybe, hopefully. Then he thought again. He called back and made an appointment. He also made a memo himself to have Johnson sweep his office for any surveillance. He then called Miller and went to his cubicle.

"Can we assure that we are not being spied on by the FBI or NSA?"

"We are fairly well shielded here. I have the latest encryption equipment and programs. But… the federal authorities probably have better stuff."

"Get with Dennett. We go silent now."

"Not possible, Chief. Unless we go off-site."

Jeffers smiled and made an okay signal with his hand.

Back in his office, he knew this was possibly a career-ending decision. He questioned why he was doing this. Then he remembered the 'thing' and the girl.

He would take this 'thing' down. Show the world.

Then he started making plans for his forced retirement.

Chapter 30

November. Friday. The last arraignment case of the day at the Clatsop Courthouse. The buff-colored Tenino sandstone of the Clatsop County courthouse shown in the low mist-filtered afternoon sun as much as it could. The building housed the Circuit Court. The suspect had been transferred to the county jail next door.

Inside, the ornate courtroom began to fill up. This murder in Seaside was a big case. There was lots of news coverage. And lots of law enforcement. Seaside police, Clatsop Sheriffs and state vehicles lined the streets. Federal black and Silver full-sized Escalade and Navigator SUVs lined the back parking lot.

Harrison and Jennifer parked in a lot off 7th near the Riverwalk path. They took one look at the traffic on Highway 30 and walked up to 8th street and carefully crossed Marine and Commercial streets separately. They made it to the massive stone building and climbed up the long wide steps to the ornate doors. Inside they were subjected to the same routine one gets at an airport. Harrison picked a spot on the benches in the first row behind the prosecution table. He sat with Jennifer near the aisle, away from the defense table. He sat nervously, continually unconsciously feeling on his hip for his nonexistent pistol.

Jennifer held his hand and tried to comfort him. She was beginning to feel a kind of dread. She mentally slapped herself. Knock it off, she admonished. What the fork do you think is going to happen here? She took a deep breath and waited. She was still unsure of why he wanted her here. She was supposed to see the 'thing' that Harrison was afraid of. Yes, he was an assassin and yes he had affected Harrison. But he was just a man. Yet a subliminal feeling of dread persisted. She waited.

The room continued to fill until there was standing room only.

The clock ticked toward three. The prosecution entered; Johnson and a woman Jennifer did not know. Both were dressed in bland business suits. Both were on edge.

The defense lawyer entered and sat like a condemned man. He was alone.

Then the accused entered. Two big marshals flanked him. They did not look at him. He was shackled by wrists and ankles. He scuttled along smoothly, without help. The room went quiet, expectant. This was the first time the assassin was in public for the media. People wanted a look, but he kept his head and eyes down.

But as he passed the Bakers, the assassin turned his head toward Harrison.

Like an insect might do.

His flat black eyes came up. He stared at Harrison who jerked and actually grabbed for his nonexistent pistol. A soft growling in Harrison's ear lessened the impact of the stare, but could not deaden it. The people around him shrank back, away from the target of the stare.

For Jennifer time stopped. The temperature dropped.

She almost cried out, but only managed to mutter, "Fork!" under her breath. That stare held the horrors of Hell. It was almost magnetic. She felt herself being drawn in even without him looking directly at her. This… 'thing,' was targeting her husband. She tore her eyes away and suddenly knew why Harrison brought her here.

The assassin then turned to the front, sat, put his eyes down, and went as still as a spider in its web. There was suddenly nothing. No movement. Except for the effect of the stare he could have been dead.

The feeling of doom eased but did not go away. Jennifer found she was squeezing Harrison's hand with both of hers. He did not notice. His eyes were now feral and aimed at the 'thing,' who did not pay attention - or care.

The judge came in and court protocol began. Jennifer sat through the procedure without paying attention. There were charges read and motions made. The lawyer at the defense table looked like he wanted to bolt. The scripted proceedings went quickly. After a short time, the court was adjourned. The assassin was lead out, eyes down. It did not turn to Harrison again, yet the black waves of hell wafted around him. The Marshals were stiff and ready. But did not look at their charge.

Jennifer suddenly thought he moved like a spider. Where that came from she did not know but it seemed apt. The court cleared while Harrison and Jennifer sat and waited until they began to breathe freely again.

"Damn, Harry. What the fork!"

"Yeah, I'm sorry."

"No! I needed this. I have to handle it. I still don't know how the 'thing' could get to us, but I'll damn well be ready. I better get a pistol too."

"C'mon. Let's wind down at that place on the dock. *Winekraft.* Remember we stopped there in May when we were looking at property here."

"Let's move, rain's coming."

They walked up to 9th and across Commercial Street and then Marine Drive with the traffic lights. These were the two one-way, main roads split east and west through town that hosted Oregon Highway 30 traffic. And there was lots of that, even in November. They made it to the Riverwalk just past the Buoy Beer building. They headed east.

It was getting colder as another front moved in. The wind from the northwest grew. The grey clouds lowered. Mist blew sideways. They made it up walking on the River Walk trolley tracks and hustled up to the boxy barn red building that was once a weighing plant and fish processing factory. Jennifer remembered that it now hosted a small mall full of memorabilia and *Goonies* paraphernalia, and a computer store. The wine bar was a separate business next to the old pier 11 weighing house. The pier had come a long way from the fish canning of the last century. Now it was a touristy fun place.

They snuck in just as a hard rain hit the windows. "Should have brought our rain gear," noted Harrison.

There were only two people there at the time. An older couple sat in the easy chairs next to the corner windows sipping red wine and talking in low tones. Harrison and Jennifer moved over to a barrel table and chairs at the window facing the parking lot. The rain sheened the window.

Harrison looked around at the warm homey place. He did not pay much attention to it when he was last here. At that time they were intent on discussing where to live and visiting various homes for sale and they sat outside on the cool spring evening. Now he noted some intricate artwork from a local artist, "paulpolson," a sign read, that played over the south wall. Racks of wine lined the area next to the short bar. Local goodies and memorabilia were arrayed under the window facing the walkway out over the Columbia River.

A cheerful bartender came over with paper menus even though the sign on the table said to order at the bar. Harrison was not normally a wine drinker. The last time they were here he ordered a Fort George ale when they sat outside in the warm sun. This time Jennifer ordered a house chardonnay for them. While they waited they watched in the dimming light as a massive ship plowed up from the mouth of the Columbia shrugging off the rain like a breaching giant whale. It was riding high. Probably headed for Kalama and the grain silos there. A Columbia River Pilot boat powered out to meet it. The pair pushed upriver past the old 11th street dock reminding Jennifer of a shark and remora.

The wine came. "So what do we do now?" asked Jennifer.

"Prepare. This 'thing' will be back."

"Harry. I saw what he was and it scared the shit out of me. But I also saw the security."

"He'll beat it. The suits will make sure. They'll screw it up." Harrison made a sour face at the word 'suits.' He meant the various agencies that were becoming interested in the assassin. "The 'thing' knows too much. They'll try to open him up or shut him down. The problem for them now is that this is too big for control by any one of the federal alphabet entities. They're probably falling all over each other to be the ones to contain it or use it. I can see it with all the suits hanging around. Sooner or later one agency will think it has the upper hand and the power players will descend. They can't control it, not him anyway. The 'thing' will survive. And wait. And seek revenge."

Jennifer thought about her experience at the courthouse, "From what I saw in the 'thing's' stare, it isn't about revenge. There was no anger, no hate, but plenty of malice. It was like being pulled into a grave. You were targeted for sure but it's about something else. A sort of compulsion to… bring an end, to finish. Like this: The thing's assignment had been interrupted by you and it needs to finish the assignment. To dispose of the body or something like that."

"Yeah, that's not going to happen. The body is in pieces now. But maybe you're onto something. The Chief says he was an assassin that made people disappear. I know I'm in the thing's crosshairs. So maybe I'm part of this perverted 'finishing.' I got in the way and need to be eliminated and maybe disappear." A light came on in Harrison's mind. "You're right it's not revenge, the thing's demented. I don't think time has any effect on it. And, hell, I shot him." He sat rehashing the shooting. Wishing he had killed it that Halloween almost a year ago.

Harrison suddenly remembered the dog barking. He had not told the police about that. "Jen, do you remember a dog barking when I shot that 'thing?'"

"Dog?"

"Yeah, a big one if his size matches his bark. It kind of woke me up from the thing's stare."

"I didn't hear that. Harry. There are no big dogs on our street."

Harrison sat confused. "It was loud. A warning. Snapped me back to the present that night. I might not have survived without it."

"You sure?"

"Now… I don't know. Maybe it was in my head. But it saved my ass."

"You didn't say anything before."

"I remembered just now. The things stare brought it back. I heard a dog growling when it looked at me. Weird."

"Well, if it saved your ass, more power to it. We'll ask around. Maybe it came from behind us somewhere toward Necanicum. I haven't met everybody yet. And there sure wasn't a dog in the courtroom."

"Let's sit here a while and relax," Harrison called for another glass of wine. "This is pretty good stuff." The rain slowed. It grew dark.

"Yeah? Careful shooter. Too much of a good thing, you know."

They sat for a while talking about not much of anything, remembering the hunt for a house in this town. The rain stopped. Then an older woman came in carrying a cased guitar and a music stand. She conferred with the bartender who came over and asked them if it were all right for them to move to a different table. The woman looked on apologetically.

"Sure," said Jennifer. "Looks like we're going to get some music." A dark bearded man came in carrying an amplifier and speaker on a stand. They began to set up.

"We need to eat something." Jennifer could hear Harrison's gut growling. And the wine was not helping.

"Yeah. There's a restaurant up on pier twelve. The *Sea Crab* if I remember right. Let's swing around to it."

Jennifer called over the bartender "Can we come back after we eat?"

"Sure, but we have food here."

"Thanks but we need to move around a bit."

"Okay. Who's name should I use?" These people did not look like "drink-and-dash" types.

"Baker. We'll be back in an hour."

"Have a nice walk."

It was dark at close to five. The Bakers walked out and then through the doors to the short mall and down to the exit. "What's that?" questioned Jennifer. To the left of the exit, there was a sign over a formidable-looking door. *Inferno Lounge.*

"Inferno, what an interesting coincidence," groused Harrison.

"Let's look inside." They had not been there before. It was a pleasant surprise. It was somewhat reminiscent of the 80s, an ornate yet modern bar, and restaurant. The sign in the entry said to wait to be seated but the waiter waived them in and sat them in a lower section right over the river with a view north and west through large windows to the Megler Bridge, across the Columbia to sparsely lit Washington side, and east out to Tongue Point, where massive ships with lighted flying decks waited in queue. Not the same view as from the Winekraft. Now from directly over the water, the bridge was more visible. Winking car lights showed through the superstructure as they crossed the span. It was scenic.

Some sort of soft rock eighties music was piped in. There were rotating crystalline chandeliers above the lower section with big windows facing the river. In the dark, these were reflecting the colored LED lights, creating beams that played around the walls and windows like silent mini fireworks.

"Wow. This is nice. Maybe we have to reassess living in Seaside." There were only two restaurants there that faced the ocean from the Prom and only Mo's had a good view. And neither had colored lights. This one sat right over the river like being in a very stable party boat.

A server came and gave them menus and asked if they wanted a drink. "Yes, coffee please," quickly put in Jennifer.

They ordered the Seared Salmon and ate in silence. The meal was delicious and the view across the luminescent dark river to the far off lights of Megler was intoxicating.

Refreshed, the Bakers strolled back to *Winekraft* out of the weather until exiting the main building and quickly slipping into the bar. The singer was in full swing. A soulful *Shame on the Moon* began to fill the room. They sat at a table near the singer. The bartender came over with their wine without being asked.

"She is good," Jenifer said. She knew this song and softly sang along with it.

"Where nothing comes easy, old nightmares are real.
Until you been beside a man
You don't know how he feels."

Jennifer felt the truth in the lyrics. She was now beside her man. She knew how he felt like never before. She knew his nightmares. She smiled when the singer got to the next part about being inside a woman's heart.

"Some men go crazy.
Some men go slow.

Jennifer knew Harrison went slow. It had been thirty years and he had kept his head the whole time. But this 'thing' changed him. He was now both fearful and dangerous at the same time. She put it out of her mind for the time being and listened to the singer.

Harrison was not familiar with this type of live music and did not analyze the lyrics but the feeling somehow rang true. He saw Jennifer mouthing the words and was intrigued by the confluence of *Winekraft, Inferno Lounge,* and this singer's song, *Shame on the Moon*. And a dog?

The singer finished the song, and people applauded. Harrison saw a setting that was intimate and personal. Similar but different from the Cannon Beach *Bistro* and the *Thistle and Rose* singers. There was not much of this kind of music in Afghanistan or most places he was stationed for his years of service to Uncle Sam. But he agreed. She was good. She sang a medley of dimly remembered older songs. Her voice was sweet and earthy and carried emotion well. Her guitar was played professionally. She made the songs live in today's world. Harrison relaxed more. He liked being carried away by the calm emotion elicited in the songs. He liked being able to forget the reason he was in Astoria.

They stayed for the full set; drinking lightly. In the end, Harrison fed the tip jar. The singer said, "thank you." When he tipped other servers Harrison often got the obligatory 'thank you.' Yet there was a genuineness in the singer's sound. She handed him a card. It read *Barbara Anne, Oregon Folk singer.* He suddenly wanted to hear her again.

"Let's go," prompted Jennifer. "Before I want to move here," she said again. The rain had restarted.

This time the rain was light and they got to their car up the River Walk without being drenched. But as they walked, the closer they got to the parking lot, the glow from *Winekraft* waned and the dread returned. They got in the Explorer quickly and Harrison pulled onto Highway 30. He passed the turnoff for Washington and Long Beach, and then under, the massive Megler bridge ramp. They moved through Uniontown and toward the roundabout. By the Youngs Bay bridge, Highway 30 had morphed into Highway 101. Harrison cruised sedately south, now with moderate traffic even at this time of the year, mindful that he was not in the best condition to be driving.

They made it back to their Seaside home. The wind had shifted. Dark low clouds were now blowing from the west. When they entered the house it felt like they were the only ones alive in the dark wet town. But they were not.

The dread from the courtroom followed them.

It took a long time to be able to sleep.

Chapter 31

Late November. Saturday morning. The Bergstroms sat around the kitchen table. Rain fell fitfully, beating against the windows. Father, mother, brother, and sister. Pancakes and eggs were gone. The dishes were cleared. Tye had a steaming cup of coffee before him. The others had orange juice.

"It's time we got to the bottom of this, Johanna," Tye said. "The therapist let us know that she's having a hard time helping you. She's offered to refer us to another one. What's going on?"

"You won't believe me."

"I'll listen. We all will listen. Just get this out in the open. What's going on?"

"I don't need any more therapy, Dad. I need to remember. I need to get rid of the demon."

"Okay. How?"

"I need to remember!" Johanna screamed. "I need to kill it!"

Tye was surprised at the intensity of the yell but remained outwardly calm. "Okay, Joh. Let's do that together. Let's go back to the party. Walk us through what happened after you left."

"You're safe here," said Jack. "Remember your feet."

Johanna's mouth twitched in a brief smile. Tye started to ask about what that meant but Pamela gave him that leave-it-alone look.

"Tell us," she softly said.

Johanna looked around at the family she was born into. They cared. But they did not know. They could not know the demon's power. She defaulted to apology.

"I didn't know the punch was spiked. I didn't know."

"But now you do. Try to remember how you got to Baker's house."

The therapist had not asked this question until recently. Johanna at first drew a blank. Now, she tried to think. "The lights. I followed the lights. They taunted me. I tripped… and went down… Broadway. Yes, Broadway." Head down, Johanna was talking to herself, eyes darting, unfocused. "A car beeped at me. I found where Downing was. Homeless man. Leaves. Another homeless man. Talking. There was talking… pleading! He was begging! Oh God!" she put her hands on her head.

She began to cry, choke. "Both feet, Joh," said Jack.

A dam broke, "The demon killed him! He's coming! He wants my head!" She bolted upright, her free hand outstretched to ward off the demon.

"You're safe here Joh," said Tye. Pamela grabbed her shaking hand.

"What happened? Let it out, Joh. Let us help," Pamela softly said. "We'll protect you."

"You can't! You can't! He's a demon! He's coming!" Johanna screamed.

An amorphous rage filled Tye. "Johanna!" He grabbed his daughter away from Pamela by her good arm and back, avoiding the sling, and shouted in her face. "Stop it! I will kill him if he tries!"

Johanna stopped screaming like a radio turned off. He let go. She looked at the stern face of her father and seemed to sink into the chair. She went silent and calm. Her head went down. Inside her, a door opened and another closed. She went deeper into her safe place.

Then without fear, as if in a movie, she saw again the demon take the man by the head and twist. That could never happen to her father. That could never happen to her brother. That will never happen to her. Now. In her vision, she saw herself running in panic. She saw the car hit her. She saw the demon grab her. She saw the other man shoot the demon. Yes, it could be done. That man did it. Her father could do it. Her father could shoot. Her father could hunt. She had seen it. His gun was much bigger than the other man's. Her mind took a twisting path. Her father would hunt this demon down and shoot him dead. "You will shoot him dead." She mumbled to herself. Jack alone heard it but kept silent.

Pamela was astounded. Never had Tye grabbed or yelled at his children. Never had he said he would kill someone. Then she realized that his "ability" must have always been there, just kept quiet because it was never needed, until now. He must have always had the ability to protect his family with extreme violence. That ability to kill a deadly threat was now on display. Right now, it was what Johanna needed. Someone to come between the demon and herself. Someone strong. Stronger than the demon. She worried that the assassin may actually come for Johanna and Tye would kill him. The legal system would be problematic. Then she thought, so what.

Better the assassin dead than her daughter. Could she pull the trigger? Without a doubt. Could she be as effective as Tye? No, but she did not need to be.

Jack looked at his father with new eyes. He knew the protective/aggressive urge. He had it. There was a little of it in sports. Especially football. But it was tempered within himself by easy living. Suddenly he wondered if he could kill someone. A queasy feeling came. He looked again at his father's resolve and knew if the circumstance came he could do it. But he saw in his father the ability to be immediately ready. Jack realized that he himself would hesitate. Then he thought about Johanna and knew if a threat came to her he would act immediately. That would be as if there was a direct threat to his own self and would trigger an immediate violent response.

But the violent response needed to be with deadly force. It needed to be immediate. The Bergstroms could not walk around armed and ready.

Inside Johanna's head, she knew neither her father, mother nor Jack knew the demon's power over her. So she entered a new phase of denial. She found this new room to hide in. She was seeing the demon blown apart by her father's powerful rifle. She smiled, but it was not entirely sane.

"Joh? You know the demon is in jail now. He can't get to you."

"I know, Dad." Johanna's eyes saw a far-off blackness coming. She knew her father would stand in the way. She knew it would not be enough. She needed to kill it. "I think I can move past this now," she said without conviction.

Jack saw the lie but was silent. The trauma lingered behind Johanna's eyes.

The table went quiet.

"Who wants Danish?" Pamela tried to lighten the mood. It partially worked. She brought up an upcoming Beach Run and they tried to get interested. Both Jack and Johanna knew some of the runners. It worked to divert the depressing feeling of not being able to completely pull Johanna out of her terror.

Johanna was turned inward, again alone in her locked room, visualizing the demon being blown apart by her father's gun.

Later that night, after Johanna went to bed, Tye, Pamela, and Jack sat in the kitchen

"Tye, our daughter is not well. That was some kind of therapy you did but she's still trapped in that nightmare," Pamela said.

"Yes. I can see that. We need help. I can't be with her all the time. I can't protect her alone."

Pamela was again surprised. Tye never asked for help in any personal endeavor. "Alright. That last therapist gave us the number of another. Let's see about that."

"Yes." Resigned. This was something Tye did not know how to handle. It vexed him.

Pamela saw, "Leave it to me, Tye. I'll get someone."

"No. I'm going to be part of this. I can't sit back."

"Together," Pamela said.

"Yes."

"Would you consider bodyguards?"

"Yes, but I don't think the school would. I'm going to take some time off. Meantime I'll contact the police Chief and see if there is any help there."

"Dad, I need to tell you something."

Tye looked at his son, "Go ahead." Guarded.

"Joh said something after you grabbed her. I don't think you heard it. She said, 'you'll shoot him dead.' I think she believes you are going to kill the 'demon.' I think that's what calmed her down. But she's not well yet. The demon must die for that to happen."

"Tye, we can't be running around hunting this guy. You can't just shoot him on sight." Pamela worried. The instinct to protect Johanna was strong in Tye. Would he actually hunt down and murder this guy?

"Thanks for that, Jack. And no I'm not going on the warpath, Pam. I do mean that I will kill him to protect us, but I would like it to be a defensive act. I'm not interested in going to prison. That said, I will kill the 'demon' preemptively if I think it's necessary. Prison is a small cost for my daughter's sanity and security."

Pamela wanted to calm the waters. "Let's get some help first. Then we'll see."

"I'll take some time off from the City Building Department. I have some time coming. Johanson's got nothing ready to be inspected yet."

Sleep was a long time coming in the Jorgenson house that night.

Chapter 32

"Do you have enough yet?"

"Theoretically. If the witnesses hold up."

Sheila Dennett and Mara Walker sat in the Seaside police station interview room. December was around the corner and Christmas decorations bloomed around the city. Dennett looked tired. Walker looked refreshed. Two junior NSA agents waited outside talking to sergeant James in low tones.

It was morning and the sky was slightly overcast. The wind was calm. In the afternoon a breeze from the north would clear out the haze. But the temperature would hover at forty-five. Dennett looked out the window and wished a magical idea would come to her. She wanted to end this.

Walker saw the impasse. "Tell me about it. Maybe I can help."

Dennett rubbed her eyes, "Why does the NSA now want to help here? The first thing you wanted was for me to stand down."

"Things change. It's now in our best interest that the accused is convicted and held here."

"There's more to this than just a murder."

"Yes, a daddy-sized clusterfuck is coming. We have managed to get control of this part anyway. The FBI is zeroing in on a Senator, but they don't know which one. They dropped the ball badly with the assassination of their inside boy and missing documents. So they don't want to have this assassin guy mucking up the works. Still, they and I need the connection to get to the bottom of how the leak happened."

"Yeah. The FBI pulled out everything they could find that implicated them in that SNAFU."

"They missed a few though, didn't they?" Walker smiled.

Dennett thought, thank god that Johnson and Jeffers had her using handwritten notes. And the Medical Examiner had backed up her autopsy report on paper. So far the feebs had not raided anybody's homes. She made a note to move the reports to a post office box from the library. But she kept quiet.

"Alright, don't answer that," Walker continued. "Here's the current status, subject to change. Normally the NSA investigates and prevents cyber-attacks. That is essentially what we have here. But they're bigger fish swimming in this pond. Assassination does that. This is becoming political and international. What they're doing is above my pay grade, but it isn't going to be pleasant. As I said, I've been ordered to help the prosecution of your John Doe so that our agency can get access to him. We need to know how the leak happened. We need a name. So does the FBI in their investigation. I think they will go ahead without one if they have to but better with one. The big boy pointy heads have two opportunities. This assassin and the Bergstrom girl. Neither is promising. But both are being pursued. So here is what I have. The assassin's real name is Dmitri Valens. Yes, that's right. A make-believe Russian/Chilean. He was mentored by this guy Ozio. Who you met before. The information I have is that the assassin will not break. There are rumors that he is a failed genetic experiment and both the name and the assassin, are manufactured."

"Okay. Both you and I know he's tough. According to reports, his musculature and skin are very dense. He is six feet two and weighs two hundred fifty for all that he looks like he's skinny. Was this a genetic experiment that did that?"

"Yes, the Russians were looking for a super soldier. They've been doing that for over a hundred years. Genetic material from apes and now insects have been used. It is unconfirmed but apparently, they made several men who were like this guy but would not take orders. They were unstable and killed randomly. They were sapient but not sentient, they were just fine at planning and executing their own plan. But they felt nothing. One of the other problems with the super soldier experiment was that their eyes appeared black. It was not because the sclera was deep brown, similar to chips and bonobos, but black like an insect. The iris was not faceted and was jet black. It easily marked the men. This was not thought to be a problem on the battlefield. Once the GRU realized they couldn't be in public and more importantly couldn't be controlled in battle they ordered their destruction. But one of their own managed to secretly get this one away and began to use him in assassinations for profit.

"The 'thing' was taught how to use contacts and keep his eyes down and shaded when in public. But that apparently did not calm the utter ruthlessness of the man. Now the cat's out of the bag and everybody wants a piece of the 'thing's' demonstrated strength.

But nobody wants to 'out' the GRU. They want sole control of the thing. If that can't happen they want him buried."

"So the Russians, the GRU, ordered the hit on the journalist to protect some spy plot?"

"We think so."

"That explains a lot."

"So it's more than just you and I who want to put him away. Big boys want this guy to kill or to use. My guess one agency will get him one way or another. But I am to assure his conviction here for this abduction and/or murder while the NSA pointy heads figure out what their next move is. We can't let him walk. So where are we? Besides dodging Hellfire missiles?"

Dennett again rubbed her bloodshot eyes. "I have given what I have to the Clatsop DA We have the witnesses to the attempted abduction. We have a witness to the murder. What we don't have is solid witnesses or a motive. And if you're right any attempt by me to find it will blow this up. Johnson thinks we can proceed without it. His first prosecution will be for the attempted abduction. For that, he needs both the Baker guy and the Bergstrom girl to be strong. Both are… shaky. The assassin has affected them, like us, but much more."

"If I may offer a suggestion, get them together. The witnesses I mean. I know we're playing close to the edge here but I think if we, you and I, and the two witnesses can collaborate it will help."

"If we're going to play that close to the edge, I want Jeffers and Johnson on board. If they are surprised this will go south faster than Biden's presidency. Coaching witnesses is not in the book."

"So let's let them in. But you will not get a conviction with witnesses that look like basket cases."

"Yeah. At first, I thought I wouldn't need anything but the thing's stare to get a conviction. The original court-appointed lawyer was happy to let the killer be convicted. As fast as possible. But any lawyer worth his salt could tear them apart on the stand."

"So let's make sure that doesn't happen."

"Okay. I'll consult with the current therapist and get Jeffers and Johnson on board if possible."

That afternoon Dennett and Walker sat with Jeffers and Johnson in the Clatsop county courthouse. The air had cleared. Now it was time for Dennett to sell their idea.

"Okay. Here's what I propose," she took a breath, "We, I and Walker, stage a scene with the Bergstrom girl. We reenact the Halloween night and walk her through the area." Now came the hard part. Another breath, "I will shoot the 'demon' for the girl. Hopefully, this will free up her memory." Dennett stopped and waited. The table went silent at the two men assessed the proposal.

"Let's see if I have this right. You want to shoot a person in downtown Seaside." Johnson said sarcastically.

"We will be staging a scene. Nobody will be shot."

"But you will fire your weapon?"

"A blank charge."

"You need more than this outline," Johnson was ready to walk.

"Okay. It will be like a movie shoot. The editor of the Signal has some experience with this. We will make it look like a movie scene to anybody watching."

"And what will Bergstrom think of this? Will she not see the ruse?"

"Okay. She will be told that we want to reenact the route from the party to Baker's to help her remember."

"What of the parents?"

"We need your approval first. Then theirs. If they balk we will think of something else."

"What do you think, Jeffers?"

"I think it's worth a try. It will be fairly easy to set up. We walk down the Downing Mall and have the girl be confronted by a 'demon.' One of our men dressed in black and made up with black eyes and big teeth. Dennett will shoot him and yell that he's dead. Hopefully, the girl will be shocked into remembering any words spoken."

"What does the therapist think?"

"She doesn't know. She's now trying to get the girl to remember, but the girl is battling her own self about this. The girl has walled off herself from reality. Hanson thinks it may work or may just drive her deeper into her trauma."

'We're playing with fire here. The girl's sanity and my prosecution are at stake. The wolves are scenting the defendant's release. This will be a disaster if anything goes wrong."

Jeffers stepped in, "We've got nothing now. The three witnesses we have will be shredded on the stand. The Bergstrom girl's sanity is our only hope. We need a name to get another direction for the investigation."

"The FBI will shut down anything I can do," Johnson griped.

"Okay. Here's where the NSA comes in. Walker can help shut that can of worms. What that will do is open the door for the assault charge. Keeping it separate from the murder. The only real witness to that is Baker. The Bergstrom girl may be called by the defense but she can claim she doesn't remember."

"Baker will be discredited on the stand if the 'thing' word gets out. And we know it will. Nothing is secret when discovery happens."

"Okay. We get him in on the ruse. We get him solid. We coach the shit out of him until he looks like the epitome of sanity."

"You're asking a lot."

"Okay. What we will do is off any record. It will be without official approval. No media help. No Signal help. We will get the therapist to stand by."

"There is not a chance in hell that this will not hit the fan with one big messy splat," Johnson worried.

"We've got nothing else, Johnson," said Jeffers. "Let's try to get the Bergstroms on board and see where it goes from there."

"Do it quickly before I have a chance to see how dangerous this is. Get back ASAP." Johnson began to see a bit of light behind the big black cloud they were conjuring.

Walker was impressed at how these small-town people worked together. In her own experience, the NSA was made up of people who were looking to advance. To do that became a game of one-up-man-ship. She knew because she played the game herself.

She also felt herself being drawn into the local mindset, where doing the right thing was a real concept. No matter how bureaucratic the system was, it was made up of individuals. Each making decisions on everything each day. The problems came with the oaths they swore to become part of that. Hell, she thought, you can't even get online without signing what amounts to an oath. Microsoft, Google, MSN, and all the social media require you to sign up to participate. How many people actually knew what they signed? She didn't. But she did know what she signed to become an

NSA agent. She knew the rules. She was close to breaking a few. The consequences for her would be severe if this went south.

Yet she forged ahead. There was something here that was outside the scope of what the rules writers knew.

For her now was just to do the job. Get the 'thing' into a federal prison where the NSA could access him. Preferably some other agent.

Chapter 33

The next day Jeffers and Dennett sat with Johanna Bergstrom's parents in the Seaside conference room. There was a lull in the seasonal storms and the air was clear.

They had brought their son Jack. Tye sat with shaded doubt. Pamela was wondering what was going on. Jack was interested. Johanna was in school and not aware of the meeting.

The plan had been laid out in outline. The therapist was involved with the planning but would stand back during the execution. There were just the Bergstroms and the Seaside police involved. From the video feed, Walker monitored the meeting.

"I don't like the idea of tricking Johanna," said Tye. "We've always been truthful with her."

"Okay. I don't like it either. But the potential benefits are substantial. Both for Johanna and the county. Now I saw the way Jack here handled the interview at the hospital. I heard the way he brought Johanna out of the coma." Dennett had played fast and loose with the intrusion into the Bergstrom's lives. "I am not going to push

on this. But I ask you to consider this as a form of therapy. The therapist thinks there is a chance to help."

"No. We're not going to further traumatize Johanna." Tye said. There was no way they were going to play tricks on his daughter. The hammer came out.

"Dad. Can I say something?"

"Go ahead."

"This is for you, Dad. Remember when we had our talk that morning and Johanna said something that I heard?"

Tye thought, "Yes. What are you getting at?"

"You need to kill the demon. Not the detective. You need to be there and protect your daughter."

The table went silent.

Dennett was the first to recover. "Yes! That's brilliant. The father saves his daughter."

Tye looked at Pamela. She had been following, and now she spoke. "Detective, do you know what you're doing? This is our daughter, not a specimen to be experimented with. Not a damned Halloween movie!"

"I apologize for seeming to be insensitive. But we have a murderer to put away. Now I have looked into the eyes of this 'thing.' The effect is horrible. And I can tell you it will kill again. I want to kill it myself. The only ones who have actually witnessed the direct, paralyzing stare and the unprotected direct threat of death from it are Johanna and Baker. Both are traumatized." She was rambling

The door opened and Walker came in. "May I?"

"Go ahead," Jeffers said. He thought better more than less.

"My name is Mara Walker. I am an NSA agent. I can tell you that I too have looked into the assassin's eyes and they are beyond anything I could imagine. I am directed to assure the assassin is convicted. We can't do that without your daughter. This is not a game - it is life and death for others. I'm sorry that you are caught in this mess. But I see the strength you have and the commitment to Johanna. I believe this charade can be a breakthrough."

"You just want to win a case!" Pamela countered. "You don't give a rat's ass for Johanna!"

The accusation stunned both Tye and Jack. Dennett and Walker had heard such before.

"Yes. I do want to win. I want to save lives. I want to protect the people of this country from enemies foreign and domestic. I do NOT want to hurt your daughter. I do think it could help her."

"Okay. Let's back up," said Jeffers calmly. "This is your decision, Mr. and Mrs. Bergstrom. We will not force anything. I ask you to consider what we have said here,"

"Mom, Dad needs to kill the demon," put in Jack. "Johanna is convinced he will. She will not be well until he does that. This is probably the only way to save her."

"Tye?" Pamela looked to her husband.

"I want the Bakers involved. He managed to shoot the assassin and save Johanna. I think he may be helpful."

"Tye? Are you sure?"

"No, but I see no other way. We've seen Joh decline. We need to do something. Hanson said that it may help. I want Jack there also."

Jeffers stood up, "Dennett, get the Bakers in here. Now!" It was what they wanted.

Dennett rushed out of the room and caught James in the break room. "Get the Bakers here. Now!"

James got on the comm and got the patrol watching the house. The officer rang the doorbell and said, "Let's go." They got up and went.

Ten minutes later the Bakers came into the tense room. Introductions were made. The Bakers sat down. Coffee came in.

"Okay. I know this is getting confusing for all involved. So I will recap." Dennett then concisely and tersely went over the case and the meeting.

"So you're thinking of a reenactment of the murder? Why do you need me?" asked Harrison.

Tye answered, "You saved my daughter that night. If we do this you need to be part of it. Johanna will feel better with you there."

"The two incidents will be tried separately. The first will be the assault. For that, we would like Johanna to be coherent, but it's not necessary. If this works the effect will be that she can testify for both trials along with you, Mr. Baker. We do need Johanna for the murder trial," offered Johnson.

"I'll do anything to help. Just don't know what that is." Harrison said.

"Okay. Let's plan. If everybody agrees we will give it a shot. Literally," said Dennett.

The conspirators planned. Each person in the room was well aware this could be a tragedy if something went wrong. The Bergstroms wanted Johanna sane again. The police and prosecutors wanted a stable witness. The Bakers wanted to help both.

They rehashed it until it was nailed down as tight as one of Johanson's buildings.

But an earthquake was coming. Would the building stand?

Chapter 34

The Editor sat in the cell. Still as a spider in its web.

Inside he continues planning. With animal cunning, he sees the actions around him and knows that there will be an opportunity to complete his mission. The contract must be fulfilled. The man who shot him must be made to disappear. He has committed the face to memory. He knows where the man lives and as if it were delivered by a letter to him, he would earn his pay.

For him, there should be nothing else. Only the plan and execution. But waiting in this cell, there is a dim glimmer of memory intruding on his plan. A memory of darkness, of confinement. Then for as long as can remember there were instructions. How to act. How to behave. How to plan. How to kill without weapons. How to obey.

A memory of failure. His mind could not accept orders. He could not obey. There was no understanding of what an order meant. He could accept instruction and could plan and execute that plan if given an instruction. But an order was not something he could understand. The difference was everything to his handlers but was a gulf across which he could not go.

At some point, he and the others like him were told to go into a closed room. It was an order. In a break of discipline, he refused. The others also refused. Then there was chaos and confusion. He could not make sense of what happened. His ordered mind could not comprehend the situation. He felt bullets hitting him. He fell and darkness covered him.

The wandering parasite saw this opportunity. Without substance, it slithered into the unconscious host as it passed by. There was no resistance. This was the most promising host it had ever used. It settled in and waited.

Then for the assassin, the darkness turned to light. He was being moved. He did not know what a helicopter was. But instinctively knew he was in a flying machine. He looked around. Across from him sat a small round man who was watching him.

The man smiled and said, "Welcome back."

He did not know what that meant.

"Don't worry John. I am your friend. I will teach you how to take care of yourself. In return, you will perform a service for me." It was dangerously close to an order. 'Johns' black eyes went dead. The abrupt change in aura caused the small man to blanch.

Hynd Ozio did not get to where he was by being afraid. But this set him back. He dropped his eyes to the floor and said "Now, John. That was not an order, this is a business offer."

For most of his previous life, 'John' had not needed to talk much. There were just instructions. Now he tried to form his thoughts into words. All he could do was grunt, "Why?"

Ozio knew he now had him. This was his ticket to untold riches. But first, the man must be trained. Instructed. But not ordered. That must be carefully orchestrated. He went to work on his plan.

The Kamov Ka-27 helicopter landed at an obscure pad on Isla de Santa Maria. John was taken down a stairway under a bunker and shown his billet. He was instructed on how to care for himself. How to prepare meals. How to dress. How to speak. And most of all how to keep his eyes shaded and his aura damped. He was given instructions on how to act in various societies. All this was done remotely. There was no real interaction with real people at first.

After a year of instruction, he was given an assignment. An instruction. Eliminate this person. Leave no trace. He had just a picture and address that he had to destroy. It was in a local city. He was given ID and lifted by helo to the mainland to proceed on his own - without orders.

He was successful. Then he was given a place to live, and more documents to aid in his assignments. For a dozen years and as many assignments, he continued to be successful.

Then in the insignificant town of Seaside Oregon USA, he was not. That the cause was a chance encounter with a civilian was not taken into account. He had failed and now was the center of a political storm. His ordered brain sought to make order out of chaos and only succeeded in making a plan to correct the original error.

He knew he could have completed the assignment even when the man with the gun appeared. Nothing alive had seen the speed at which he could move. Or his ability to weather bullet wounds. But the man fired faster than any other before. Something had alarmed the man. He had recovered from his stare faster than any before. And the first shot had hit a nerve rendering his arm useless. The odds against all that happening at once were astronomical. He saw the man's intent shoot for his head. He could not repair the arm in time. Then he just had to survive.

There was no consideration of failure in this instruction or any instruction. All he needed was a chance. It would come sooner or later. He settled into a suspended state and bided.

Like an insect might do.

Yet he was more than an insect. He was more than a man. He was more than genetically enhanced. He was more than an instruction.

There was a parasite that chose this body. It would work just fine for what it wanted. It was not interested in mass casualties. It was not interested in politics or power.

It was interested, indeed, wanted, needed, and fed on hopelessness. Up close and personal. It wanted to see the effects of this host's eyes on victims as they saw their death coming. It needed to feed on the fear, the terror, the hopelessness. It wanted to drive their souls into the void where it could torment them. The alternative for itself was endless wandering in the void in constant hunger.

The last victim was beautiful in his suffering. The one who got away would have been even better.

The one who shot him was alerted by something the parasite did not, could not feel. But it knew there was another presence at work. That presence must be eliminated for it to continue without constraint. It thought the man with the gun was the cause. The other presence would die with the man.

It pressed its thoughts on the host. The empty of a soul body it inhabited. The host's programming changed, just enough. The parasite could continue.

Chapter 35

On a late Monday afternoon under partially cloudy skies, the group of Sheila, Mara, Harrison, and Johanna stood outside on the front lawn of Baker's house.

Inside, Jennifer, Tye, Pamela, and their son Jack watch.

"Okay," said Dennett. "First thing, for this exercise we use first names. It makes it easier to relate. I am Sheila, this is Mara and this is Harry. Second thing, if at any time it becomes uncomfortable, call for a time out." She was talking to Johanna. "We will be with you. We will protect you." Sheila and Mara openly wore their Glock service pistols. Harry wore his Sig.

"I want my father. He will shoot the demon." The sight of the pistols was not enough to calm Johanna. She remembered her father's pledge. The rest of these people were not capable of knowing or killing the demon. She did not care about first names.

Dennett worried that Johanna was on to the ruse. But she waved to the house. Tye came out as agreed. He carried his rifle slung over his back. It would still work even if Johanna knew.

"Okay, Joh. Your father will be with you." So far, so good. Johanna had to think she was in control.

Police lined Downing Street from 5th to Broadway. Placed at every intersection to control traffic and calm any visitors that might be worried about a band of armed people walking down the center of the street. Two plain-clothed officers held video cameras. This had taken a considerable effort by Dennett to coordinate. The attempt to jump-start Johanna's memory hinged on this working.

Every powerful agency out there wanted a piece of the assassin's or victim's words, and Johanna was the key. She was also the key to Johnson's prosecutions. So far Johnson and Walker had succeeded in officially keeping other agencies away. Unofficially they, of course, were here.

Dennett now had three civilians to control. Two of which were armed and with unknown abilities. She knew Harrison could shoot and that Tye was a hunter. But this was not that. She took a deep breath. There was no real danger here, she reasoned. But she and Walker had seen the thing. Baker and Johanna had actually felt the thing. The residual dread was real and affected all of them adversely, to varying degrees.

Walker had managed to secure NSA protection for this experiment, but that was always subject to political winds. If discovered by the defense, this action would be an open door for any that wanted to use it. For now, it was holding. The group stood ready.

"Comm check!" Dennett said into her mic. The dozen responses came in by the numbers. Johnson and Jeffers waited at the restroom building. They were set. "Okay, Joh, ready?"

Johanna looked at her father and nodded. It was close to getting dark. Hanson thought that if conditions were approximately the same as that Halloween night it might help. "Let's go," Dennett said and they stepped across the rutted lawn, across the sidewalk, and down to the street, moving in sync with Johanna's tentative steps. Inside the Baker house, the remaining family watched the group move slowly away toward the place of Johanna's trauma, then they stepped out onto the porch and waited. They were not part of this.

Yet they were.

Evalyn Hanson waited inside the tavern. She had never been so nervous. This was another potential end to her career. She owed it to Johnson and Jeffers to help as much as possible. Both for them and Johanna. And mostly for herself. She had contributed to Johanna's problem while under duress from the threat to he career. Now the leak at the Clatsop courthouse had been plugged. The records of her plagiarism were archived again. The criminal who masterminded the threat had been effectively neutralized under the threat of prosecution.

This attempt at helping Johanna and Johnson was the most awkward, out-of-the-box effort she had ever been a part of or ever heard of. All of her long education did not include actual shooting for therapy. There was role-play of course. But not like this where the patient did not know what was happening.

She stood ready to help calm Johanna if she reacted badly. But there was something here that seemed under control. She watched the interaction between the police and the families. There was serendipity here. A calmness despite the circumstance. Or was she projecting what she wished for?

She watched the approach through the tavern window. She saw the families move off to the side of the Mall.

At one point the group stopped. There seemed to be a problem. She saw Mr. Baker kneel and talk to Johanna for a minute. Then they started back up to a make-or-break trial by fire.

Gunfire.

Jack, Pamela, Jennifer, and Katrin moved behind the group by fifty yards. Ready to help. All this to help a single young girl remember a paralyzing event.

And much more.

The group started up 5th the short block to Downing then down the street toward the Beach Club tavern and the shark mural, with four armed adults surrounding one young girl. And a dozen police officers lined the way. Spectators began to gather, watching what they believed was an actual movie being made. Those who had seen real movie sets knew this was not real, but it was interesting anyway, maybe a theater production promo.

In the crowd were men who did not resemble tourists or vacationers. Police spotters on the roof of the Heritage Square Mall and Carousel Mall noted them and took pictures with telescopic cameras.

As agreed, Tye walked beside his daughter.

As they progressed, Johanna pressed to the front. Dennett allowed it. Maybe Johanna was coming to grips with the trauma. Maybe she would remember.

Give me a name, Walker thought. Just a name. Something to give her superiors to officially use. Something to sic the FBI on. To get them out of her way as she went after the cybercriminals.

Johanna's mind was a cauldron of conflicting emotions. A path through the parked cars, pickups, and vans had been cleared to the tavern wall. The shark with its eye and teeth was visible. To Johanna, the eye, and the teeth appeared like in a dream, swimming toward her. Unstoppable, inevitable. Blackness, pain, and death. Her eyes began to water. She faltered.

Tye noticed the change in his daughter. He readied himself for the planned intervention.

As they entered the parking lot she began to shake. Tye moved the Remington 30.06 to his side. He took Johanna's hand and showed her the rifle. She stopped at the parking lot entrance and looked around at her father and then at the mural. The shark was coming. The demon was here. This was it. Her father must kill it.

"Shoot it," Johanna said in a flat monotone.

The group stopped with her. Tye was at a loss. This was not in the plan. Dennett felt the beginnings of failure. Johanna stared at the mural like she thought it would attack her. She was not sane.

Then Harrison stepped forward, bent down, and turned to face Johanna. Between her and the mural.

"Remember me?" he started. "I shot the demon a while back. I saw its eyes. I know what it is. But the mural is not the demon. It's just a picture. Your father can shoot a picture but that will not kill the demon. But he can shoot and kill the real demon. Understand?"

Johanna looked at Harrison. "But you didn't kill it."

"I could have. I should have done it. But I was stopped by the police. They didn't know what it was at the time. Now they do. The demon is in a bad man but can be killed by your father. The mural is not the demon."

"The demon is still alive."

"Yes, but not for long. Your father will kill it. To do that we need to remember. You and I need to make sure of that. We need to tell what we know. We need to remember what happened."

"You know, but I don't."

"Not right now. But if we can retrace your steps maybe we can. Together."

"Joh," Tye said. "We can do this."

The discourse was back as planned. The use of "we" was paramount. The use of the words "kill the demon" was the hard part. Johanna had to believe that they killed it. That her father blew it to pieces. She had to feel safe enough to remember.

Johanna nodded. Stared at the mural and then started forward again.

"Okay," said Dennett. "Let's go past the tavern to Broadway and walk the way you took from there to Baker's house. We are all here." It was getting dark. A glimmer of hope arose. She wondered how Harrison came up with that. Then she remembered that Harrison had looked into the 'thing's' eyes and survived. She knew that if the assassin were free at the time she confronted it, she could not have done what he did. The stare paralyzed her for a second even with the killer being restrained. That's all it would take. She knew from her training that a man with a knife could cover six to eight feet before she could decide to pull the trigger. That one second and the 'thing' could have her head in its hands.

Johanna and Harrison were forming a bond that could not have been forged any other way. A bond that was going to save them, and her, Dennett hoped.

When they got to Broadway, out of their sight, a black SUV backed up under the shark mural. The driver and passenger got out and waited. Both wore body armor. An officer made up like a homeless man took his position next to the restrooms. The scene was ready. The critical act was coming. As they came back up the mall, Tye got ready. The rest of the group dropped back a step. Out of sight on the other side of the Heritage Square Mall on Oceanway, Pamela, Jack, Jennifer, and Katrin waited, ready for anything. Hanson held her breath. Cameras recorded.

Time slowed. Johanna began to shuffle like she was drunk. The escorts dropped further back. She came to the corner and stopped, waiting. She saw the homeless man. She saw two men in the space behind the SUV facing each other. One was talking.

One man fell, the big one turned to her, black eyes and big teeth showing. Johanna screamed. "No! No! No!" She started to run but Tye stepped between her and the grinning man. There was a tremendous blast and the man fell. Johanna's ears rang. Instantly Dennett ran over.

"The demon is dead," shouted Dennett, then, "Stay down until we say," she whispered to the dead demon. Miller couldn't hear her well but knew what she meant. This was something they could not practice. He had seen Tye shoot but had to trust Tye not to hit him in the face with the speed he had to use. Despite the round being a blank quarter-power and the ear protection, his hearing was still ringing like bells in a church steeple. He had closed his eyes when Tye pulled the trigger, but he still saw the flash of the round and felt the wad hit his vest. There was a fake blood bag there in case Johanna noticed. And then the detective had gleefully rolled him over in the slimy concoction. He spit out the irritating demon fangs. He would stay down for a while all right, even though the close contact dark swim goggles, which he couldn't remove, were grinding into his face.

"Johanna, what did he say?" Harrison asked quietly. To ask this now was not part of the plan but Dennett was happy he did the asking.

Johanna stood blankly staring at the inert body, leaking a pool of blood. "Didn't you hear? He said, 'We have the stuff on Trask, you can have it.'" Then she looked around at the growing group.

Walker had her name. And so did every other agentcy there.

Pamela came running over and held her. "Good going. You were very brave."

Reality came sneaking back.

"What? What happened?" Johanna said.

"You've beat the demon, that's what," crowed Jack. "With both feet." He grabbed her and spun her around.

Johanna broke free and glared at Jack. "The demon's not dead. You tricked me!"

Jack still was close. "Yeah, we did. Felt good, didn't it? Do you want to do it again? You can shoot the demon next time."

Dennett watched with concern. This was another tipping point. She remembered the name but would need to repeat it on the stand. If she reverted they were at square one again, even with the camera's video and audio recording.

Hanson came out and faced the girl. "Johanna, this was my idea. We needed you to remember. *You* needed to remember. You needed to kill the demon, and you did just that."

From somewhere in a dark memory Johanna remembered the words she threw at her family that one Saturday; *I need to kill it!* But it was not her that fired the shot.

"Wasn't me," she mumbled. Then she remembered what she said to her father, words that only Jack heard, *You'll shoot the demon dead.*

"Was too, Joh. You did it, you remembered. You didn't let the demon win. It was you!" Jack was adamant. Johanna was stunned. But she felt the truth in her brother's statement. Just a little, but enough to move her past resentment and into acceptance of the effort. But this was not over.

"Okay. Let's clear out this movie crime scene," said Dennett. "Back to Baker's place." She turned to Johnson and Jeffers who were at the tavern door, "You heard? We have it on tape too."

"Yes, it's another piece in the puzzle. It will help only if she gets straight. The video is not admissible proof." Johnson was concerned that this little charade could be a means for his dismissal by a smart lawyer. He had the cooperation of the court-appointed counsel and therapist, but this act was loaded with problems if a real defense lawyer ever got hold of it.

And that was a dead bang certainty.

"She will." Dennett broke in on his thoughts.

"Keep her sane, detective." Johnson began thinking of a rebuttal to a defense claim that the testimony was coerced or coached. Maybe Hanson could help.

"Okay," Dennett said in the comm. "We're done here. Dismissed."

The walk back was on the sidewalk. As they neared the dogleg at 5th, Johanna began to remember again what happened on the front yard. She saw the fight and felt her arm tear and the demon's hands on her face. She heard the shots fired by Harrison.

She turned to Harrison, "Thank you," she said.

"You're welcome, but you saved yourself," Harrison instinctively knew what she was saying. "You fought the demon like a whirlwind. It gave me time to get to my gun." They walked back side by side. The police guard disappeared.

As they approached the front yard, Harrison again heard the dog growling. A deep rumbling sound. Not aggressive. A warning. He looked around, but nobody else heard it.

Then someone did.

"What was that?" Johanna said.

Harrison smiled at her. "You heard?" he thought quickly, "That will be our secret for now."

"What will?" asked Jennifer.

"I'll tell you later. Otherwise, these people will think we're crazy." He winked at Johanna.

Johanna looked back and shrugged. "Okay," she said uncertainly.

Jennifer saw the interplay, frowned, and vowed to find out.

They got into the house. A cabal of conspirators, successful in their charade. Jennifer broke out the wine and pastries. Harrison got the glasses for the Jameson. A discussion of how to proceed commenced.

Johanna and Jack moved away and sat off to the side and talked in low tones about demons and how they were excised. Jack had been doing some reading. Katrin drifted over.

The parents and Bakers talked about the event and then the talk went into the 'thing.'

"Harry, what was it like? I need to know for my daughter's sake, what she's feeling?" asked Pamela.

"You sure? I don't know if I can put it in words. But it's the worst thing that I could ever imagine."

"I need to know."

"I'll try," Harrison felt the doom descend. A portal to Hell opened.

"Harry!" interrupted Jennifer. "Harry! Don't go there. Stop! Stop!"

Pamela, Jennifer, and Harrison were suddenly talking over each other.

"It's okay…" from Harrison.

"Harry stop…" from Pamela

"I can do this…"

"You don't have to…"

Then Jennifer took control "All right! Everybody shut up!"

The entire group did just that. Silence. "If we're going to go that way I want Harry to know that he is safe here. A show of force. Weapons out. You talk to me, Harry. Like you did before. Everybody here can listen."

"I can do that," Harrison shakily said. "This little reenactment put me back a step."

"Listen," said Pamela. "I got enough. I never got this from Johanna. She kept it so reserved, hidden. I felt the doom second hand but this was real. And I'm sorry I did. I'm sorry Harry."

"Don't be. Just know that Johanna beat the devil today. She and I will be okay. I have Jennifer as my rock. You have your family. I see the strength there. And Johanna is… I don't know… a miracle."

Tye and Jack had an inkling now of what Johanna went through. They also knew it was not over.

The Johansons felt the air clear a bit. Katrin smiled. There was a subtle glow that no one noticed, except Johanna. She also smiled genuinely for the first time since Halloween.

The parents conferred for a while about legal issues. Johanna, Jack, and Katrin drifted over to the fire and had their own discussion.

Chapter 36

During the parents' discussion of the problems they faced, the Bergstrom siblings and Katrin discussed demonic possession. They sat apart from the grownups in comfortable chairs near the fire. They faced each other closely and talked in low tones. Harrison noted this. He knew the conversation and was concerned that Jack may try to 'cure' her. If he heard about barking dogs things might get messy. Occasionally he would look over at the pair and observe. After a few times, he felt that it was beneficial and stopped worrying.

He did not need to worry. Pamela watched Harrison to make sure he did not interfere with the trio. She knew them. It was a healing moment. Harrison had helped immensely. But now he should not interfere.

Jack had been reading up on the matter. Most of the online sites on demonology referenced religious themes. They quoted the Bible. Like a demon was a physical thing. He knew his parents were Lutheran but did not go to church regularly. For this part, he relied on information found on the internet, not necessarily the definitions and religious beliefs found in the Bible.

"Near as I can understand it, the demon possesses a person, a host, to cause problems for the host and others. There are levels of possession that only people with ESP can detect. These levels are 'mild, medium, and severe.' My guess is the killer is possessed by a major demon."

"I don't think the internet and religions have it right. Remember this demon is also a hitman. It kills for money. But that's not all. It needs to feed on the terror it makes when killing. I saw it. There is no way for anybody to know without seeing the demon's intent. The eyes…" Johanna shivered. "The… doom."

"Feet, Joh! You survived, you're strong."

"No, there was something else. I was frozen. I knew it could catch me, I felt it! But it didn't try at first. Something stopped it. When I talked to Mr. Baker, he said that a dog helped him shoot the demon. I believe that I survived in the alley because something stopped the demon there." She thought for a minute. "I heard a dog barking. Yes! Telling me to run. I think it was the same dog that saved Mr. Baker." A revelation.

"Well, I'm glad it did. I think I know what it was." Katrin said. She had been doing her own research. "I know that we as humans see only a small percentage of the electromagnetic spectrum. And only hear a small percentage of the sound spectrum. There's so much we don't know. Even with all the scientific tools we have, we don't know much." She believed Johanna had seen or heard something outside the normal ability of humans. She was the only one that stood by Johanna in school when others were distant. She knew that what happened to Johanna had scarred her. She felt it when Johanna came in on Halloween when she tried to hold her. It had affected Katrin too.

"Don't forget quantum entanglement theory, multiple dimensions," put in Jack.

"It had to be something greater than the demon that protected me. But why me? Why did it pick me?" Johanna said out loud ignoring the scientific discussion.

"The something that helped you must have helped Mr. Baker too. Why him? There's only one answer to that. You both deserve it!" Katrin answered quietly.

"What about all those this demon supposedly killed? Did they deserve that?" Johanna moaned. Katrin did not know and remained silent. Then she felt a warm blast of knowledge.

"No. But they were part of secular, hedonistic endeavors. Part of the power players. They were not seeking this kind of help. Whether you know it or not - you were."

"Alright, I don't know. Maybe it's not 'deserve,' it's to do with purity, sinlessness, God I don't know," Jack had been listening and suddenly realized. "We've been avoiding that word, God. I think it's the answer. When I was reading about possession, one of the examples given was Hitler. It was supposed he was possessed by a severe demonic entity. According to the internet, such a demon is not detectable by anyone other than a top-level priest." Jack veered off topic. To invoke God now would beg a load of questions that were unanswerable.

Johanna stiffened. "This demon doesn't wish for Armageddon, it doesn't care," she stated with conviction. "It's personal. I think this demon is like all demons. They don't care about anything but their own satisfaction. They are sustained by feeding on pain and terror. Serial killers are probably possessed, but this demon was not. What I called the demon was not a man possessed by one. It *is* a demon. But not that exactly. The man was without volition, he was empty." Jack gaped. "Yes, a big word, I've been studying too. I've heard the talk about genetic experiments. This 'man' was not a man. He was part insect; it was in his eyes and movements. He was a host for the demon but he was empty of a… soul. The 'man' was doing a job. It's the demon that wanted pain and suffering. It wanted to feed on terror the mutation inspired without having to share."

"Joh, that was amazing. How do you do that? How do you stay sane in all this?" Katrin asked. But she knew. She just wanted Johanna to also know.

"We've been sitting here talking about demons and maybe angels like we know. Maybe we're not completely sane. Only I do know what happened firsthand. It nearly killed me. Something stopped it when I was under the shark. Was it an angel in dog form?

How does that work? Do angels possess humans or dogs? When I was saved the second time, Mr. Baker credited the invisible barking dog. I and he heard it growling tonight, but nobody else did," Johanna added absently.

"I don't know how that works; I just know it did. You've grown up fast. I think you're smarter and stronger than most." Jack wondered about the barking dog. Was it real? Or a figment of Johanna's need?

"Not smart, just more experienced," Johanna then almost cried. "Jack, tell me how this ends!" The events this night caught up with her. She almost went back to her locked room.

"You've got good people on your side, and if you help with this, then it ends with the demon dead."

"Yes, Dad will kill it!" She sat in the chair holding her knees. Folding in on herself. Then she did go back to her safe room. But now she knew where she was and could leave at any time.

Jack and Katrin did not know what to say about that. Johanna had slipped back into the fantasy. Or was it fantasy? He knew his father could shoot. He knew he would without hesitation. Maybe his Dad really would kill the demon. Maybe a barking dog would help him.

Jack did not actually know about the pop demonology expressed by Johanna. The only thing that stood out was that she believed it. He vowed to stand by his sister in all this.

He did not know the demon or need to.

Katrin struggled to help Johanna but felt left out. There were forces here she could not understand. She thought maybe even Jack did not know.

She threw a question to the wind of her mind. What should I do? *Just be there,* an answer whispered back to her in her mind. *Yes,* she answered, *I will,* as Harrison turned to the discussion.

Over at the grownup's table, Harrison thought he heard whispering from the teen's table. Janice did also. But they were quiet. They both looked at her daughter and thought they saw Katrin momentarily glow. A beautiful ethereal color not found in nature. Harrison and

Janice looked at each other in puzzlement and then at the beginning of understanding. Then they returned to their discussion.

Later as the group broke up, Johanna called Harrison aside out on the porch, away from the others. "No one else heard the dog, did they?" Harrison and Johanna now shared another bond. Both had survived the demon. Both had heard the dog.

"No."

"It was there when the demon looked at me. Telling me to run. I didn't remember till now. I wish it were real."

"I do too. But it saved us. Are you all right with what happened here?"

A cloud crossed her face. "I didn't like being tricked, but I don't know how else it could've been done. Kinda like being scared straight. Now I remember what happened and what was said. But I know the demon is still out there. I don't know if I can face him alone. It's not just a bad man. There's more."

"I know that too."

"This is bad, really bad."

There was nothing to say about that. She was going to have to face the demon when on the stand during the upcoming trial. And maybe again at a murder trial. Harrison took her hand and said, "Remember your father's gun."

"Remember your wife, Mr. Baker."

Chapter 37

When they had gone and Jennifer was done cleaning up she called over to Harrison, "Come here, we need to talk."

He came in from the porch. He still had on his pistol. "Yes, dear?"

"Don't give that forking 'yes, dear' stuff. What's the secret?"

"You already know it. It's the barking dog. Johanna heard it when we got to the yard. It was only growling this time. So did I. But nobody else did."

"You care to explain that?"

"I don't think I can. I thought maybe it was just me warning myself when I shot the thing. But Johanna and I both heard it when we got to the yard and there was no danger at that point. But the sound was not the same. It was like a warning about the future. For right here."

"Yeah? So it's supernatural? Or maybe God letting you know or waking you up. But why now? Why you?"

"Johanna and I share a bond. We saw the absolute … pure… evil… of the 'thing,' the demon close up, it was going to kill us both. With nothing between us and it except a barking dog. If it was God then maybe He wanted to save us."

"What the fork is happening?"

Harrison was not religious. Neither was Jennifer. But both were quasi-deists. Harrison because of his past and she because of the fertility problem. Yet Jennifer knew there was something out there besides them. Now she realized there were things outside her ability to see or hear. Harrison had convinced her that at least this one 'thing' was more than a man. Now she was sure her husband heard a dog no one else could hear. That it was real to him.

Harrison thought for a moment, what about the glow? "You want to hear another strange happening?" he continued before she could answer. "I saw a glow on Katrin when the kids were talking. I think Janice did too. Johanna seemed to relax a little after that."

Jennifer knew the beliefs of her parents who were also Lutheran. She also knew the history of the Norse. A pantheon of gods. She knew the legends. But never had she known any god to actually interfere with *her* human activities. Yet now it sure looked like it. Demon's eyes, a dog's bark, and a glow. She took a breath.

"Harry, what do we have here? A real demon? Devine intervention?"

"Jen, I don't know. I don't think we can know the why about barking dogs or glows, but I do know about the 'thing.' I'll accept the fact of it. He is not just a man, and not just dangerous beyond any other. Dangerous beyond all. Walker explained the failed Russian experiment. The 'thing' is tougher than any other human. He is also obsessive. He will seek me out. This I know like I know the barking dog."

"So we, all of us conspirators, need to make sure that he winds up in a super secure prison waiting for the injections that will put him back to where he came from." Jennifer was accepting the impossible.

"We, I, will do my part."

"Both of us, Harry."

"How did I ever manage to get you?"

"Just lucky. Or something else."

"I'll take it. Let's try out that Thai place. I'm getting hungry. Pastries were good but not filling."

Later that night after making love, Jennifer lay staring at the dark ceiling. "Harry. I want to ask you to do something I don't want you to do.

"I recognize this. I've heard it before. So here's my response: Well fork Jen, that was about as clear as mud. You want to explain that?"

"I want you to promise me something." Deadly serious.

"Anything I can." Sobering.

"That's my man. You don't want to promise."

"I will do my best."

"Harry. I don't care about your best. I know you will do that. I know you hate making promises you might not be able to deliver. But I want you to promise me that you and I will survive this. Promise me!"

Harrison heard the need and did what he had to do. "I promise." The words almost caught in his throat.

Jennifer rolled over and gave him a kiss. "I know that was hard for you. Thank you. Now tell me what's really going to happen."

"Well, I think that somewhere down the way, the 'thing' will come for me. I shot him before and I'll shoot him again. Like I've said, I will shoot him until he's dead."

Jennifer noted that Harrison had reverted to the use of the words "him" and "he." Maybe the 'thing' was becoming human and killable. She smiled in the darkness, then hoped that he was right. She knew the reality. If indeed the 'thing' came it was a tossup who would die. Jennifer did know one thing. She was going to be as ready as her husband.

"Harry, tomorrow we go to a shooting range. I need to be ready."

"My Annie Oakley. We'll find a place."

The next day Harrison got on the internet to find a shooting range. The nearest ones were an hour away. He looked for national forests that allowed shooting and found none close. Then by luck, he asked the local gun shop. The guy said that the local private tree farm offered passes. They did not prevent shooting on the property. And it was private property so they could open carry.

He applied and got passes. They scouted around for a good place to shoot and found several. They narrowed it down to a logging road near Twin Peaks.

Chapter 38

Out in the Greenwood Resources Forest near Twin Peaks, Jennifer squeezed the trigger. The bark of the Sig sounded over the twenty feet to the bullet trap. The ejected brass casing spun out to the area cleared by Harrison. The trap rang with the impact.

They had obtained passes to the private property. Their name tags were on display. They hiked far enough away from the gate to a clear-cut area to be isolated from others who might be out here.

"Yow!" she exclaimed.

"Good shot!" commented Harrison.

The day was overcast. A light mist rolled between the peaks.

"That hurt my hands."

"Hold on a sec. Let me." Harrison took the pistol and checked the round in the barrel. He stood and fired off the remaining rounds. Brass spun. The trap shook. The gun locked open.

"Wow!" Jennifer said again. "I want to be able to do that."

Harrison ejected the magazine and loaded another. "Here, take it like this. Hold your arms straight. Now get stiff."

"Yeah? Get stiff? You never liked that before," she chided.

"Hah. That's a different kind of shooting. This kind takes life, not gives it." Harrison hurriedly moved on before the 'gives life' miscue settled in. "Keep your finger outside the trigger guard until you are ready to shoot. Lock your elbows. Put your off hand cupped like this. Like you're scraping crumbs off the table. Now pull with your left and push with your right. Squeeze the weapon's handle hard and squeeze the trigger gently. Pretend the trap is the 'thing's' ugly face." He did not for a moment think she would actually have to shoot at the 'thing.' But better safe than sorry. And she wanted this.

"Let's see. Push, pull, stiff, hard, aim, and gently. Right?"

"You got it."

She set up and squeezed the trigger. The report rang out and was filtered through the trees and eventually into nothing. The trap jumped.

"That's better," Jennifer said. She sighted and fired off several more shots. "I could get to like this. It makes me feel powerful."

"You are powerful. But careful, too much of a good thing, you know. The thing about shooting is that bullets do not discriminate. I was taught that I am responsible for the bullet from the time it leaves the barrel until it comes to rest. And they can go a long way."

"Yeah? Well, mine are going in the trap or the 'thing's' head. I learn from your mistakes."

"I'd be offended if that weren't true. Next time in the head."

"You know what I meant, Harry. Don't you?"

"I know. Let's make this bullet trap earn its cost."

The trap was five magazines worth of lead and brass heavier on the way back. Jennifer rubbed her sore hands and smiled. She could shoot.

Harrison watched her. He saw the glow. She was happy with her newfound power. He too smiled. They would make this a regular event. Jennifer needed to be ready, just in case. For her sake, Harrison suddenly decided. For her own safety.

Life and shooting went on. For Harrison, it was sort of relaxing to be preparing to be ready.

They had Thanksgiving dinner at Twisted Fish watching football and lots of other sports features on their multiple screens. Jennifer wanted time off from the chef's duties. Then they got ready for Christmas and New Year's. This would be the first time they could be traditional. They got a real tree at a local lot.

Reality intruded. The 'things' assault trial was slated for December.

Chapter 39

December. The rains came sudden and often. Harrison and Jennifer sat in the office of DA Johnson. He had asked them here to prepare for the trial.

"Thank you for coming here in this weather. I would like to prepare you for the trial. I cannot coach you, but I can show you what it will be like."

"Seems pretty straightforward to me," Harrison said.

"You'd be surprised," deadpanned Johnson. "For instance what do you say when the defense asks you why you didn't warn the victim?"

"Victim?"

"You see, already you're off balance. Let me tell you how it will go. Then we'll do what we can to make you ready."

"Let him help, Harry," Jennifer stepped in, seeing Harrison start to complain..

Johnson started off, "You'll take the stand. You'll be sworn in. You'll first be asked questions by me. These will be softballs. I will set the stage by asking you to describe in your own words what happened on the night of October 31st. You will do that as clearly as you can. I cannot tell you now or then what to say. I'm confident that you will be coherent and straightforward. I will ask a few questions about your state of mind and clear up any points I see that need to be answered. You must answer honestly. Now when I'm done, there will be a cross-examination. Assume the lawyer will be well versed in what happened." Johnson paused. "I cannot stress this enough. Answer with yes or no if you can. Do not explain. The defense attorney will not ask anything they don't think they have the answer to. If there are questions asked that require more than yes or no I will try to object and there will be arguments made. You will remain silent."

"Sounds fair," Harrison said.

"It won't be, Mr. Baker. There will be nothing fair about it. If the defense uses the little charade we did, this could blow up my case. What will you say when asked about that?"

"I'll wait for your objection."

"Good. If the question is allowed, what will you say?"

"That it was an attempt to help the assault victim to heal."

"Good. Now if this gets technical like what are your credentials? Then wait for my objection. We will present professional testimony later."

This went on for the morning. By the time they were done, Harrison had just a taste of the real thing. He thought he knew.

Johnson then sent them to Schiefer.

The drive back to Seaside and the office of Hunt and Kindler was stormy. The wipers had a hard time keeping up with the sheets of rain and traffic spray. The Bakers were silent while he concentrated on driving.

They parked in the blustery lot and ran to the door. They were let in by the same cheerful paralegal and more good coffee.

"We're set up in the conference room. The attorney will be in shortly." She left them sitting in the brightly lit room. Outside the rain continued its assault on the building. The day was mimicking Harrison's mood. He was in full battle mode.

The door opened and Schiefer came in with a short, broad woman. She was flat-faced and without expression, dressed in a drab pantsuit. Her dark hair was cut short, her eyes were shaded, and held some kind of secret knowledge.

"Mr. and Mrs. Baker, this is Brenda Sikorsky, she will act as attorney for the defense. This is to help prepare you for what's to come."

"Johnson briefed us."

"Mr. Baker, this will be like nothing you've ever done. It will not be pleasant. We are also playing at the edges of the law. There will be no recording here. I'm sure Johnson could not do this. He told you to answer any defense questions with 'yes' or 'no.' And not to offer any explanations. This may not always be possible. For instance, how will you answer an open-ended question like: Why did you shoot without warning?"

"Johnson said to wait for an objection."

"Good. He will object on the grounds of 'assumes facts not in evidence' or whatever he can think of. But the judge may allow the question."

"Then I will say: 'I did not shoot without warning.'"

"Let's play that out, Ms. Sikorsky?"

She stepped forward and came within a few feet of Harrison so that she filled his vision. Her face went stony.

"You say you didn't shoot without warning, yet in your testimony here in this trial you stated, 'I shouted halt.' That is not a warning is it, Mr. Baker?"

"It is." Harrison's mouth twitched; his hands clenched. He began to look like he had something to hide.

"No Mr. Baker, it is not. A proper warning is, "stop or I'll shoot.' Is that not so?" Harrison had to give the woman respect. She played the part well and he was getting heated even though this was practice. He started to engage.

Jennifer looked on with concern. Harrison was off balance and beginning to look deranged.

Schiefer interrupted, "You see what's happened? The defense has drawn you into an argument. You appear petulant."

"Yeah? So how do I answer then?"

"Here is where we depart from the not answering too much rule. The question is about the definition of 'warning.' You have the floor when the question is asked. Then the defense will be looking for something to discredit you. You must remain factual. Here is how I formulated an answer: 'I stated that I gave a warning. I shouted 'halt.' The man holding the girl by her head turned and looked at me with my gun pointed at him. That was the warning.' Now the defense may persist. Ms. Sikorsky?" She grinned like a hunting cat.

"Oh come now, Mr. Baker. You say the man should understand the threat simply by looking?"

"Yes," Harrison bit off a reply that would have started "Are you crazy…"

"Good, Mr. Baker," said Schiefer. "Now the other weak spot in your testimony will be the fear factor."

"Mr. Baker. Is it not true that you were afraid of the defendant?" Sikorsky's voice became tinged with scorn. Mocking.

"Yes."

"You were holding a gun on the defendant. You were in control, yet you were afraid. Why?"

Schiefer let it play out. How would Harrison handle the reference to the eyes?

"I saw that he was not afraid of the gun. It made me fear that I would have to shoot him before he could hurt the girl."

"And how could you tell that? Are you trained for that?" she scoffed.

"As I testified, he did not stop what he was doing. He did not care. He was not doing what a normal person does when a gun is pointed at them. He just continued what he was doing."

No eyes yet. Schiefer continued to let it go on.

"So your answer is that you do not have any training. How long did you wait before shooting the defendant?"

"I testified that it was a second or two."

"A second? Not much time for the defendant to react is it?"

"The man was in the process of assaulting a young girl. He had her by the head and did not change his activity even with the gun on him."

"So you say, Mr. Baker. And what training have you had in threat assessment? How many times have you been in this position? You were just afraid and pulled the trigger out of reflex. The defendant did not have a chance to comply, did he?"

"He did."

"In one second? You shot an unarmed man without warning, did you not?" snidely accusatory.

"I did not."

Now Schiefer interrupted. "You see how this is going. The defense is trying to make you into a bad guy. So far you are holding your own, but she will continue to dig at you until she can provoke an outburst. Do not let that happen. Do you understand?"

"I think I got it." dryly spoken.

"Then let's continue."

For the rest of the afternoon, Harrison and Sikorsky sparred. Occasionally Schiefer offered a comment. Harrison became better at remaining calm and alert. This was Johnson's questioning on steroids. Jennifer relaxed a bit. Finally, Schiefer called a halt to the session.

"I think you've got the gist of this, Mr. Baker. I would like to thank Ms. Sikorsky for her help here. She is one hell of a prosecutor for the DoD. And after being briefed on this trial was more than willing to help."

"You did well, for a civilian, Mr. Baker," she said in a conversational tone. It was like a switch had been thrown, the lights went out and when they came back on a new person was now in the room. The flat-faced brutal woman was replaced by a kindly mother. "I wish you well in this."

"Thank you," Harrison managed to say. Then "DoD? NSA? I get it."

Sikorsky smiled, "We're on the same side here."

Jennifer had been silent but now had to ask, "This is off the record. Why is the DoD concerned here?"

Sikorsky laughed, "I could tell you but then…"

"Got it. Thanks." Jennifer snorted. Then, "Is Sikorsky, like the helicopter, even your name?"

"I could tell you but…"

Even Harrison chuckled a bit.

Then Schiefer added, "Just for your information, the Chief got your service records. He was concerned that it may be an issue in the trial. You know, like how sure were you to be able to shoot with the girl so close? He's a retired Marine. Well, after laughing about the difference between Marine and Air Force qualifications, he begrudgingly gave props to the Air Force pistol training. And on top of that, he said that you would have made a good Marine. Particularly that you had only a few misses and actually one in the head at twenty-five yards during your qualification. High praise from one who knows."

Sikorsky offered, "I took the FBI course. The training did not include headshots."

"I don't know how much my training had to do with it. I wasn't thinking very well. I wish I'd used that shot first. By the time I thought about it I was too unsteady."

"Thank you for that," said Jennifer. "I know what you meant."

The Bakers left. The rain subsided.

"No lunch. I'm hungry. Let's go to that Mexican place. I feel like a Nacho," Harrison said.

"Yeah? That's funny, you don't look like one."

"Ha, ha."

They stopped at *The Stand* and ordered at the counter. They sat at a table looking out at the Holladay Boulevard traffic and up 1st toward the Convention Center. The rain started again.

"So what now?"

"We wait. We live as best we can. I keep thinking about the dog. This is one of those things where I question my sanity. Even when Johanna heard it I don't know whether it was me projecting or her actually hearing."

"I don't think we'll ever know in this life, Harry. But I think we can trust whatever it is to warn you. We have nothing else."

"Right. You notice that nobody today brought up the eyes?"

"Yeah. I wonder why?"

"The defense is going to have contacts for it!" At least they would not have to weather the stare. Especially Johanna.

The Nachos and Coronas came and they dove in.

Chapter 40

The classic revival Clatsop County building was both imposing and dour at the same time in the meager sunlight. A north breeze cleared out the last of the clouds by ten that morning. But it was cold.

Jennifer again watched the ornate courtroom fill up with news people and gawkers. From second-hand knowledge, and the training session with the lawyers, she thought that trials were like a civilized but perverted Roman Coliseum game. Where someone is tied to a stake in the middle of the arena and armed men in teams try alternately hack them to pieces and or protect them. While a judge watched, ready with his thumb.

Before Harrison retired she had watched some of the hyped trials of police and vigilante events. She had never seen a real trial, and the televised events lacked the intensity of the real thing. Nevertheless, she felt for the witnesses who testified. The lawyers were so cold and calculating. It seemed there was no morality in the courtroom. Only win or lose. And to win the lawyer must destroy witnesses who are metaphorically tied to a stake. Easy targets, who have no defense. Witnesses who tried to answer beyond the question were censored. It was even possible that the judge would join the blood fest if the witness proved to be a problem.

With that mindset, she entered alone into the massive stone building with the antique cannon outside which, she idly noted, was aimed at the city proper, maybe for a reason.

Harrison was sequestered as a witness. Soon he would be tied to the stake in the ornate courtroom. A small arena with bloodthirsty spectators, inquisitors,- and men with knives.

She was sure Harrison would tell the truth about what he did and saw. She was sure he would keep his cool. He would leave the dog barking part out though. The prosecutors had promised that no charges would be filed but she knew that the defense would seek to make him seem like a criminal for shooting an unarmed man. She had a rubber band around her wrist. Her friends thought it would help her control her emotions. She was to snap it when she felt like yelling out. She put no faith in it but something was better than nothing.

Harrison and the Johanna girl had been escorted up earlier by Seaside police. The assassin had been held in the Clatsop jail just across the street. Dennett was also now separated from the other witnesses. Walker sat in the front row behind the prosecutor's desk. She would not be part of the effort to convict the thing. Next to her sat an officer whose name tag read James. She recognized him from the Johanna trick. He was the 'thing.' Both looked tense.

Security around the building was again tight. County, state, and city police cars lined the roads around. FBI and US Marshals vans were in the secure parking lot. She noticed discrete NSA and even Interpol cars also. The hierarchy was defined by the status of the SUVs. Chevys and GMCs up to Cadillac Escalades and Lincoln Navigators. And one stretch limousine. This was going to be a "clusterfuck" as she heard Jeffers once say. Of course, he was not talking about the trial. He meant that the number and diversity of agendas of the many entities involved were going to create confusion and jurisdictional clashes. Harrison thought so too, but for a different reason. And it already had. In the middle of the storm, Harrison and Johanna had persevered, partially protected by the Chief and Clatsop DA

Now would come the test by fire. There would be metaphorical blood spilled. Harrison and Johanna would have to sit facing the 'thing' while being questioned under oath. The things stare would be direct and insidious. Jennifer was sure Harrison would bear up. But Johanna would have to face the nightmare without her father between them. Johnson told her he thought that just her reaction, along with the transient's testimony, would be enough to show that she witnessed the crime.

Nevertheless, there would be only a temporary conclusion. Who would survive this round?

She knew that Harrison would survive. After all there were no real weapons here. But she worried about Johanna. Even with the help of Dennett and the NSA agent in the reenactment and with Katrin's and Jack's help, she was not well. She was better but had that lingering taint of fear. Johanna's family was here for support. Her therapist was here but could not interfere.

But the young girl would be alone on the stand.

Harrison's attorney, Schiefer, came in and sat next to Jennifer. He looked worried. It was not so much about the proceedings. He was sure about his inoculation of Harrison against an aggressive defense attorney. But he had been told about the effect of the thing's aura by people who knew. Would Harrison react with aggression to that? It cast doubt.

While she waited for the onset, Jennifer idly recalled a story in the Astorian about a decade-long legal saga of an Astoria shooting in 2012. The legal dithering continued for ten years. One character, Stavisky, had been convicted on two counts of attempted first-degree murder. The moron then tried to put out a contract on both an officer and Stavisky's ex-wife who were witnesses against him. Again he was convicted. Then the legal BS began. The wonderful lawyers got some evidence thrown out as inadmissible. The matter was finally resolved by agreement, ten years after the fact. Jennifer thought about that. Ten forking years.

And there was another recently where a killer had a sentence changed because he claimed he was possessed. The courts actually allowed that defense. Could it be used here?

She should have let Harrison finish the assassin on that first Halloween night. It had already taken over a year of their lives. And this was a relatively fast prosecution. The only upside was that the assassin had not said a word for all that time. But she felt the blackness ooze out of him at the arraignment hearing. He was just waiting.

She knew the 'thing' had a chance of winning here. The high-priced team that came in at the last moment was oily and impressive. Something else was happening. Something dark and dangerous. Harrison and Johanna were going to be on trial here in a small arena populated by men with knives.

And the 'thing.'

Johnson came in alone and sat at the prosecution table. The judge came in.

It began. The case file numbers were read.

She watched as they brought in the prisoner. He did not look around. He kept his eyes down. He sat with a trio of those recently imported high-priced but nervous lawyers who did not look at him. Then there was the protocol that Jennifer paid no attention to.

Before anything else, the lead defense lawyer stood and requested a sidebar. Jennifer did not have a clue as to what was happening but she could feel something devious slithering behind the faces of the lawyers. A different kind of chill filled the room. Spectators wondered what was happening.

Johnson knew. At least as much as he was allowed. What he did know was that the Oregon judicial system had been steamrolled by the US judicial system. The US system had been steamrolled by the International courts. The POTUS had signed off on a deal. The NSA agent had warned Johnson of the coming storm. He did not want to believe it, but here it was.

A number of agencies from the DoD to the DoJ had been ordered to stand down by POTUS. Right here, right now, suddenly the United Nations and International Law prevailed. How this happened he could only guess but nothing good was happening here. He listened as the arguments were made and he was not allowed to respond. Clatsop County was a bug to be flicked off of the International Court of Justice's back.

The lawyers stepped back. Motions were made by the defense. The judge so ordered. The defendant was to be turned over to ICE to be deported to Chile. The cadre of International Jurists breathed easier.

To Johnson, it became apparent that the Chilean government had given this assassin a sort of diplomatic immunity. Whatever battles had been fought in the airless halls of the International Courts were now over. The men who sat in that ivory tower, looking down on the clueless plebians, had spoken. The dead journalist was forgotten.

None of the elite saw the real 'thing.' None would bear the consequence of the crimes he would commit. They would go to their multimillion-dollar palaces and drink expensive wine and dine on expensive foods. They would sleep on expensive beds with expensive escorts. They would have expensive security. They simply were so disconnected that they did not, could not, care about reality. Their lives were just fine. And the money continued to roll in.

Johnson wanted to call them out in an editorial, but he knew, even with his position, neither the Astorian nor any local paper, including the Oregonian, would print what he had to say. It was not politically correct for a prosecutor to criticize the courts. Especially to criticize the POTUS, which was not allowed. That was left to outraged uninformed morons.

Johnson at this point was not afraid to vent. He did not care. But he knew that the editors feared the power of the political elite and their minions in social media and cable news. The danger was that they would be canceled. Their advertising funding would dry up and only a change of leadership could save their papers. That leadership would be assigned by the current woke political power. This was like a death threat to them.

The Astorian and the Oregonian would print the bland facts. "Accused Seaside murderer remanded by International Court to face charges in Chile." There would be no follow-up.

Johnson was livid. The defendant was about to be released to ICE. The men who did this had not met the defendant. They did not know what Dmitri Valens was. They did not care. Enough money and favors were passed to ensure that peace was kept and their elite lives were made easier. None of those were here now. Their lawyers were terrified but would not let that be known. They would retire and try to forget.

The marshals stood stiffly.

The 'thing' radiated doom and did not care.

"Remove the shackles." The gavel came down. The judge left the room. He wondered what just was let loose. He had seen the eyes. That night he would require several shots of Jack Daniels Blue before passing out on his bed.

The 'thing' did not care.

The parasite rejoiced.

Jennifer watched in horror. This was Harrison's nightmare come true.

Johnson turned and left the room in a huff. The marshals carefully did as told. The ex-defendant stood still as an insect - waiting. Several ICE agents entered and escorted the freed man to an ICE van parked at the back of the building. A long sleek limousine waited behind the van. They pulled out together. The top floor of the Elliot Hotel was abandoned. The concierge breathed a little easier. The Chilean envoys who had not left the hotel during the negotiations had done their job. Now they headed to the airport.

Two private jets waited at Astoria Airport. One had the official Chilean logo the other had none. Inside the unknown jet where the pilots spoke Russian, Hynd Ozio waited with his bodyguard. The van and limousine pulled up to the Sukhoi S-21 and the ICE agents escorted the man to the boarding stairs. They breathed a sigh of relief when the assassin left their care. At first, they were not comfortable with ICE being used this way. But once they were close to the assassin they changed their minds. Better to let this 'thing' go somewhere else.

The Chileans thought that they had sold the assassin to the Russians. But it was the oligarch Ozio who waited in the jet. Now he could cut his ties to this man. For good. It was a shame that he had been caught. He was the best Ozio had ever cultivated. But business was business. The man he created as Dmitri Valens would not make it to the mother country. Ozio's bodyguards had their orders.

Inside the Clatsop County Court House FBI agents carefully retrieved all the DA's evidence. Scrubbed the computers and left the stunned prosecutors, sheriffs, and medical examiner to wonder what could have possibly subverted a simple murder investigation, and why. The agents then again descended on the Seaside police station. Jeffers let them root around for a while then shut down the station, turned off the lights, and locked the doors. The on-duty officers waited in their cruisers. The FBI agents got tired after a while and left.

Dennett's personal notes were not known or found.

Harrison and Jennifer left in a daze. She found him standing in the hall. He was outwardly calm. Inside he was screaming. By the time they made it back to the house, he had calmed enough to be coherent.

"Harry, the 'thing' was shipped out to Chile. He's gone." Jennifer tried to help.

Harrison strapped on his pistol. "No, he's just away for now."

Jennifer felt the truth in that and said, "Let's go shoot."

"How did I manage to get you?"

"Just lucky. Or something else. Bring your best. I feel like showing you up again."

"The 'thing' doesn't stand a chance."

The bullet trap was going to take a beating.

Chapter 41

The Sukhoi S-21 banked and descended into Havana's Jose Marti International airport to refuel. The landing was smooth. The plane taxied to a secure hangar and disappeared inside. The hanger door closed and the S-21's door opened. A tall straight man in a Russian colonel's uniform and expensive sunglasses exited. He ordered a cab, went directly to the Chilean consulate, and entered. After a short time, he returned to the airport and boarded an American Airlines Boeing 727, through the Cubana de Aviacion agency for a flight to Mexico City.

During the flight he planned.

No one else exited the idle Sukhoi S-21. When the National Revolutionary Police finally entered the motionless plane, they found the pilots sitting in their seats, afraid to move. The Russian colonel assigned to escort the assassin back to Russia was dead along with a short balding man. Both had their heads twisted almost off. There was no evidence of the bodyguards. The flight recorder noted a momentary cabin pressure loss somewhere over the Gulf of Mexico.

An investigation by the Ministry of the Interior agency found no one willing to testify to any facts. But witnesses did give the same description of the suspect. Not his size, shape, skin color, or any physical attributes. They only remembered his eyes and then tried to forget them. Portals to hell, one man said. The lead agent assigned, traced the suspect through the forged documents, to the airport and his flight to Mexico City. The agent then decided not to further pursue the suspect. This was better handed to the Mexicans. He did not want to meet the man described and the Mexicans deserved him.

Chapter 42

Just a week after the surprise intervention of the trial by the International Courts and ICE, Jessop Johnson met with Frederik Jeffers, Sheila Dennett, Mara Walker, Harrison and Jennifer Baker, and Tye and Pamela Bergstrom in the Clatsop County DA's conference room The day was clearing, a slight breeze came from the west. It would be warm in the afternoon. But the room was chilled by the DA's serious tone and abrupt news.

"He's escaped," Johnson said.

"Fork!" Jennifer shouted. They all looked at her in surprise.

"That's as profane as she gets," explained Harrison. "I'd have said something a little more direct."

"We all would," Johnson said. "Now here is what I can gather from the various complicit entities." There was no doubt as to his feelings here. If the responsible people were in this room, they would be held as accessories. He continued. "Due to the bungling of our heavy-handed FBI and our weak administration, the assassin was transferred from us to ICE, then to a Chilean delegation. The Chileans delivered him to a Russian oligarch in a private plane right here at our own Astoria Airport in Warrenton. All in the cause of a perverted form of 'international diplomacy.' From there we have unsubstantiated reports that he killed his handlers in Cuba and disappeared."

"He'll be coming here." Harrison declared. "No doubt about it. How much of this meeting is on the record?"

"None," said Johnson.

"Then I'll say this, the 'thing' is coming for me. When I see him I will kill him. In the street, on the Prom, in a restaurant, or in City Hall. Any-fucking-where." This was said with such bitterness even Jeffers cringed. Jennifer was afraid for him. Was he about to sacrifice others?

"What about Johanna?" Tye asked, breaking the silence that descended. "Will he come for her? If he does I get the first crack at him."

"It's me he wants, Tye. Johanna is safe. I'm the one that shot him and spoiled his plans. There will be another killing is Seaside soon. This time I will shoot him when he's down, in both of his black eyes."

"Alright. Before we get to that point, we should assess the situation. Here is what I know about his tactics." Johnson began to lecture. "He traveled under various fictitious names, using well-crafted documents which indicates he had a very high-level employer. Probably the Russian oligarch with the complicity of the Chilean government. He no longer enjoys that protection. He still has protected access to one of his secret accounts the Chileans have not found or are not now looking that hard. He is not in their country now. He pays all expenses in cash sent to PO boxes. He used to stalk his victims for weeks or months. He used no weapons and left no viable evidence. We have a pretty good idea of this from the timeline for the assassination of this Billings person."

"So the 'thing' is in the wind? And can travel?" Harrison said, ignoring the information, and getting to the bottom line.

"Basically, yes. We are now in a defensive position. We, the County and Seaside police will provide round-the-clock protection for you and the Bergstrom's daughter until he is arrested or killed."

"Arrested for what? Does he have any warrants out? Didn't the pieces of shit that run this pile of bullshit scrub all charges? The alphabet agencies aren't here anymore. This 'thing' could be here right now. I said before and I'll say again I will shoot on sight." Jennifer was astounded at the vitriol but vowed to stand beside her man. She had seen the eyes.

"Mr. Baker, are you saying that if you see this 'thing' on the streets of Seaside, say on Broadway, that you are just going to open fire regardless of collateral damage? Maybe a child getting a stray round," said Jeffers with exasperation. "Calm down. Think this through. Our best option is to use the police. Assuming he uses his preferred methods, he will have no weapons. It is highly unlikely that he will approach in daylight.

"For how long, and how many resources are you willing to use?"

"We have access to assistance from County Sheriffs and Oregon State Police. The NSA has offered agent Walker."

"You going to camp on our front lawn, agent?" Harrison snarked.

"No, I'll be in the Beachside Motel. For the people in this room, the White House has issued an AUMF for the assassin."

"Knock it off Harry," butted in Jennifer, getting her footing back. Harrison was just blowing off steam. "What's an AUMF?"

"Authorization for the Use of Military Force. It's a kill authorization. It exempts government agents from prosecution and subsequently any others if the 'thing' needs to be put down. You should know the Russians and Chileans have a hit order on him also. The oligarch apparently was a rogue. The CIA has an arrest and detain order out. They would like to see what there is about the assassin. It theoretically can't be used inside the U.S. but... "

"How are we to know who and when the players are here?"

"I'll know them. This isn't rocket science. Seaside is a small town, and strangers here are noticeable. And they will not make a difference unless they kill the 'thing.'"

"Seaside is a resort. People come and go."

"The hit squads will not look like tourists no matter how hard they try. But the assassin can blend in if he turns down the gloom and doom stare. We have pictures of some 'alphabet' agents from the Seaside demonstration. They are not dangerous to you except as collateral damage. They will not care who gets in their way," Walker said. "Our esteemed POTUS is covering his butt. He wants this assassin dead."

"I need a concealed carry permit. I can't run around with the Sig on my hip," Harrison said.

"I'll see to it," said Jeffers. "But this assassin does not operate in the open. It will come in the night."

"I'll be ready," grunted Harrison.

"We'll be ready," asserted Jennifer.

"Yes, we will." Harrison looked at his wife. A feral gleam showed through her fear. He hoped he had the same confidence.

Jeffers noted the determination and worried they might shoot the wrong person. Then he thought, no. Nobody is going to mistake the 'thing' for another human. The problem would come if there were anybody around when the shooting started. But he himself just said it would come in the night when nobody is around. That was its modus operandi. He knew this was a problem for him. His own people were going to be around and in danger.

He made a note to let his people know what was going on. AUMF! His own people could put the assassin down if they saw him.

Chapter 43

The Bakers went home. The sky was a filtered overcast. The wind was calm. It was a Friday in December a week before the winter solstice and Christmas. The city was gayly decorated. A high-pressure system inland kept the temperature mild, in the low-50s. Rain was predicted for the following week but today was calm and beautiful, but wintry cool.

No hit squads showed up.

"What do we do now?"

"Let's take a walk. We need to stretch our legs and clear out the fog of this… spot we're in. This weather won't hold for long."

"Lead on."

They put on their hiking shoes. Jennifer had a new puffy nylon coat that made her look overweight but was considered fashionable. Harrison wore a hooded sweatshirt under his coat and they of course had on their armament. Jennifer started at their house and turned north on Downing. They settled into a steady leisurely pace. Harrison's eyes swept the path ahead and occasionally looked back. Jennifer began to look in sync. They made the turn at Franklin passed the Johanson's Christmas-decorated place and continued through 12th and out to the bluffs overlooking the Necanicum bay and estuary.

Harrison stopped and stood looking over the bay which was at low tide. The expanse looked like a desert scape with rolling sand and occasional clumps of grass. He seemed to Jennifer to be calmer. The look in his eyes was clear as he gazed over the bay to the Gearhart bluffs over a half mile away. She remembered how they looked at that city for a home. But Gearhart was expensive beyond even Astoria or Cannon Beach, and it offered no nightlife except *McMenamins*. The place seemed to be somewhat exclusive with the Golf Course 'leave us alone' mentality.

They stood not far from the Seaside water treatment plant over a lot of massive rip-wrap rocks that Jennifer learned were deposited in the 90s to protect the houses and the plant from storm erosion. It was hard to envision. The build-up of sand in the last thirty years had pushed the Necanicum bar a half mile out.

They slid down the steep path to the sand and trudged toward the ocean. Seagulls soared overhead. A light breeze ruffled Jennifer's hair. The sound of the surf grew. The fishy smell of the sea blew over them. The high tide wrack line was rife with crab and razor clam shells and sea born sticks and debris. Earlier king tide storms had left more heavy chunks of driftwood almost up to the dunes. They made it to the hard-packed sand near the surf and started south.

They strolled and did not talk. The beauty of the sand, surf, sea, and sky was filling up their senses. The unusually soft wave crunch was muted. Jennifer's grey-tinged auburn hair floated in the cool breeze. Harrison wanted to reach out and run his hands through it. Jennifer tossed her head like she read his mind and laughed at the sky.

They continued south toward the Tillamook Head promontory. At this time of year, the arc of the sun barely cleared the Tillamook Head and it sank well to the south at dusk. The low sun occasionally shown in their eyes through some accumulating clouds building over the Head. The offshore breeze held a bank of storm clouds out over the Pacific looking like a black mountain range – or maybe a coming tsunami.

The "Terrible Tilly" lighthouse gleamed for a moment as the cloud mottled sky gave way to a passing light shaft. They passed the turnaround. Now there were a few people setting up firepits, and digging in the sand. Harrison could not understand the need to dig. But lots of people did. Fathers especially turned into children again in the summer. Maybe if he was a father… He let it go.

They looked up at the Shilo, the eight-story Wyndham, and the six-story Sand and Sea Condominium as they walked. This was a small city and the skyline was not impressive but it seemed to be diminished by the distance. They were over three-quarters of a mile away. It almost seemed like another world inhabited by a few singular nomadic families.

They headed toward the Cove. At Avenue U there were a few more families digging fire pits.

They were still silent.

At the Cove, a few surfers were testing their skills on the now easy incoming tide. They hiked up the path toward the Unknown Sailors Grave and sat on a log watching the surfers and the rolling tide increase.

"This is what it should be like," said Jennifer. "Calm, peaceful."

"Yeah. I like it here." The sky parted for a moment and the surf lit up like molten silver.

"C'mon. Let's walk the Prom."

They walked back on Ocean Vista street, which had no ocean views. Instead it offered a view of big money houses with occasional glimpses of dunes through vacant lots. They made it to the Tides Hotel parking lot and the start of South Prom. There were a few more people here. Some of the houses were decorated with bright Christmas lights. They traded smiles with the few couples and singles as they walked with their shadows stretching out ahead of them. This was a friendly place and most did not know their problems. Hopefully, they never would.

The late day was clearing, as a soft cold north wind rose, but daylight hours at the 45th parallel in December were short. They stopped by *Maggie's* for a drink before returning. They walked through the brightly colored Christmas tree lined patio. It gave a view of the dunes obscuring the surf but allowed a look at the Pacific horizon. The area looked cozy and comfortable. The iron tables were sturdy, but the air was cooling rapidly. They got seated inside.

"You did good," Harrison absently noted as they sat down.

"What are you talking about? Did what good?"

"Did I say that out loud?"

"Yeah? Don't fork with me, Harry."

"Okay. This town, the beach, our house. All the things you took care of after I retired. You did good."

"Nice of you to notice. You've been kind of absent in all of that."

"Yeah. Sorry. I left the service in a snit because of the bullshit politics that has gotten into it. But it was a big part of my life. You stood by for all of it. I love you more than the Air Force, but it was a big part of me that went away.”

“So I did good even though I planted you right between a murder and a ‘thing.’”

“Even so. Look at where we are. Sitting in a great restaurant, on a nice day, with a view of the vast pacific - if you stand up. Great food and better booze. Who could ask for anything more.”

“If you burst into song I’m gonna whack you,” Jennifer laughed.

“You’re in luck, I can’t sing.”

“You know I also put you in a Tsunami zone.”

“That’s alright I know what to do.”

“Yeah? What?”

“Grab beer run like hell.”

“You saw the sign at the house on the Prom.”

“There’s more than one around. And I don’t care about Tsunamis. I have you.”

“Nice save. It’s getting late, let’s eat here. A while back the chef here won the Iron Chef award.” The westering sun turned the sea horizon to gold. Then left for its long winter journey. It got dark.

Harrison called over the server and asked for menus. “So much good stuff,” he mumbled.

“Let’s splurge. I’d like a Hellcat Maggie’s Manhattan to start.”

“Me too.”

They had the Honey Dijon Glazed Local Salmon. “It doesn’t get much better than this,” said Harrison.

“Yeah, it does. Server!” Jennifer called, “A couple of Gooey Butter Cakes for me and my friend.” The young woman smiled and took away the empty plates.

The deserts came and they savored them. Then they sat with another Manhattan and watched the darkness fall. The air cooled into the low 40s.

Then it was time to walk back to their home. Harrison's wallet was a lot lighter, but from the look on Jennifer's face, it was worth it. They walked back out to the Prom. The light poles were wrapped with strings of colorful red and green led lights. It was Christmassy. The night was clear and even from sea level with the Prom lights glowing, stars were visible.

As they walked down the starfish-lit Broadway, Jennifer was getting cold, she looked up Commercial and spotted a new sign on the sidewalk. Live Music Tonight from 7 to 9. "Hey, it's almost seven, let's take a look." It would be warmer in there

Inside the *Hop and Vine* was a dazzling array of wines and beers colorfully backlit. The singer was setting up. There was not much to it. A guitar, a simple chair next to the pay station, and the tip jar. This guy sang without amplification.

"Let's listen for a minute," enthused Jennifer. She went to the bar and brought back a couple of house chardonnays. Harrison sat down at a low table and got ready to handle a little more alcohol.

In the afterglow of the calm day, the singer was great. He sang a mix of older and contemporary tunes with a lot of energy and a strong baritone voice. Jennifer wanted to know who he was because the sign did not mention a name. So she asked. He was friendly and too good-looking for Harrison's taste. Not so for Jennifer. She started a conversation that went on a little too long for Harrison. But he did not interfere. She was having fun. Turned out the guy's name was Jason Lambert. Another local singer. Too bad there were not more in Seaside.

They sat and listened for a while then turned to home back down Broadway to Downing where the city Christmas tree glowed with the noel tunes played from under the stand.

A feeling of calm came as they walked. The calm before the storm.

Things were about to heat up in this December, but not the air.

Chapter 44

It was amazing to Jennifer how friends were made outside of the military. The proof was in the willingness to help neighbors and friends, even against the power of the federal government. When the Bakers were eating a light lunch at home the next day, a black Chevy SUV pulled up on 5th and parked. Two men got out and approached the house. Both wore the standard federal agent suit and tie. Both were immaculately crisp and clean. One was perhaps six two the other five ten. Both were armed. They strode up to the door and knocked.

"What are we going to do about this, Harry?"

"Answer the door, I guess. But don't let them inside. And don't answer any questions." He went to the door and opened it. The two men flashed badges at him and the taller one said, "I am FBI Special Agent Print and this is Special Agent Cho. May we come in?"

"No."

"Mr. Baker, we are FBI agents. We simply want to ask a few questions."

"Jen, come over here, please. Special Agent Print, please produce your ID again so that my wife can take a picture of it and verify your identity with the local authorities. This will take a few days. Come back on Wednesday."

"This is not a joke, Mr. Baker."

"That's debatable. What do you want?"

"May we come in?"

"Asked and answered. What do you want."

Sigh, "We are not a danger to you. We just need to know a few things about the events of October 31st. For instance, why were you armed that night?"

"No comment."

"This can be easy or hard, Mr. Baker."

"Is this you being not dangerous to us?"

"This is an official FBI investigation into the death of one of our agents. We will continue until it is resolved."

"What agent? There was no agent killed here that I know of. There is a current Seaside police investigation into the murder of a journalist."

"Mr. Baker, you shot an unarmed man right here on this property on October 31st at about ten o'clock in the evening. Why did you do that?"

"No comment."

"You are about an inch away from being taken into custody."

Harrison could not stand it anymore. The pent-up stress exploded. "You tools! Someone tells you to go there, do that, and you go there, and you do that. You don't think for yourselves. Was that beaten out of you at Quantico? It's sad. But right here right now you are wrong. You are threatening a citizen of the country you've sworn to protect. Why? Because some bureaucrat said to."

"Nice try, Baker. You don't know what's going on, but you can help us." This was old hat for them.

"Yeah. Need to know. The real question is: do *you* know what's going on? Do you know about the murderer? His strength and speed? Do you know where it came from? Do you even care?"

"I don't need to know. We have our orders."

"Yeah. Bureaucrat city. Harass the citizens until something breaks. I wonder what they know and are keeping from you. Why can't you just interview the accused? And what about the NSA, aren't you infringing on their territory? They have been assigned something to do with this case. It's cyber-related if I understand correctly. The FBI can only investigate federal crime not exclusively assigned to another agency. And what federal crime has been committed here, anyway?"

"We're not here to discuss politics. We're here to ask a few questions, that's all."

"You'd lie to your own mother, wouldn't you?" it was almost a snarl.

Jennifer stepped forward and put her arm on Harrison's. "Slow down Harry, I am sure these fine gentlemen are just doing their job." She smiled. But in that smile were Harrison's words.

"May we go inside? It will be more comfortable." Print tried again.

"No. Ask what you want."

"Very well. Let's start with your names and address."

"Are you recording this?"

"It is required."

"No, it's not. We will record it for you. Live and in color." Jennifer stood with her cell aimed at the men.

There was movement on the sidewalk. Bjorn Johanson walked halfway up the path to Baker's house and stood watching. The FBI agents took notice.

More neighbors were gathering.

A news van pulled up and broke out their gear.

"There will be another time," Print growled.

"Threats again, agent? Look, we're aware that you and the NSA think this is a matter of national security. But I know that making any damned statement to the FBI can lead to federal charges for lying! That charge will be used to extract the information you think we have about the murderer. You could not care less about us. I will make no statement of fact to you."

"You can be arrested."

"For what? Disrespecting you?"

"How about detained as a material witness."

"To what? This is a local investigation into a local murder and assault. Do you want to make it bigger than that? Do you want to air your damned SNAFU? If you're the ones that got this journalist killed, don't blame me."

"Mr. Baker, we are trying to do this in a civilized manner. This is a matter of national security."

"Yeah? National security in a local murder. For what are you fishing? A nuclear weapon around Seaside maybe? Terrorists hiding in the bushes? There is an ongoing official investigation by Seaside police. A rare occurrence here, and it is also being investigated and prosecuted in Clatsop county. If you have information relevant to that, then present it to the prosecutor. I have told them what I know."

"Local politics do not stop FBI investigations. There is more to this than your local politics." Looking at the reporters.

"So you say. So the public needs to know."

"No, they don't."

"Right. So here we go again around this SNAFU bush. Don't open this can of worms. Better yet why don't you go and interview the suspect himself. Maybe you'll get a taste of what is really happening. Or won't the bureau let you do that?" He saw the puzzled looks. "I wonder why?"

Jennifer was recording. The news cameras were rolling.

The two agents looked around at the crowd and the news camera. They knew this could be handled, but like Walker before them, it was not worth it. They backed away and went to their black Chevy SUV, and drove to their hotel to call it in. Their superiors did not want them to interview the prisoner. Like Walker, Print wondered why for a moment. Then he did not. He had his orders. He awaited further orders.

The scene cleared out. The news van left with a page three story. The neighbors went back to their homes and jobs.

The Bakers and Jorgensons stood on the porch and tried to make sense of the effort the FBI was putting in on this murder. The NSA had the name, why did the FBI not? And what could the Bakers add?

"Let's go inside," offered Jennifer.

They got comfortable at the kitchen table. "Coffee?" offered Jennifer.

"Tea for me if you have it," said Janice.

"Green Tea with elderberry okay? You guys have lunch yet, I have a DiGiorno pizza in the freezer," offered Jennifer.

"I have some Buoy IPA beer," offered Harrison.

"I could use one," Bjorn said.

"Set us up Jen," said Harrison, "I'll get the dishes. I think we need that beer." They sat and discussed the tea and beer for a while.

Teacups were refilled. The beer was slowly being consumed. Janice stuck with the tea. The people sitting around the kitchen table were waiting for the pizza to cook. The discussion went the long way around from the food to the weather, to the current situation.

"You don't think much about this kind of stuff until it lands on your doorstep – literally in this case," said Bjorn. "I get the NSA, this might be a secret stealing event, but this FBI and assassin… I don't understand."

"Yeah. It's about the 'thing.' I've looked into its eyes close up and I can tell you there's something more than human in that 'thing.' I bet that's what the FBI wants to know." Harrison's haunted look came back.

"Whatever it is, we'll deal with it." Jennifer broke in, "Meantime we need to navigate the forking 'suits' agendas. The FBI is tiptoeing around. At any other time, my guess, they would have simply taken us in using whatever force was necessary. The NSA seems to be in control of itself. Detective Dennett has made a 'friend' of the agent Walker. They have the name of the senator involved."

"Let's line out what we know," offered Janice. "We know that Johanna saw and heard the murder. We know she is the subject of the NSA investigation. They have the name of a senator to chase. But why is the FBI harassing you?

"We know that she saw what you saw, Harry. We know it traumatized her." Janice was staying on track. Bjorn was secretly proud and surprised at her ability to reason. He didn't marry her because she was shy. He knew her strength and now he witnessed her ability to reason. But then again, this was unprecedented.

"I can only imagine how that was for a twelve-year-old drunk and scared girl, and I saw it first-hand – sober," Harrison said.

"Yeah. We know that she and you, Harry, are now the subject of multi-agency investigations. We know that the DA is moving forward as fast as he can to prosecute the 'thing' for the assault charges. Then comes the murder charge." Janice stopped and gathered her thoughts. "I and Bjorn are watching this from the spectator's seats so to speak. We see the effects on you guys. The Bergstroms are in pain and are our friends, we will help in any way we can."

"Thank you," said Jennifer. "We thank you for being here today when the FBI arrived."

"Well, they came to our home first. Asking about you and what we knew about the murder. We were just dumb grunts and knew nothing except what the papers wrote." Janice smiled.

"That was hard," put in Bjorn. "I wanted to throw them out."

"Yes, when the Bergstrom girl came here after the murder and assault we really had no idea what happened. The police came and took her away," Janice then smirked. "Those FBI boys were so tied down they couldn't have a thought of their own."

"Don't be too sure. Yes, they have their protocol, but I could see them trying to manipulate us into saying something 'actionable.' Something they could use as a wedge or lever to force more information from us."

"Yeah, we saw that too. But why?" asked Bjorn.

"Back to the 'thing' what do you think it is?" Janice was interested. This was the crux of the matter.

"I don't know but there is something more to it than genetic engineering. When I first saw it, it looked like it was trying to kidnap Johanna, but when it looked at me a bunch of emotions hit me. First, there was the emptiness, the lack of emotion in it. It looked like it was just doing a job. Then there was a malignancy that came. There is a need in it. A need for terror, for pain." Harrison suddenly realized, "It wanted to feed on it! It wanted to feed on me!"

Jennifer put her hand on his arm. He was shaking.

Harrison calmed. "It was so sure of itself. It looked like it was calculating. It was going to kill me and the girl. It was sure there was nothing I could do about it."

"Tell them about the dog."

Quizzical looks from the Jorgensons.

Harrison was hesitant. He liked the Jorgensons but did not want to appear even crazier than he just did. But he went ahead. "Well, when the 'thing' looked at me I nearly froze. But there was a dog. It barked and shocked me into shooting."

"What, a dog?"

"Yeah, a big one. But there's nobody around that heard it or owns one."

"Tell them the truth, Harry."

"Not sure what that is, Jen. The dog barking caused me to shoot before the 'thing' could move. I first thought it was real but was probably just in my head."

Janice was intrigued, "So you're saying without that 'dog' you might not have survived. That Johanna would be dead." She ended the statement on a decidedly worried note.

"Maybe. This can't get out in public. The police already think I'm crazy. There's no use in proving it."

"No one thinks you're crazy, Harry. Just a little traumatized." Jennifer offered.

"You mean just a little crazy," Harrison laughed. "But something happened that helped me. I'm going to hold on to it. Whatever it is."

"I think it was an angel," asserted Janice. "I think you're protected. That means Johanna is too." Hopeful.

"I think you might be right," agreed Jennifer. But I also think Harry is right. The 'thing' is mad at Harry, not Johanna. I saw it at the arraignment. The dog did not come to her when the 'thing' grabbed her." Jennifer did not know the truth yet but had an inkling. A glimmer of what happened to Johanna. She thought Janice might shed some light.

"No," said Janice, "It came when it was needed. Who's to say how Johanna got to Harry? The 'thing' could have caught her before she got there. Something saved her then. Circumstance? There was that transient there. There were people in the tavern. Somehow Johanna got to your place, Jennifer. Somehow the 'thing' got stopped here."

"Tell them about when we reenacted the event." Jennifer pushed forward.

"What are you doing, Jen? I'm not crazy. You don't have to… you're trying to help, aren't you?'

"Tell them, Harry." Jennifer smiled.

"Okay. Maybe a little catharsis is due. When we did the reenactment and came back here. I heard the dog again. It just growled a warning. The thing is, Johanna heard it too. No one else. So whatever it was, it was watching out for Johanna too."

"An angel," asserted Janice again. "A barking dog would have helped her get away when the 'thing' chased her. It helped her to get to you too, Harry. You were armed, capable and dangerous. Whatever it was, it helped Johanna to get to your place after she saw the murder. It had to be the 'dog.' Then it came to you to save both of you." This was a simple statement of fact by Janice. Bjorn just gaped.

"You know what? I'll take all the help I can get. I know it's coming," Harrison said.

That killed the moment.

The timer dinged. Bjorn recovered, "Well, for the time being, we have friends, beer, and a pizza."

The discussion turned to politics and power. So far Seaside was mostly unaffected, but Bjorn was sure that fascism was just around the corner. The last three presidents were proof.

Finally, Janice shushed him, "Stop it, Bjorn, these people have a lot more to worry about besides the political problems."

"Thanks, Janice," said Jennifer. "We appreciate the help here for sure. And we'll be prepared for the 'thing.'"

Bjorn tried again. This time to lighten it up. "Let me tell a joke I heard on the job," he went ahead without waiting. "Biden and Putin meet. They size each other up. Biden says 'Mr. Putin, I don't think you have a soul.' Putin answers, 'Ah. Then we understand each other.'" He chuckled to himself.

Harrison laughed. "Good one, I'll remember that. Probably could be said about a lot of recent top-level politicians."

Jennifer and Janice smiled and feared that it might be true.

Again the conversation stalled. They said their goodbyes and the Bakers settled into the coming evening. The glow from the Johanson's visit remained.

Chapter 45

For most of the rest of December Harrison and Jennifer tried to live like they wanted to. They decorated with a real tree. Something Harrison had not done since childhood. They had a nice Christmas dinner at the Jorgensons with good cheer. Another thing the Bakers had not done for thirty years. They watched a movie that Janice picked out. *The Christmas Lodge.* It was a calm reverent offering. It left them with a good feeling.

They did New Year's Eve at the Chinook Winds Casino with good music and a long winning streak on the Roulette Wheel before their luck ran out and they began paying for the lights.

January through March was cold and rainy. Most nights were spent in front of the fire listening to music, reading, movies, and reminiscing. Some days they spent dodging rain storms on the trails and beach. Then the weather turned, the rain got warmer, and summer peeked in. The temperatures went into the 60s. The sun leaked through more and more. They traveled and hiked more. They visited the *Hop and Vine, Winekraft,* and *Bistro.* Listened to that good live music with good wine. Visited the Farmer's Markets on Wednesdays in Seaside and on Sundays in Astoria. More good food and music.

They had leisurely dinners at *Maggie's* and *Inferno.* They hiked the Northwest Coast's magnificent trails and found spectacular views from over a thousand feet up of vast sweeps of the Pacific and Cascade ranges.

They saw great performers at the Chinook Winds and Spirit Mountain Casinos, and at the Ilani Casino in Ridgefield, Washington they saw the much-delayed Celtic Woman concert. The afterglow from that one went on for a long time.

Except in the casinos, all the while they carried their pistols. Jennifer now carried hers in a sling purse. She had not done that before and it was awkward until she got the hang of it. Harrison carried in a special holster under his belt. His shirt untucked. It made him appear fat. A practiced eye could tell what they were carrying but the average person did not care to look. Both weapons were loaded with one in the chamber.

Harrison got tired of lugging around the trap. So once a week now they shot at a local range outside of Astoria. Stopping by the *Inferno, The Sea Crab,* or *Moe's* afterward. The range owners became impressed with their speed and accuracy but did not ask why. They knew. It was not a secret there.

The dog remained silent.

August. The weather was mild. Jennifer wanted to hike the Cathedral Trail to the Astoria Column. They were getting better at this. When Harrison was in the service there was not much time to sightsee. It had taken a while to get used to physical hiking, up and down thousands of feet at a time. But now they could do the trail through the quiet primeval forest with ease.

The top of Cockscomb hill that day offered a beautiful view from the mouth of the Columbia and the jetties to Saddle Mountain. All the way to Seaside's Tillamook Head. They sat at a picnic table with bottled water and enjoyed the view.

On the walk back to the Explorer, Jennifer suddenly said, "Hey, remember the *Rogue Public House* at Pier 39. We're close. Let's eat, I'm hungry."

"So am I." Harrison drove down to the highway found 39th and out the planked wooden dock to the restaurant parking area. "Hey, look at that," Jennifer exclaimed. "The *Vineside*. Another wine bar."

"Let's eat first." Harrison wanted real food before wine.

"Alright, but we're going to see what that's about. Remember the museum here? We have time."

The Rogue Halibut Fish and Chips with a local brew Dead Guy Ale were good. The view was terrific, and they left feeling satisfied.

They walked up the cavernous remnants of the fishing cannery trade building which was set on pilings well out into the Columbia River. It now housed the *Public House*, the *Hanthorn Museum*, a *Coffee Girl,* and *Vineside*. They found the door to the wine bar. It was a cozy place with a short bar and living room type comfortable seating. Jennifer looked around at the décor and spotted an advertisement for *Barbara Anne*, playing here Thursdays. "Hey, look at that. Barbara Anne is here today. It's after three right now let's come back at five."

They backed out and went to the Explorer.

Suddenly Harrison stiffened. A far off sound interrupted his thoughts. He turned to the south where deeply forested hills rose up and obscured the source. He automatically put his hand on his weapon.

"What? What's wrong?" Jennifer reached for hers.

"The 'thing' is coming. I hear the warning… but it's still far off. We have time." Harrison partially relaxed. Trusting the dog to get louder if the 'thing' got close. "Let's walk a ways."

They walked the planked causeway to the Riverwalk path. Then west. The day was calm and the views across to the Washington side were spectacular. Sealions barked, having their own loud conversations, their voices traveling a long way, not caring who heard.

"Harry, what are we going to do?" The warning had awoken her instincts for protection.

"Before I said 'prepare.' Now I say 'live.' We can beat the 'thing' by being happy. By being unafraid."

"Yeah? Turn on the good, turn off the bad?" Jennifer snarked. "You have a hidden switch somewhere?"

"Something like that," laughed Harrison. "You know I've been doing some reading and investigation into what's happening to me. How do I sense the 'thing?' What is the dog? I came across a quote that stuck in my mind. It read:

The day science begins to study non-physical phenomena, it will make more progress in one decade than in all the previous centuries of its existence.

Nikola Tesla"

"Yeah? So you're saying this 'thing' and the dog are non-physical phenomena that only you can sense? Are you becoming a warlock, Harry?" chuckled Jennifer.

"Well, why not? It makes as much sense as anything else. Let's go back, it's almost five." They were almost to the Columbia River Maritime Museum on 18th.

They hoofed back, through the barking noise, to 39th, up the wood-planked roadway, entered the *Vineside*, and at Jennifer's request the bartender set them up in the corner area with a couple of chardonnays. This was another intimate setting with the singer close to the patrons.

Barbara Anne was in full voice. Her songs cut through the pending return of the 'thing' banishing the dark. Bringing a light calm to the air. Then she sang another, prophetic to Harrison, song. *Stand by Me*.

Jennifer softly sang along. Harrison watched her face as she sang. He would never get tired of that. 'Stand by me and I won't be afraid,' he marveled.

The set ended. They left and drove in the slanting sunlight back to Seaside and spent a leisurely evening watching a movie Jennifer picked out. *Murphy's Romance.* Harrison thought it was just fine, a calm respectful movie with a sweet message.

There were no more warnings that day.

The rest of the summer passed without incident. The dog was now grumbling occasionally without threat. If the FBI and NSA were around they were silent.

September equinox. Today the Bakers sat in Moe's restaurant on the Prom, with a clear view of the concrete walkway, the sand-colored balustrade, the bronze statue of Lewis and Clark, and the vast Pacific ocean. The American flag fluttered high above the turnaround as cars lazily circled, enjoying the view. The sun was setting on a beautiful clear fall day.

The Hood to Coast Relay was over. The End of Summer festivities at Fort Stevens was over. The smoke from the Cedar Fire in central Oregon had diminished along with the earlier east wind and heat wave. Seaside had taken down the lifeguard tower. Things in Seaside were slowing down while the Oktoberfest parties in Astoria were warming up.

The 'thing' had not been caught nor heard from. According to Jeffers, the intel from the various agencies was that a GRU or CIA hit squad had taken him out. Walker was recalled. The FBI disappeared. The Oregon State police were pulled from permanent assignment to standby. Police departments in Astoria and Cannon Beach were aware but not concerned now. Only the few Seaside police who had seen the 'thing' up close were still on guard. And Harrison who continued to hear the dog.

Outside Moe's, on the turnaround, an officer on patrol walked past the restaurant without looking up at the Bakers. Her eyes were moving over the people strolling on the Prom.

Johanna was in school and doing as well as could be expected. She still had nightmares but they were diminishing. Katrin remained at her side. Most of her tweener BFFs kept their distance now. Johanna was viewed as troubled.

"This is beautiful right now," sighed Jennifer.

"It is." The tuna melts came and they ordered another 67 Honey Ale. "Let's watch the sunset. Maybe we'll get the green flash." It was rare that the horizon was this clear. The lazy breeze from the east made the sky high, dry, and crystal-blue for the second day in a row. The sun was still brilliant yellow as it neared its rendezvous with the sea.

"Harry. How long now? Do you hear the dog?"

"A little. Off and on. My guess is soon. It's getting quiet now. The 'thing' will be moving with the silence. I don't hear the dog actually growling for real yet."

They moved to the outside patio and sat in the calm air. The leeward side of the Shilo Inn was comfortable even though the flag at the turnaround stood flapping out to sea. Broadway would be a wind tunnel between the Shilo Inn and the massive Windham Resort building even with the slight wind.

The moment came. The sun sank slowly into the azure sea. Due west. Without a ripple, it moved silently down. It was amazing to Jennifer that they could actually witness the world turning.

"There! The green flash did you see it?" Jennifer was a kid again.

"Sure did." So was Harrison.

The sky showed with brilliant reds, yellows, and oranges clear across the horizon, as the sun progressed on its journey somewhere below the Pacific horizon. Twilight came and darkness would follow.

They sat for a while. Enjoying the calm. The flag now twisted leisurely as the temperature and pressure gradients eased.

Then they left. Walked down through the diminishing breeze on Broadway aiming for Downing Park and home. Despite the warmth of the evening, Harrison suddenly felt a chill, he became uneasy. He could not say why, the dog did not growl, but he felt like the 'thing' was coming. Had the dog abandoned him? He reached down and took Jennifer's hand.

Was she ready for this?

There was a movement across the street in front of the Times Theater. Harrison let go of Jennifer's hand and put his hand on his Sig. Jennifer saw the move and put her hand in her purse. A figure headed their way in a hurry. Harrison pulled the weapon out and held it against his leg. People began to notice and move away.

"Harry! It's Jeffers!"

Harrison did not put the pistol away. Jeffers was moving at double time. Something was up. He came up to them quickly.

"Harry, Jen, come with me. Put that away for now." Motioning to the gun.

Harrison holstered the gun and followed Jeffers into *Sam's Café*. He headed to the back bar room and motioned them to sit in the corner booth. An officer came in and moved past the video machines and disappeared through the back door. Harrison saw another at the front entrance.

"What's up?"

"We've found a body in the Mill Pond. It was Harvard. His neck was broken. The 'thing' is here."

"Why Harvard? He was harmless." Jennifer wanted to cry.

"My guess is that he recognized the assassin. We made a sweep of the area without finding anything. No one else there saw anything suspicious. We showed the picture around. Nobody recognized it although several said they knew it from the trial and reporting."

"He's in disguise," said Harrison. "He killed Harv for nothing. The broken neck is like a signal flare."

"No. The assassin had to do it because Harv would be broadcasting a warning. We'd be all over it in a hurry with a new description. As it is we have the time of death at over a week ago.

And no description. So it is likely it's still here and in disguise." Jeffers shook his head. "But how does he hide those eyes? We took his contacts." During its time here the assassin had been without its contacts. The inventory and his gear had been confiscated by the FBI.

"Whatever. Harv must have seen through the disguise. Probably because he was one who saw it before."

"Alright," Jeffers said. "You need to know this. The Chilean government has finally come around. Apparently, they didn't like the way the GRU and their oligarch treated them. The Carabinos de Chile raided a place on Isla de Santa Maria in the Golfo de Arano, not far from the thing's house in Talcahuano." He paused. "That I even know the names of these places makes me wonder about what else is out there," he worried. "Anyway, this place was thought to be the training facility for the 'thing.' It was abandoned, but the computer cloud backup survived. The NSA cracked the code. There was a trove of information about the genetic experimentation. But here is what you need to know."

Jeffers became deadly serious. He made direct eye contact with Harrison. "This 'thing' moves very fast."

"Yeah. I could tell he thought he could get to me before I pulled the trigger."

"Harry. He could! He could! I saw the video. NSA saw fit to give me a viewing. I don't want to see it again."

"Chief, I had him pinned at fifteen feet. He was a dead man."

"Aside from the fact that you hit him three times, center mass, and he could have walked away from that… he could have covered that fifteen feet in the blink of an eye."

Harrison doubted that. "I can shoot Chief. A bullet is faster than the blink of an eye."

"Harry, let me tell you what I saw," Jeffers persisted. There was a haunted look in his eye. "It was a video taken in the lab where the assassin was being trained. The 'scientists' wanted to see how he related to women."

Jennifer stiffened. "Maybe I don't want to hear this."

"You're not in danger. This is about the 'thing's' abilities. They sent various women into his cell. Nothing happened. Then one of the observers from the Russian GRU was admitted to a viewing room to watch a demonstration of some sort... she was ovulating. The NSA let me see that. And only that."

Jeffers stopped and let that sink in. "The state-of-the-art video was shot from several angles. The 'thing' moved like an insect in a National Geographic special. Still one moment on its prey the next. The cameras could not catch the movement except as a blur. The assassin went through a locked the door like it wasn't there, caught the woman, and raped her all in a few seconds. No one had a chance to intervene. Even if someone tried they likely would not survive. The woman was not hurt except for bruising where she was held by her hips. She hardly knew what happened. The 'thing' simply went back to the observation room... thirty feet away! It had moved that distance through a closed door in less than a second. The door was steel reinforced. It wound up flat on the concrete floor."

"Why are you telling us this?" Jennifer was feeling sick.

"I'm sorry, Jennifer. You, Harry, need to know that what I saw was real. This 'thing' can move like nothing I've ever seen. No animal, no man, could beat it. If he can get to within a... hell, probably within eyesight he has a chance. Please, understand this. I am afraid for you. I can't guarantee protection. I advise you to move." Jeffers knew that was not going to happen but he had to try.

Harrison sat back. His heart was racing. The tuna melt rolled in his gut like a bag of rocks. Jeffers thought he was dead if he stayed. He believed the Chief about its ability, but did not want to hide. The 'thing' would just continue until it found him. He would just have to adjust his strategy.

"Wait a minute. If he was that dangerous how did he manage to assassinate so many people? Surely there must have been ovulating women around during his travels," Jennifer asked.

"That was classified and not explained to me, but the video was taken over twenty years ago. My guess is that they programmed that out of him. They did not want him to be distracted by sex."

"Castration?"

"Maybe. It doesn't matter now. I am ordering more surveillance and recalling Walker if I can. No one else has seen the thing's eyes directly. You need to be on guard."

"So now I can shoot on sight."

"Yes, try not to hit anybody else. Your gun will not shoot through it for sure."

"If your sense is right, he will come in the night. He will come to our house. He will die there," asserted Jennifer. "There will be two guns firing."

"I will double the guards."

"Don't put your men between me and the 'thing.' If you're right they will just be collateral damage. Let me kill it," Harrison said.

"Or let it kill you? Not a chance. If you don't like it… move!" Anger flared in Jeffers's voice and eyes.

"Slow it down guys," said Jennifer. Harrison was mixing 'he' and 'it' again. "Harry, let the Chief do what he has to. You have your own early warning system. Remember."

"What system?" wondered Jeffers.

"He can sense when the 'thing' is near," explained Jennifer before Harrison could blab about the dog, there was no reason to make Harrison seem any crazier than he already did.

"Really? Well… Okay. But the guards stay." There was nothing to be gained by pushing Harrison too hard. The shit was about to hit the fan and the mess would happen no matter what he did. He began to worry about Harrison's sanity again. And maybe Jennifer's too.

He ordered a patrol officer to accompany the Bakers home. The cruiser parked out front.

The Bakers would just have to put up with it.

"We need bigger guns," declared Harrison."

The next day they sat at the kitchen table near the window with their guns on the table. The first light of the day glowed down the street, reflecting off the idle cruiser.

"What do you have in mind?"

Harrison pulled out his cell and activated the voice command. "Large caliber handguns."

They scooted together to look at the small screen. A list of sites came up boasting the most powerful options. He picked the first one. A bewildering array of revolvers came up. They spent an hour looking through the options. In the end, Harrison decided to consult with the gun shop owner in Cannon Beach.

"You gonna be Dirty Harry, Harry?" smirked Jennifer.

"Ha, ha. What we can see from the list of revolvers is the 44 Magnum is no longer the most powerful handgun in the world. There are a bunch of contenders out there. I think one of them should be enough to kill the thing."

"Then I need something too, besides the nine millimeter," said Jennifer. "We know how well that works."

"Let's see what the Cannon Beach guy says."

The owner of the gun shop was skeptical. "A Smith and Wesson 50 caliber magnum? Four inch barrel? Are you sure? This gun and the 440 grain bullet are made for shooting grizzlies or maybe rhinoceroses. It is not a casual weapon. It kicks like a mule. Its side flare will curdle your innards at close range. Its blast rivals a jet engine."

"Order one. You know what I have to shoot. I hit this guy center mass with three rounds from my Sig and it could have walked away. It will not again!"

The owner knew the situation from newspaper stories, but not the 'things' abilities. "How do you know the rounds were center mass?"

"I saw the medical report. The bullets barely penetrated the 'thing.' It has a genetically enhanced thick skin." Harrison was not going to get further into this. "Order one for me and a Springfield 45 ACP for Jen."

The gun shop guy had looked askance at their choices but said nothing past his warning. He just hoped that if Harrison actually had to use it, the area was clear for about a mile.

"You got it. Takes about a week. I'll let you know." He hoped that this guy did not shoot an innocent bystander with this cannon. He did not want to have anything to come back to him.

A week later, back at their old shooting site in the forest, away from civilization, Harrison set up the portable bullet trap. This was not guaranteed to stop more than a 45 but it was better than nothing. He staked it down as best he could. They brought enhanced ear and eye protection. The Sig was noisy but the Cannon Beach guy warned them about the kick and noise of this Smith and Wesson 50 magnum with the four-inch barrel. Plus Harrison remembered the warning "Do not stand next to the shooter. The side blast alone will curdle your innards." He had said it twice.

Harrison would shoot first. He took the standard Weaver stance. His left foot forward, his arms in the slightly bent push-pull grip. He held the sixty ounce weapon like it might not just try to bite him but that it might try to get away.

Twenty feet separated him from the trap. An easy shot. He cocked the nearly four pound weapon, and sighted. It was heavy but easy to use in that regard. It was a beautifully crafted precision tool, he reminded himself. It would do what he wanted it to do. Kill the 'thing.' It was not alive. It would not bite him; it would not try to get away.

Right now, however, he needed to prove that, and to test its strength. And his also. He looked back at Jennifer. She was out of the effective curdling range, twenty feet back. He nodded. She had on ballistic ear muffs and eye protection. "Ready," he called. He expected a significant blast. The four-inch barrel was his idea for portability and to allow for an extreme close encounter.

He was planning on that.

Jennifer nodded. He sighted and pulled the trigger.

Several things happened at once. The trap deflector blew off. The recoil shocked Harrison from his hands to his feet. The gun really did seem to try to leap out of his grip. He actually felt himself slide back a bit. The shock of the blast dulled his ears even through the ear protection. And the luminous flame that bloomed in the humid air obscured the effect on the trap for a microsecond. They stood numb for a minute, then removed the muffs.

"Fork!" exclaimed Jennifer.

"Damn!" echoed Harrison. "If this doesn't do it we'll need a howitzer."

"I can't shoot that cannon!"

"We'll get that 45 you ordered."

"The trap is toast."

"I think I'm almost done here. But I have to be ready." He fired off the remaining four rounds into the ground. He was getting the feel of the gun. But he had no intention of using it for anything but the 'thing.' "The next time I use it will be the last. The 'thing' might be tough but this will even the odds," he said rubbing his hands. He picked up the remnants of the trap to carry back.

Back to the gun shop. They picked up the Springfield for Jennifer. The owner thought that she could use it in the Chapman stance Harrison taught her. If she could shoot the Sig, she could shoot the 45. They were building an armory. The gun guy wanted to know how Harrison liked the 50.

"It's a cannon all right."

"Look, I know you were military. And the chief at Seaside vouched for you but this 'cannon' is unforgiving. This is not a pull-and-fire weapon single-handed unless you like wrist braces and off-hand writing for a while."

"Got it. I suspect it will only be used once more."

The gun guy left it at that. Make sure there's nobody else within a mile, he thought again.

The Bakers left to set Jennifer up with the 45. And headed to their range with a new trap.

Chapter 46

The Editor sat outside his tent in the Seaside Mill Ponds camp. Away from others. He is now bushy blond haired and bearded, with blue eye-colored contact lenses. No matter how he is disguised, others still avoid him. He prefers it that way.

He now had a bicycle with a trailer. He has been scavenging cans and bottles along with several others. He did not need them and leaves his bags where others can steal them. The trailer is big enough to hold a body. The Necanicum river is close to the edit's house and the murky water is deep enough so that a body held in a weighted body bag with enough room for crabs to get in would not be found for a long time. He would complete the assignment and be gone long before any pursuit.

He watched how the edit moved and tracked. Unlike his previous edits, there was no particular pattern. He noted the police protection. Yet every edit has one moment when they are vulnerable. He would find it. He noted the nighttime habits of the edit. He noted the holiday coming up.

A plan formed. The edit will be where he wanted him. When he wanted him. When he does not expect him.

A weighted body bag waits buried next to the designated hedge. A rental Civic waits on Necanicum drive. The Editor relaxed and remembered. Being on his own was interesting.

It was relatively easy to disappear in Mexico City. The people who did his bidding tried hard to please him and to change his appearance as best they could. Nothing could stop the dread they felt even though he had no designs on them. They worked quickly.

He attached himself to a group of migrants for the walk to the border. But he crossed the Rio Grande near El Indio alone in the middle of summer. He did not need to pack much water. And the heat kept the coyotes and polos inside. Not many of the coyotes tried to march their polos during the hundred-degree days.

He bought an old Nissan from a local shop owner for more cash than the man had seen in a long time. He up drove 277 to Del Rio then up Highway 90 to Van Horn and caught Interstate 10. The car broke down after he passed El Paso but now he had internet access to his secret bank account in Chile. Where the owners of the bank had only one very particular and very dangerous client. He rented another Nissan and was on his way. He passed through San Diego and caught Interstate 5. He ate at local diners. He did not need to sleep. He made it to the Oregon Coast and the city where he was shot. He parked the rental in a local neighborhood. Moving it every once in a while.

For half a year he stalked the man who shot him. It was a difficult hunt. The man moved without any pattern. He moved without any time schedule. He was most of the time with others. There were guards. He made a plan that would work for him. He had narrowed the place of capture to the house the man lived in. He had narrowed the time to evening, before the man locked the doors when he stood on the porch and scanned the area. The Editor could easily breach the house but had no idea of the layout or any defensive traps. He knew the man was aware he was being hunted.

Then the homeless man at the last edit recognized him and had to be eliminated. It was easy to dispose of him. But he had no body bag and the body did not stay submerged. It bloated and was discovered.

The authorities had been alerted. Police canvassed the camp without seeing him. Now he must move carefully. He had to recalculate. There was a holiday coming up. The man would be at his house for that. The Editor scouted a path and fine-tuned his plans.

The Editor had no plans for after the completion of this edit. Without the control of the mentor and the letter instructions, he would be a loose cannon. He did not care.

Nor did he know it, but inside the parasite was rejoicing. It could feel all control slipping away. Random mayhem and murder were coming. This host's victims and their hopelessness was beckoning. The parasite could taste the feasts coming. It hoped for many before the host was brought down.

Chapter 47

Oct 29th. The day dawned misty clear. A low fog remained offshore for the time being. Harrison and Jennifer watched the annual "Witches Paddle" at Quatat Park. They laughed at the costumes and children having fun watching the pumpkin carvers do their magic. The carefree atmosphere almost dispelled the lingering taint of the 'thing.'

But a purposeful growling now periodically invaded Harrison's thoughts. It was nearing.

The 30th dawned grey and threatening. By noon a light rain arrived. The Bakers braved the October weather and watched the parade and pumpkin drop. A massive thousand-pound pumpkin, that had been on display next to the carousel, was dropped from high over the seawall at the turnaround, into a wading pool filled with water and rubber ducks and beavers. The Bakers made their bets as to which would fly farther, the rubber ducks or the beavers. It was fun but they lost their bet when the pumpkin blasted a duck almost a hundred thirty feet.

And just as the duck hit the sand the growling suddenly grew close. Then waned. Harrison scanned the crowd. Was the 'thing' here?

Harrison grew more concerned. Yes, it was near for sure. The dog would let him know.

In the crowd watching were the Bergstroms. Johanna was having a good time despite having to be with family instead of friends. The pumpkin dropped; water splashed over the laughing people who stood too close. The officials went to measure.

Suddenly she stiffened. A soft growling filled her ears. She looked in the direction of the sound. After a minute she saw the Bakers up on the turnaround. The growl followed them for a minute then was gone. The dog was protecting them.

Tye noticed his daughter stiffen. He saw he look in a direction toward the turnaround. He stepped in front of her and said, "What is it, Joh?"

Jack then moved with his father. He scanned the crowd.

"It's the Bakers, Dad," he said.

"Is that it?" Tye questioned his daughter.

Johanna thought for a beat, she saw the Bakers react by quickly scanning the area. They reacted in synch. They knew. They were protected. She did not have to tell them. But she knew the demon was near.

"Yes," she said, as the Bakers moved away toward Broadway. The demon was close, and was not here for her, but her father protected her anyway. She felt that warm glow. Her mother came and put her arm around her. Johanna almost melted with the care.

Nevertheless, an invisible dark cloud gathered around Harrison that further dimmed the already dark day. For a while, Harrison felt the pressure increase. The soft growling came and went with purpose and was never far off. He was being hunted. He said nothing to Jennifer or anyone else. This was his problem. If someone got in the way they could be hurt or killed. He looked but could see no threats. The heavy 50 got even heavier.

He no longer drank any alcohol. Coffee and tea were the drinks for the season of the 'thing.' Jennifer brewed up a pumpkin spice tea that helped break the monotony. He missed being able to have that soft relaxing glow from the devil rum. And it was a devil's drink at this time. He was not about to be dulled until the 'thing' was dead.

Outwardly he got into the holiday. Inwardly he knew… it was close. The steel wall inside him was going to be tested. This time the 'thing' would not affect him.

Meanwhile, the Bakers set out to enjoy what they could

Oct 31, 2022.

The Downing Park had been torn up by the city for some reason. Only a couple of trees remained. The stumps of others stood amongst the destruction. Caution tape surrounded the area like a crime scene. It added to the spooky Halloween décor. All it needed was gravestones and disembodied arms reaching up from the torn ground.

Throughout the last few days, Harrison heard the rumble from the dog. Sometimes he felt that tickle that raised the hairs on his arms. He would then make sure the 50 was ready to go. He remembered the gun guy's admonition about drawing and firing it one-handed. It did not make a difference if that was what he had to do. People would just have to get out of the way. Speed was of the essence. Yet he knew the 'thing' would not come in a crowd.

Evening came. Clouds and rain were in the forecast. The Prom lights were on all day. Harrison and Jennifer stayed home. She knew the 'thing' was near. She knew it because Harrison knew it. He would not talk about it. But she was tuned to him like he was tuned to the danger. The difference was the dog. She saw it warning Harrison in his sudden quickness. His tilted head. His attention to his surroundings. She read him like a book and let him be, because she loved him and did not want to distract him. But she could not understand the dog. Why could Harrison hear and not her? Sooner or later she would find out.

Meanwhile, she would do what she could to help. But it would be without him asking or her volunteering. She waited with him in the front room for the kids to start their annual sugar fest. Her 45 rested on the kitchen table. The 'thing' was close but she thought it would wait for Halloween to be done with. No witnesses was its modus operandi according to Jeffers.

At six o'clock The-Trick-or-Treaters were on the streets trying to get ahead of any heavy rain. This street celebration was less than in previous years. Nevertheless, on South Prom in a big house, another party was set to go. This would be a real bash.

Johanna would not attend. She was with her parents watching the comedy *Ghostbusters* at home. The *Halloween* franchise was banned.

Katrin would not attend. She was being the candy girl and calmer of Bjorn's antics at the Johansons. Tweener parties were a thing of the past.

Halloween candy fest came and went.

At close to ten o'clock, after the small rush of Trick-or-Treaters waned up on Huckleberry. The Bergstroms began to take down their rain-threatened decorations. Rather, Johanna and Jack did. Their parents were not big on Halloween like the Johansons. They were inside watching the news.

As ten o'clock approached, Johanna suddenly stopped pulling down the fake ghosts from the front yard tree, turned to the northwest, and went still.

"What are you doing?" complained Jack. "Let's get this stuff in before it rains." Then he stopped and paid attention. "What's going on Joh?' There was concern now. The echo of Halloween past intruded. He looked at his sister.

Johanna stood in a trance. From far off, she heard a low rumbling. She heard a muted barking.

"Joh?" Jack stepped closer to her.

"The demon's here. There's a fight going on," she murmured.

"Dad! Get the gun. It's here!" yelled Jack. He stepped in front of her, but she stood looking right through him.

Tye reacted immediately. He grabbed the rifle from the front room closet and burst through the door, releasing the safety as he moved. He went to Johanna and looked in the direction where both she and Jack were. From up on the hill, he could see nothing but the empty street, the far off downtown and the coming rain. Pamela came out. The four stood looking at nothing they could see. Pamela broke the silence, "What do you see, Joh?"

"I can't see. I hear. I hear a fight. I hear the dog." Suddenly she jumped. Tye almost pulled the trigger. Johanna made a little sound that was almost sorrowful. Then she jumped again. Tye's sharp ears knew the barely heard soft pops that made Johanna jump were gunshots. A double tap it was called. Yet she jumped well before he heard the pops. He knew it came from a long way away, but he did not break his protective stance. Who was shot? And more to the point, who survived?

"What's happening, Joh?" Jack said in her ear. He believed she was hearing and reacting to something far away. Probably at the Bakers. Then he knew, "The assassin is at the Bakers!" he said. Over a mile and half away as the crow flies.

"I hear shots, bullets…dog." A short time passed. Another pop. This time Johanna did not react. The Bergstrom family waited.

"It's over," she mumbled again, staring into the night. The family stood looking with her. Waiting.

Tye held his Remington at the ready, as if the 'thing' may come for his daughter. Was the assassin dead or Harry? He wanted it to be the 'thing,' but he would only believe it when he saw its ugly carcass. For now, he would be ready.

After a while, inside the house, the landline telephone rang.

Chapter 48

On 5th and Downing, owing to their friendship with the Jorgensons, the Bakers had set up decorations for this All Hallows Eve holiday.

Harrison and Jennifer had tried to get into the spirit of the holiday. Down the street, the big spider was not back up. That house was under repair. Harrison had hung a skeleton off the eave. He could make it rattle by pulling on it with fishing line from inside. He had learned something from the Jorgensons during the time he had known them.

But that did not stop him from remembering the 'thing.' Even when the growling stopped.

The Trick-or-Treaters were few. When the traffic stopped Harrison began to take down the decorations.

He carried his sidearm in a holster under his belt within easy reach. Right now even with the special over the shoulder holster, the heavy 50 made Harrison's gut sore and left a growing bruise. He set it on the porch table while he worked.

Just off 5th near Necanicum Drive, The Editor waited. Bundled like a homeless man. Invisible to the revelers. His bike and trailer were disposed in the river. The waiting was over, the children were gone. His plan was now activated. He moved up between the houses like a ghost. Silent and swift. Success assured. Quiet as an insect, he quickly slipped up between the houses and got close to the edit's house concealed by a hedge. An observer would note that it moved the three block distance in just a few seconds.

Walker sat in the Beach Side Inn and watched the front yard of the Bakers through the bedroom windows as the last of the Trick-or-Treaters walked the slick streets. Then she watched Harrison begin to pull down his decorations.

Dennett was the police watch tonight. She sat in her cruiser parked on 5th down from the Prom with a view of the south side of Baker's house. The candy hunters were scarce where she was next to a vacant lot.

Harrison was intent on pulling the fishing line from the eyehooks in the eave when he was jerked to awareness by the sound of the dog growling growing from a faint sound to louder, then in a split second, to a full throated roar. He heard the words.

Wake! Wake! WAKE UP!

Then rumbling urgently.

Look! Look! LOOK!

He snatched up the gun. He looked in the direction of the sound. The dark laurel hedge? The growling moved to the left of his stare. Then to the right. He followed the sound holding the magnum revolver close to his chest.

This was for sure not a preferred stance to shoot this weapon. But Harrison suddenly knew… he knew it was necessary. He knew it like he could hear the dog, like he knew the 'thing' was there. And at least it was not being held one-handed. He was as ready as he could be. Eisenhour would be proud.

This time The Editor was not encumbered. He would not hesitate. Nothing alive had seen how fast he could move. And nothing ever would. The man was pulling down decorations. The woman was inside. He watched the man. Waited for him to reach up again. Got ready. But the man did not reach up. He instead reached down to a table and pulled up a hand weapon. The man looked in his direction. The Editor soundlessly moved to his left. The man's eyes and stance followed. He moved back and the same thing happened. Something was warning the man. The same thing that warned him before? It did not matter. He recalibrated.

The time it would take him to close the gap was still less than the time it would take the man to decide to pull the trigger and then to actually do it. Even if he did, The Editor could easily weather one hit.

The needful parasite inside The Editor pushed him forward. It lusted for the doomed look to feast on. To know and taste the other's defeat. So close now.

Inside the house, through the window, Jennifer saw Harrison pick up the revolver. She saw him look at the hedge. A prickle of fear ran up her spine. It was here. She reached for her 45.

Across the street, Walker saw Harrison heft the heavy revolver and stare at the hedge. "He's here," she said into her comm.

Up on 5th, just above Downing, Dennett heard the transmission and got out of the cruiser, drew her weapon, and ran toward the house.

Chapter 49

The Editor came through the laurel hedge as if it were made of paper, exploding it with a shrapnel of twigs and branches. The gap between he and his prey was closed in a split second. He covered the distance in a storm of hedge pieces, tearing-up the ground, before the man could even blink.

Walker shouted, and opened the window to shoot. But it was over.

Dennett heard the noise and called for backup as she ran to the house. But it was over.

While Jennifer watched, something blurred across the yard. Her eyes could not follow it and the 'thing' appeared as if by magic directly in front of Harrison. She tried to aim through the window, but instead, she screamed. It was over.

For Harrison, time went away. All outside sound was lost to him. All he could hear was the deafening bark of the dog.

SHOOT! SHOOT! SHOOT!

He pulled the trigger without being able to see what he was shooting at. Then in slow motion he saw the black eyes coming. Framed in a bushy blond bearded face. He felt the massive hands closing on his head.

Then he felt the concussive energy of the 50. The force of the blast stopped the 'thing's' forward motion and set Harrison a step back. It also dislocated his right-hand thumb and trigger finger.

The Editor stood paralyzed; went still as an insect. This was a new sensation for him. There was pain greater than before. His voluntary movement was stopped. The heavy bullet had penetrated his skin and ricocheted off his ribs and hit his spine near his neck. The nerves to his hands were numbed.

The Editor could not move. He was paralyzed. He was now as his prey. Standing helpless, ready to be killed. For the first time in his existence he panicked.

This could not be. Desperately he tried to reroute the nerve pathways. Inside its body, repairs were being made automatically. Just a little more time to reanimate his hands. The man appeared to be stunned. There was time.

Harrison tried to cock the double action gun with the dog still barking at him. The 'thing's' eyes boring into him. Something was trying to feast. His wall was failing.

The dog broke through the paralysis.

SHOOT! SHOOT! SHOOT!

Harrison could not cock it. So he pulled the trigger with his left hand. The cylinder turned. The hammer ratcheted back. He struggled to aim. He placed his bent right hand under the barrel because his thumb was not responding to his commands. He steadied the weapon and tried to raise the gun barrel to aim for the 'thing's' head.

He could not raise it.

The hammer fell. The blast was louder this time. Pain radiated up his arms. The side flash burned him. The recoil this time hit his chest and knocked his wind out. The gun hung from Harrison's numb hand by a single finger.

Time came back. The 'thing' fell.

But this was not over. The dog quit barking and emitted a continuous intense low growl.

Harrison tried to catch his breath and began to stagger to the 'thing's' body.

Jennifer heard the first blast of the 50 fire as if from far off, muffled by the wall and proximity to the 'thing's' body. It was a contact hit. She blew through the door like it was not there. Harrison stood with the 'thing's' hands on his head but nothing was moving.

The monster looked like it was going to kiss him.

She aimed her 45 but Harrison was partly between her and the 'thing.' Then she heard the click of the 50's hammer and this time a deafening blast. She felt the reflected muzzle flash off the 'thing' as a warm gust of air. Both shots came with a miraculous speed she could not believe before, but now knew, that Harrison had.

The 'thing' fell away. Harrison staggered. She went to him. He was shaking, barely hanging on to the gun. She looked down at his broken hands. The 50's kick from being held in that awkward grip made a mess of them. His trigger finger pointed in a random way it should not do naturally. There was a tear in his shirt and blood seeping from where the hammer had hit him.

She tried to take the gun. "No, Jen. I need to finish this." She knew he was still trying to keep her out of it. Not a chance.

The 'thing' was now twitching, scrabbling. Its arms and legs randomly moving in quick time.

Like an insect might do.

The first blast shocked The Editor into a paralytic stupor, severing its spine. The second crushed his heart. The Editor took a step back and fell. The essence of his life force was snuffed out. What was left fell with a wet thump onto the torn grass.

Inside the dead host, the parasite tried to go with the host's soul but there was nothing there. No soul to ride into the void and torment. Its exertions caused the body to jump and twitch. It tried reaching out for another host. But there was nowhere to go. The souls around it were secure.

Then there was one that might be receptive. The parasite spun its seductive web out. But the soul retreated and was gone. It suddenly realized it could not even have entered the one who might have been receptive. The parasite was bonded to the host that carried it, a host it had picked because of the ease of possession. A host without a soul. It was trapped in the body.

It screamed its frustration, but there was no sound. Then it knew it could yet escape. The body would be examined in detail.

During that time, before the body began to rot, as it was dismembered it would be able to escape. It could reside in the eyes and spin its seductive web at those who came near.

Harrison shuffled over to the spasming 'thing.' Jennifer followed. He tried to cock the 50. He tried to aim and pull the trigger with his left hand. He could not. His numbed hands were not capable. Jennifer again came to him. "Harry, let me help you."

The dog was now softly growling in Harrison's ear.

Finish! Finish! Finish it!

He physically could not function. His body had taken a hit from more than the pistol. The 'thing' had his head in its hands and had stared into his eyes. His wall held but was battered. The effect was catching up to him. The rage he had bottled up could not help him. It dissipated with the barking. The gun fell from his hand.

Jennifer felt Harrison's need like it was her own. But he was silent. He was quivering with effort. She picked up the hot weapon and cocked it. Then she went to his side and put the gun into his bent hands. She held it with him, placing her hands around his. She stiffened her arms like she had been taught as much as she could. The 'thing's' twitching weakened and now it was barely moving.

Together, wordlessly in sync, side by side, the Bakers aimed at the thing's skull. Together they steadied the heavy weapon. Together they pulled the trigger. There was another blast and the head no longer looked like a head. The brain pan was splattered into a fine mist, most of it well into the sandy sod.

What was left was also now tilted like no head could achieve naturally. Even an insect's. Yet somehow the eyes were unaffected.

The blast knocked the weapon out of their hands.

"Ow!" complained Jennifer.

"Yeah. Ow for sure," confirmed Harrison. He tried to reach for the gun but stopped. He wanted to shoot the eyes but the dog had gone silent. Was there no more threat or was there something else going on?

"I think you got him this time," mumbled Jennifer, holding his hands.

"We got him, Jen." Harrison was panting and sore like he had just run a marathon. He felt like he had just touched a live wire.

Sirens and lights closed in.

"Time to stand down," said Jennifer. They left the 50 where it fell, she put the 45 on the porch and then she helped him up the steps and they sat on the chairs watching for the coming clusterfuck. This time it would be a spectator sport.

Inside the 'thing,' the parasite saw a door close on its plan to escape during autopsy with the terrible blast that blew up the head of the dead host. It saw the intent of the shooter to kill it's eyes. If that happened it could escape immediately into this reality. It would not need to wait. But something stopped the shooter. One last chance remained. It hid in the eyes and waited.

Chapter 50

The body lay crumpled, meeting the ground temperature challenge. In the misty rain, it looked smaller than Harrison remembered. The head was smashed but the black eyes were open and even in death seemed to emit an aura of evil. This couldn't be true but the residual effect of the hands and eyes closing on him was too recent. It always would be. His battered wall that he thought helped him to shoot continued to deny the truth.

Walker was the first official to arrive. She ran out the hotel room door to the parking lot and around to the Baker house. The first thing she did was call for support. The second was to do a visual examination of the body of the assassin. She did not move it but looked carefully with her penlight. There were two 50 caliber holes in the torso, one low in what would be an abdomen in a normal human. And one over what would be a heart in a normal human, but unknown in this body. There were no exit wounds. The strength of this body must be phenomenal. She knew ballistics. She knew what the 50 magnum could do. The body should have no internal organs left. They should be scattered over the grass. Yet it was largely intact. Except for everything above the missing C1 cervical vertebra that is. Yet those eyes remained. She looked away.

The back of the head of the assassin was blown away at the base. If there were a bullet remaining, it would be deep in the sandy soil. The third thing she did was confer with Dennett who arrived just after herself. And the next thing was to ask Harrison how he did that.

Dennett was the second person to arrive. And the first police authority. She had called for support. She examined the body, noted the same wounds as Walker and conferred with Walker for a moment, then together they went to Harrison, and Dennett asked for an account, she had not seen the 'thing' move.

Walker, however, was in awe. "How the hell did you do that? I couldn't even see it move. There was an explosion and then it had your face in its hands."

Harrison answered both Dennett and Walker at the same time. "I was lucky. I heard the hedge move and pulled the trigger. The 'thing' was on me by the time the gun went off. It seemed to freeze. I shot it again and it fell. Then I shot it in the head."

Jennifer stepped in, "We both shot it in the head," she knew Harrison wanted to deflect any murder charges. Not a chance. Both or neither, she reasoned.

"I could not have done it without Jennifer's help," Harrison admitted, smiling at his wife.

Walker and Dennett looked at the Baker's hands and understood. "How about the wound on your chest?" asked Dennett.

"Self-inflicted." Like that explained everything. "It's not serious," he added.

He was not asked how he knew the 'thing' was in the hedge and did not volunteer.

From down on 9th, Bjorn came running. He held his Swedish Model 1896/38 Mauser rifle at port. Janice was right behind and Katrin followed. The gunshots had awakened the whole neighborhood, but Bjorn, with his family, was the only one who ran toward them. They gathered around the dead 'thing' and looked at the body and Harrison's hands. He was sitting on the porch steps with a blank stare. Shock had set in. Jennifer was sitting with him and cradling his hands in hers.

"What the hell happened?" Bjorn was the first to speak. "Are you alright?"

"Little shaken," said Jennifer. "God that was close!"

Bjorn looked around. "It came through the hedge? You know how tough these Laurels are?" he said in awe.

Janice went to Jennifer, "How can we help?"

"Just being here is enough."

Janice sat next to Jennifer and put her arm around her. Jennifer sagged in the comfort.

"The police are coming, Mr. Johanson, put that antique away," Dennett said.

He took the weapon inside the house chafing at the term.

"It shoots just fine," he mumbled.

Dennett did not hear; she was on her comm trying to order up a body transport; reaching for that gold star on her record.

"We should get the Bergstroms here now before the police take him away. Johanna needs to see him dead." Janice said.

"You sure?" Bjorn was concerned that Johanna may be further traumatized.

Janice was already on the phone. "Pamela, you want to hear this. The demon is dead. Harry killed him. If you think Johanna is strong enough, this could be the end of her torment," pause. "How…?" pause "Baker's house," pause, "Got it." She turned to Bjorn, "We have to keep the body here. Tye, Pamela, Jack and Johanna will be here in a few minutes. Johanna knew it was dead. They all knew when and where."

The Johansons and Bakers knew something other than a routine assassination attempt had been foiled. There was a lot more. There were forces at play that were beyond human ability to understand. Yet the feeling of awe faded in the building police presence.

"It's not going anywhere soon," Harrison wearily said. "There will be a lot of police and feds here shortly fighting over it." He was coming around. Jennifer stood.

More Seaside police showed up within a few minutes. Sirens and lights split the night. Everybody wanted to get a look at the 'thing.' Those who got too close would turn away and leave quickly. Crime scene tape spooled out. Dennett finally called the county Medical Examiner to stake claim to the body.

The two junior NSA agents arrived next and conferred with Walker. They were also here to stake claim to the body. This was a jurisdictional dispute with the FBI. NSA did not have the expertise to evaluate the body, but wanted the gold star for retrieving it. Calls were made to superiors asking for authority to commandeer transport.

FBI showed up next. The two agents who tried to interview the Bakers came to stake claim on the body. Calls were made to superiors asking for authority to commandeer transport.

This was the first time Print had actually seen the assassin. Like Walker and Dennett, he looked closely - and suddenly reacted. Something in the dead body seemed to seductively reach out. The eyes held a somehow beautiful low black fire. He stumbled forward for a step and then jumped back.

Cho looked on with concern. There was a sudden prickle at the back of his neck that made him also take a step back. Was the body not really dead?

Print looked at Harrison and wondered just what the hell happened and what did that guy know? A few minutes later he decided not to pursue that knowledge and to not be so OC about it. It served him well when operating within the rules and regs of the FBI, but out here - right now - not so much.

If his superiors wanted to get the body he would see to it that they got it. But Baker would be left to the local police.

Then, in his head, he filed the experience under "Don't need to know" and retreated a distance.

Jeffers arrived next, saw the problem coming, and was first to act. He did not need to confer with his superiors. The Seaside police were the first to get transport. An SUV unit was dispatched and got there within minutes.

Then the real battle for the body began.

The Bakers and Johansons sat and watched the clusterfuck. The Seaside SUV Unit arrived with a heavy tarp and the officers stepped out. Jeffers conferred with them and they moved toward the body. He called over a couple more officers to help with the heavy load.

"Wait for a minute, Chief." Harrison moved from the porch steps and stood over the body. Jennifer went and stood with him. Bjorn and Pamela came over.

"What's going on Harry?" asked Jeffers. Had Harrison gone over the edge? His mangled hands and wounded chest attested to the fact of a fight. Was he experiencing PTS symptoms already? Was he going to shoot again?

"The Bergstroms are coming with Johanna. She needs to see this." Harrison clearly said.

Jeffers got it. Harrison was sane enough to care about the Bergstroms – at least for the time being. He turned and held up the officers with their cart.

The FBI and NSA agents watched. There was no show of force or threat that would work here. The County sheriffs and State police were arriving. None of the new arrivals would listen to them. Their calls made to superiors were answered by clerks who would get back to them. It was one o'clock am on the east coast this Halloween night, and no one of authority was immediately available. They were happy about that. There would be no good way to obey an order to confiscate the body. Interdiction would have to take place at the Clatsop morgue. That was for another day. For now, watching the small town's support handle this was impressive.

The Bergstroms arrived a few minutes later. Tye, Pamela, Jack, and then Johanna stepped out of the sedan. Tye held up his hand and stopped his family. He then surveyed the yard and came over to the body and looked at it. He did not flinch. "You got it," he said to Harrison.

"I and my wife, Tye."

Tye nodded and gave an okay signal to Johanna. Katrin held her hand as she approached, Pamela trailing and watching her daughter and Tye. Johanna moved to within six feet of the body over the muddy ground. She stared at it. She wanted to move closer and poke it to make sure, but there was still something in it. The demon was still there. The flashing lights made it seem to move. She turned to her father.

"You didn't kill the demon," Johanna said without inflection. Just a statement of fact.

"No. He didn't come for you. He didn't care about you. Harry was right, he needed to complete his assignment. Harry was always the target." Tye thought she meant the 'thing' but she really referred to the demon. He turned away. Johanna saw the hurt.

"Dad, you stood in front of it for me. You saved my life before when it haunted me. You saved my life."

She paused, "But Mr. Baker didn't kill it either. I have to see the demon." As if the body were not enough. "I have to kill it myself." Tye did not understand.

Katrin took her hand again. Jack came forward. "No, Jack, Kat. I have to do this alone." Jack looked at his father. Tye was puzzled but nodded. It was dead was all he knew and could not hurt her anymore.

Alone, with small tentative steps, Johanna walked the six feet over the wet grass to the torn-up area that held the body. The Johansons and Bakers gave way. But Katrin followed her. Johanna sat on her heels and looked into the undead eyes, the aura Harrison denied, remained.

The parasite was still hiding in the eyes. Unable to affect the body now. As Johanna approached, it cast out an undisguised malignancy but was unable to feed on her fear. She was protected. Its ability was diminishing. The other had won. It would have to go back to the void again. Hunting. Hungering. Without end.

Johanna did not react. "I know you're still in there. I know you can't escape. I know what happens during an autopsy. I know you will be there till the end. Then you will be no more. I know you were just the result of some sort of Frankenstein experiment. I don't fear you anymore."

She did not hear the wailing of the parasite. Nobody alive could.

Behind Johanna, Katrin stood like a protective angel. *'You are there,'* a thankyou whispered in her mind. *'I am, you're welcome.'* she answered. She seemed to glow for a moment, - for those who could see.

Johanna stood and looked at Katrin, "Thank you," she said, took Katrin's hand and turned to her family.

Harrison looked at Katrin, then at Janice. He was amazed, Janice smiled and nodded. She heard. She saw. Johanna also smiled with a faint glow.

Tye was astounded and just beginning to understand. Pamela was proud. Jack and Katrin knew that Johanna had rid herself of the trauma. She had killed the effect of the demon.

Jennifer was happy for Johanna. She also saw the interaction of Harrison with Janice. She knew that Harrison and Janice saw something that she did not.

"Harry, what was that all about?"

"Jan, we just had a whole lot of help here tonight. I'll tell you later."

"Yes, you will." Of that there was no doubt. Harrison heard the finality of that statement and knew he had better come up with the reason, whatever it was. He was just going to have to wing it. He had no logical reason.

The full clusterfuck of Seaside police, Clatsop Sheriff deputies, Oregon State troopers, NSA agents, and FBI agents conferred. The Clatsop Medical Examiner arrived. She took one look and said, "Yes, it's dead." And turned away from those eyes. She was not looking forward to having this body in her morgue. Then she looked around at the needful eyes of the NSA and FBI people and relaxed. She would not have to house it for long.

The immediate jurisdictional fight boiled down to Clatsop county ownership – for the time being. The Seaside Unit left for the morgue with a blast of sirens and lights. Nobody alive rode in the back. The driver received orders on the way and detoured as instructed.

In Portland, private charters were readied awaiting orders directly from the DoJ and DoD. Warrenton was about to become crowded with federal power.

Jeffers called Johnson. The upshot was "Who cares now. Let the big boys fight it out," and went back to formulating an article to be published. The locals did not care for sure. The county sheriffs were told to stand down unless the feds started shooting at each other. Then to just pick up the pieces.

Harrison's gun went away with the meager evidence packets. There was not much else left but the body and echoing gunshots and vanished smoke. The hedge and torn ground were inventoried on camera.

Jennifer's 45 remained though. Resting on the kitchen table along with Harrison's Sig. Ready for anything now. Johanson's rifle also rested next to the door. Bergstrom's rifle waited in the sedan. Just in case.

Jeffers suddenly made a snap decision. He reversed his original aim to out the assassin, Chile, GRU et. al. There was no good that could come of that. He called the Unit's driver and had him re-route the body. He climbed into his cruiser and followed. The gold star for the return of the body would go to him only in his own mind. He was suddenly calm about the deception. Something told him it was the right thing to do.

Then he started to formulate an official report of this incident. It would need to be carefully worded. His handwritten account would not. His retirement plans were next.

All this occurred, in the firestorm of lights, oblivious to the misting rain.

Chapter 51

The carnival-like light show, cameras, and multiple agencies waned and died. Inside the Baker house, the cabal of survivors sat in muted silence. Savoring the ending of a terrible time.

Then Bjorn looked at Harrison's hands. "Doesn't that hurt?"

"Now that you mention it," he deadpanned.

"Looks dislocated. I can fix that. I have EMT training. This kind of stuff happens on the job every once in a while. Or we can transport you to Providence emergency."

Harrison looked at his bent fingers which were already turning black and blue, and nodded. "Go ahead, it can't get worse."

Wanna bet, thought Bjorn. Before Harrison could say anything more, Bjorn took his wrist and grabbed the thumb. This was a strong man, noted Harrison, just before a white hot pain from his thumb shot all the way up his arm. While Harrison gritted his teeth and tried to get his hand back, Bjorn deftly grabbed the index finger and another white-hot bolt shot up Harrison's arm. This time all the way to his toes. Bjorn let go.

"Now, how about the wound on your chest?"

Harrison's eyes were watering and he struggled to say 'hell no' but could only make grunting sounds.

Jennifer saved him. "I got that, Bjorn. You want an aspirin, Harry?"

Harrison struggled to say 'hell yes' and actually got it out this time. "Hell yes," he growled. He looked around at amused faces, was everyone getting a chuckle from this? Then he had to see the humor. It wasn't for what caused it, it was for how it was fixed. He let himself smile.

The air calmed. Jeffers cleared the area, came over and said he would take their statements tomorrow. He did not want to bother these people tonight. And it was pretty self-explanatory. Also, he had plans to make.

Print, Walker, and Dennett et. al. went to file their reports. Harrison got his aspirin and sat carefully testing his hands for movement and with a new bandage over his wounded chest. Now he, Jennifer, Tye, Pamela, Jack and Johanna, Bjorn, Janice, and Katrin rested in the silence. An unlikely crew that defied the NSA, FBI, and the 'thing.' And anybody else who threatened them. They randomly sat and stood on his porch looking at the bare lawn and the churned-up sod between the torn hedge and the faint outline of a heavy body. There was a deep hole in the ground near where the head was, where a deformed bullet had been excavated along with whatever brain material they could find. This done by the Seaside police, the first ones there with a shovel and a garbage bag.

The gold star was theirs but they did not collect it. The bag was sent with the body which would not make it to the morgue.

Then the yard was empty.

In the ringing silence, Jennifer had to know what Johanna meant when she said, 'I know you're still in there.'

So she bluntly asked, "How do you know the demon is still in the body?"

"You don't know, do you? I thought maybe Mr. Baker would. But I see it's just me," Johanna sighed.

"Both feet," reminded Jack.

"I'm okay Jack. It's just that there is a real demon in the 'thing.' It's still there."

"I remember this from our research into demonology. I thought at the time that it would help you to believe that it couldn't get out and you were safe from it," said Jack.

"It did. More than you know."

"How is it that you are the only one to see or know the demon?" wondered Jennifer out loud. "All I saw was a demented man. With scary eyes, but still a man. Even when it was explained to me that it was a genetic mutant, it was still a man-like thing. With a powerful evil stare."

Johanna shivered. Katrin took her hand protectively.

"Don't answer if it makes you uncomfortable," butted in Pamela.

"For sure," said Jennifer.

"Don't worry Mom. I know the demon is trapped and will… cease to exist soon. I have killed its hold on me. I can't say how I know this. Maybe it's because I'm young and haven't grown up yet."

"You know," offered Harrison, "When I looked into its eyes when it was holding you last Halloween, I saw death. There was some sort of power there besides a man, besides damned misbegotten experiment. But I could not name it. I knew it was a 'thing.' I knew it was deadly but even though I myself described it as a demon, I denied the truth to myself. I did it to stay sane and not go off the rails. Even with that, I could not have done it without Jennifer. You are strong beyond belief to weather the stare, accept the truth and survive."

"It nearly killed me in more ways than one," murmured Johanna. "Those eyes were like looking into Hell. Like *being* in Hell. I was trapped for a long time. Without this irritating brother of mine and my not-so-irritating father, and my beautiful mother, I don't know if I could have made it back by myself."

"You had more than us, sister. Look around you."

Johanna looked around at the Bakers, Jorgensons, Dennett, and Walker. She smiled. "Yes, thank you. But most of all I have a strong father, a comforting mother, an irritating brother," chuckle, "and a loyal understanding friend. And something more." Then she looked at Harrison, "The dog was here. I heard it." A statement of fact.

"Yes. It was. Right up until the last shot." It made me do that. And stopped me from shooting the eyes. I don't know why but it was necessary."

"I know," Johanna said.

Now it was the Bergstroms turn to ask, "What dog? How could you hear it?" Tye asked Johanna. "We were miles away. We could barely hear the shots." He marveled that Johanna reacted in real-time to the shots. The weak sound was several seconds behind but he accepted that she was tuned to the fight. But a dog? Not a chance.

Harrison almost laughed. The Jorgensons knew but the Bergstroms did not. Before Johanna could answer, he said, "Okay, here's the latest hallucination from crazy Harry. When the 'thing' was attacking Johanna on the last Halloween, I was surprised by its horror. I had the gun pointed but now I think it could have killed both me and Johanna at that time. I had no idea it could move so fast. Anyway, a dog started barking and I pulled the trigger. Just now when I was being stalked by the thing, the dog growled. I followed the sound of the growl and pulled the trigger when it barked. Goddam! It still got to me." He felt the hot grip, the gloating eyes, he shuddered and continued. "There is also this, I held the 50 close to my chest," he pointed to the bandaged gash. "The gun broke my hands but… if I'd have stood like I've been trained, the 'thing' would have hit the gun before it went off. I don't know why I did that." Harrison slipped back into some sort of depression.

Jennifer got in front of him and said, "Buck up Harry, whatever warned you, whatever you did, it worked. You're here. It's over. You're okay, Johanna's okay. I'm okay. Now you can let it go."

"How did I ever get you?"

"Just lucky, or something else," she smiled that knowing smile. The protective wall he had built up, which was damaged by the 'thing's' assault, crumbled. The remaining horror and rage were banished by this beautiful girl he had married. Harrison came back from the edge.

"I heard it when we got back to the Baker's place from the trick you played on me," Johanna said in answer to her father's question. "Both I and Mr. Baker heard a soft growl when we were on the lawn. I think I remembered it because I was freed of the fear and felt safer. It is now with me. I hear it inside, like Mr. Baker. I think it is a force… the opposite of the demon. It was there when I saw the murder too. Telling me to run."

Johanna thought that what she heard during the murder was much more important than the name everybody was after. Much more important. She would hear it long after the name Trask was forgotten. A comforting rumble of strength. A reverent feeling came. To those who could see, she glowed with an ethereal light.

"An angel," chimed in Katrin. "It has to be."

"Well, the strange thing is that I don't… didn't think much about angels and demons before. Even when in combat areas." Harrison said.

"They're real," asserted Katrin. "We don't have to believe. They are what they are without us needing to know."

"Over my pay grade," laughed Harrison, wincing. "I'll take your word for it." He kind of expected, even wanted, to see Katrin or Johanna glow again.

Then he thought back to the Eisenhower quote. None of any of the preparations he made would have saved them without the dog.

"So wait a minute," Tye cut in. "You say the demon is trapped for now," he turned to Johanna. "Can it escape later? Should we make sure the corpse is cremated?" He was now a believer.

"I don't think we need to worry about that. The people who finally get the body will take it apart, piece by piece. Right down to the DNA. There will be nothing left," ventured Harrison.

"That's what I'm talking about. Once they tear this body apart, what's to stop the demon from… doing whatever demons can do?" looking now at both Jack and Johanna.

"Well, it will be a long way from here for sure," Jack offered.

Johanna had been thinking, "There were two 'things' here. One was the assassin. The other is the demon. The assassin was the one that wanted revenge. The demon is just along for the pain and suffering and horror the assassin generated. But the assassin had no soul for the demon to control. It was a man-made 'thing.' The demon didn't really control the assassin. So, I think it became the 'thing's' soul so to speak. It became the assassin and was bound to the body. It's now in the eyes. It can't leave. It has nowhere to go."

Everybody was watching this young girl speak like a professor. She looked up. "I just feel this," she explained.

"So this demon, this entity, is without form and can't move?" wondered Tye. "I hope it gets taken back to Hell."

Johanna shrugged, "I hope so too. But that's beyond my knowledge. All I know is what I feel. The demon will cease to exist. Not die in the sense we think but simply cease to exist."

"I'm going to take your word for it, I'm through with it," Harrison said again.

There were sounds of assent.

Chapter 52

The group finally broke up with lots of handshakes and hugs. Harrison carefully used his left hand. Each family went its own way. Yet a bond was formed. Jennifer knew they found a true home at last. She watched their friends depart. Then she brought Harrison a Jameson double. Harrison took it with both hands. Neither was working well on its own.

"Alright. Talk. Tell me about Katrin and Janice."

"God. Another mystery. I'll tell you what I saw and heard. It was similar to the dog," Harrison took a breath. Wing it, Harry: "When Jack and Katrin were comforting Johanna after the scene we did, I heard a whisper that came from near the trio. But was not *from* them. It came from somewhere or something else. It was talking to Katrin. She apparently had made a plea that was answered with '*Just be there.*' She whispered back without actual sound '*I will.*' How I heard that is, I don't know, a miracle?"

"This was not like the dog, was it? The dog was like a guardian, this was like a comforter?"

"Yeah… right! That makes sense. I think so. Anyway, it happened again tonight when Johanna confronted the dead 'thing.' Now, the other part is that Janice heard and saw what I did."

"What did you see?"

"Yeah. Katrin seemed to light up for a moment during the whispering. Janice I think saw it and Johanna felt it. They all believe in angels."

"What did it look like?" Jennifer was leaning close. Wanting to know. Wanting to understand. Wanting to believe.

"The color was nothing I've ever seen. Even the sunsets here do not rival it. Even the green flash. Even the rainbows we have here. Even the aurora borealis sky when flying over the pole. It lit her entire body. I am going to say it reminded me of what a halo should be."

"Fork, Harry. How did I ever get you?"

"Just lucky I guess, or something else," he laughed and cringed as the ribs complained.

"Yeah? I'm guessing we're both lucky, and something else."

"I'd say it's something else. I don't think luck had much to do with it or this."

"Harry?" Jennifer got serious.

"Yes."

"Why a dog? Could you picture it?"

"You know I thought about that. Look at it like this: if a human voice told me to shoot, the first thing I'd do would be to look for the source. Knowing the ability of the 'thing' that would be a disaster." Sigh. "I have no vision of what it looked like. I just had the impression it was… I can't describe it other than… big, beautiful. And loud!"

"I have my own idea of that. Maybe we should get one."

"Maybe we should."

"Yeah?" Jennifer's eyes twinkled, "So what if it was me telling you to shoot?"

"Hell, Jen. That's easy. I'd immediately pump the full load into it with two in the head, and start looking for more mags just in case." laughed Harrison.

Jennifer smiled and then sobered, and got to the real issue. "Why can't I see and hear what you can? What Katrin and Janice can?"

"I don't know. Maybe it's to do with being targeted by the demon/thing combo. It leaves an impression all right. Like a disease. Maybe the dog is the antidote. It made me, and then both of us, shoot the 'thing' in the head even though I thought it was dead. I think it closed some kind of door on the... demon."

Harrison thought about Janice and Katrin. They had not seen the 'thing' like he or Johanna. It came to him, "Janice and Katrin are mother and daughter. They believe in angels. I think they accepted the 'angel' dog without question because of that. I see what they see because the dog sees."

"God, Harry, I'm in awe. I heard Johanna say that the dog was with her now. Do you believe that?

"Yeah. I think I have it too."

"What do you think it is?"

"Something good. I didn't ask for it. It just came."

"Why?"

"I think because of us. I think it intervened because of us and the Bergstroms. Maybe just for Johanna."

"Yeah? Because we're what... good?"

"Partially... maybe. Maybe there is stuff going on we can't fathom. Maybe love has something to do with it."

"Can't argue with that." Jennifer suddenly had an idea. Was love the key? Time to find out. "Come here for a minute," he leaned over and she kissed him. And for just that moment in time, she heard the contented gruff rumbling of a big dog in her mind. Then a comforting rumbling in her chest. It was the most beautiful sound she had ever felt. It made her feel warm and safe. It was interesting that Harry was driven to action by it, and that she felt… comfort. Maybe someday she would tell Harrison about it.

Jennifer then had a flashback to when they listened to Barbara Anne at *Winekraft,* right after she first saw the 'thing.' The song was *Shame on the Moon.* The last lines were:

Until you stand beside a man
You don't know who he knows.

Prophetic, she thought again. Then and now. Harrison knew people all right, but he knew the 'dog' too. And she stood beside him and now knew it right along with him. She was proud of herself and her husband at the same time.

Tomorrow they would be giving statements to the police. Tonight they would celebrate. As much as Harrison's ribs and hands would allow anyway. She brought out another Jameson for him and one for herself too. She wanted to hear the dog again.

What she heard reverberated in the air that night and allowed Harrison to be free of pain. And allowed Jennifer to feel the power of the contented rumbling. He would pay in the morning. She would remember this night forever.

What she heard allowed Johanna to be free of the demon. She slept well for the first time since before the last Halloween. A comforting soft rumble was never far off.

Denouement

"Assassin shot dead in Seaside," was the Daily Astorian headline. The five "W's" were attended to in a sterile clinical story. There was a passing mention of a genetic anomaly creating black eyes. There was no detailed examination of how the assassin was released or managed to escape. Just that it happened.

The witness interviews were superficial. The main people involved did not answer questions.

There was no mention of a dog. There was no mention of a halo. There was no mention of a demon. There was no mention of angels.

In the same issue, there was a lengthy story decrying gun violence and promoting gun control.

In a related story, for some reason, the body of the assassin did not arrive at the county morgue. The County officials claimed it was confiscated by Homeland Security agents that same night. There were no records.

The FBI agents secretly thought this may be best and filed their reports. The NSA agents stayed a few days and conducted debriefing interviews with Dennett and the Bakers. These were conducted over dinners at *Maggie's*. Their reports were factual and bland. The dinners were interesting.

There was also a story about an unapproved slash fire in one of the piles in a clear cut, off Highway 101, south of Warrenton. The Fire Department noted an exceptionally hot burn. An accelerant was used. A Halloween prank was suspected. It burned for three days. Nothing but ash was left.

The FBI raided Senator Elmond Trask's offices in Washington D.C. and Salem Oregon citing a plot by Russians to spy on the White House, and the assassination of a Journalist in Seaside Oregon. There was a storm of partisan stories about the event as the media lined up on one side or the other. The White House blamed Trump. The Republicans blamed the corrupt Biden administration. After a while, another event hit the stage and the media went after it like coyotes on a rabbit.

No more letters came to the small ornamental post office box in Talcahuano, Republic of Chile. No more plain white envelopes. The post office box lay dormant.

The news hit Talcahuano several days after the killing of the man who once lived up Avenida Tumbes. It noted that it happened in another seaside town in America. The town breathed a sigh of relief.

Both towns were once more easy places to live.

Jeffers did not have to resign despite losing the body. From the reports written by the FBI and NSA, no one was that interested. Homeland Security did not answer any questions. They all had their facts. The case was closed.

In Seaside Oregon, In January of the next year, a hack novel writer got a thick packet in the mail. The return address did not exist. Inside were handwritten notes from various law enforcement agencies. Including a secret dossier from NSA. There were transcripts of testimonies from several of the primary people involved in the recent assassination story and the killing of the assassin in Seaside. All handwritten. There was a treatise by a Providence Hospital doctor detailing the trauma of one Johanna Bergstrom. There was a letter and notes from a therapist. There were photos of agents and the assassin.

There was a letter written by a Clackamas DA speculating on the massive amount of institutional corruption evinced by court rulings from top to the bottom. It included a lament about the lack of morals in top politicians.

But the best was a copy of a diary written by the young girl, detailing the personal events and what she heard on two Halloween nights. What she heard was a lot more than a name.

He began to formulate a story. After a while, he knew it would be a novel. Fiction, of course – based on an actual event. One that would be entertaining but no one would believe.

What She Heard

He first thought that the story would end on a sour note in the last words of the denouement:

"Out there somewhere, more labs were working on creating better super soldiers. And legions of parasites were drifting outside of time. Forever hunting, hungering."

"Son, the greatest trick the devil pulled was convincing the world there was only one of him."

David Wong

The author decided not to do that.

Or did he?

Thanks from the Author

I have to thank those who helped me with the local music scene. Even though I live here it always amazes me how much wonderful local talent there is.

I thank the wonderful people of Seaside, Astoria, and Cannon Beach who own and operate the businesses that offer a place for local talent to showcase. There are too many to mention but here are those that are locally owned that I used in this novel:

WineKraft in Astoria. Great bartender, and live nostalgic music from Barbara Anne folk singer. Thanks, Rebecca Kraft.

Bistro in Cannon Beach. Great food, and live oldies music from the Rose and Thistle singers. Thanks, Chef Jack.

Hop and Vine in Seaside. A wonderfully lit array of wines and beers, and live eclectic songs from Jason Lambert. Thanks, Tim Welsh.

Vineside at Pier 39 Astoria. A cozy calm wine bar, and songs from local talent. Thanks Nathan and J.R. Alvarez. (Sorry that it had to close in December.)

At the time this printing, *Burly and the Bean Coffee House* was hosting more great talent. The great voices of Chelsea LaFey and Segrid Coleman. Thanks Vanessa and Justin Boone.

And here are those mentioned that just offer great food and service.

The Inferno in Astoria. Great view, and great bartenders and servers. Great atmosphere. Thanks Rich Ewing.

Maggie's on the Prom in Seaside. Fantastic cuisine, great view, and friendly servers. Thanks, Sadie Mercer.

The *Rogue Public House* at Pier 39. Great food, great views. Thanks Jack Joyce.

Also and certainly not least (indeed worth the most thanks) are the people who aid and abet this guy's hobby. Family.

My sisters, Diane Jette and Susan Ripley, and daughter-in-law Tammy Liddycoat, who know more about grammar than I ever will.

And Eve Marx, I enjoy the constructive criticism.

As always, any bloopers are mine. As I may or may not take the advice from any of the above. I am, after all, an admitted egotistic novel writer.

A parasite has not found me yet… I think.